THE
REGGIE WARFORD
STORY

THE
REGGIE WARFORD
STORY

INTEGRATING BASKETBALL
AT THE UNIVERSITY OF KENTUCKY

SCOTT BROWN
FOREWORD BY JACK GIVENS

UNIVERSITY PRESS OF KENTUCKY

A note to the reader: Some of the anecdotes and quotations printed in this volume contain racially insensitive language. The author has chosen to document the original terminology to provide full historical context for the events under discussion. Discretion is advised.

Editorial and Sales Offices: The University Press of Kentucky
663 South Limestone Street, Lexington, Kentucky 40508-4008
www.kentuckypress.com

Unless otherwise noted, photographs are courtesy of Marisa Warford.

Cataloging-in-Publication data is available from the Library of Congress.

ISBN 978-1-9859-0105-6 (hardcover : alk. paper)
ISBN 978-1-9859-0106-3 (pbk. : alk. paper)
ISBN 978-1-9859-0107-0 (epub)
ISBN 978-1-9859-0108-7 (pdf)

This book is printed on acid-free paper meeting
the requirements of the American National Standard
for Permanence in Paper for Printed Library Materials.

Manufactured in the United States of America

Member of the Association
of University Presses

To Dr. Tom "TB" Brown III. TB is a first cousin but has always been an older brother to me. He and Reggie were close friends, and he got all of this started. I hope this book does both proud.

Contents

Foreword

Reggie Warford taught me an important lesson shortly after I arrived at the University of Kentucky in 1974. I was a homegrown kid, having played basketball at Bryan Station High School in Lexington. If Reggie had been a different person, he might not have welcomed me the way he did. He had arrived at Kentucky two years earlier as only the second African American scholarship player in the program's history. He eventually became the first African American basketball player to graduate from Kentucky and helped pave the way for players like me.

But he had not played much in his first two years because he had to wait his turn. Now I was coming in with a highly touted recruiting class and as Kentucky's reigning Mr. Basketball, the award given to the top prep basketball player in the state. He could have seen that as a threat, but we hit it off immediately.

One day Reggie said, "C'mon, rook, let's play H-O-R-S-E." I went first and took a shot around the free-throw line. I made it, but Reggie walked to another spot on the floor. I said, "Reggie, I made the shot here." He said, "No, you didn't make that." I said, "Reggie, the ball went in. I made the shot." He said, "No, no, you didn't make it." I'm thinking, *Man, am I playing a different game?* He said, "Listen, man, on this level the only shots that count are the ones that go in that do not touch the rim. Your ball went in, but it hit the rim, so that doesn't count. You've got to hit all net."

From that day on, I really thought about how to shoot the basketball, to make sure I got the arc on it right so it would drop in and hit no rim. I tell people to this day that the reason I learned to shoot the ball well was because of Reggie's lesson that day.

Reggie, in his mind, was always the best player on the court. You could tell that by the way he competed in practice against guys like Jimmy Dan Conner and Mike Flynn, guys who were playing the guard spots above him my first year, and then Larry Johnson as he moved into the point guard spot. You knew every day in practice that Reggie was trying to prove that he was the best guy on the team. This tells you that if Reggie didn't have the makeup that he had, if he didn't think of himself that way, he would not have made it at the University of Kentucky. He would not have been able to carry the torch for all of us who came after him.

To do what he did at Kentucky required absolutely the right guy, a guy with confidence, a guy who was able to be thick-skinned at times when he had to do things he didn't necessarily like or agree with. His mindset was *I'm not backing down, I'm not quitting. I'm still coming at it head-first.* That's the way Reggie approached every day at the University of Kentucky. I learned from Reggie the importance of working hard, believing in myself, and standing firm.

His perseverance paid off in 1976. He became a starter early in the season and led us to the National Invitation Tournament Championship. Reggie just flat took over down the stretch that season and became the man. For the first time in his career, he was in the position where he knew that we wouldn't win games unless he contributed. That didn't necessarily mean he was going to score the most points every night. It meant he had to make plays. I don't think we would have won the NIT without him, not just for the plays he made but for the leadership he showed.

Anytime you can be the first in something deserves a lot of credit. For Reggie to be the first African American basketball player to graduate from Kentucky, that's special in itself. I don't know that young players coming through the program now think that it even matters who that first guy was, but it matters. It makes a big difference.

Whether Reggie got a fair chance to really exhibit what he could do, I don't know. But I know my transition at the University of Kentucky would not have happened as easily as it did had Reggie not endured everything he had to go through, had he not hung in there.

Reggie dealt with unimaginable health issues in the twilight of his life. How he and his family weathered them, with unyielding strength and faith, is truly inspiring. I suppose it is another lesson that Reggie taught me and so many others. Reggie didn't know that if I was having a bad day, I called him so he could lift me up because he never complained.

He always had a positive thing to say. He always asked about the guys that we played with and wanted to reach out to any of them who were struggling. He did not say, "You could have it as bad as I have it." If anybody had reason to complain and feel sorry for himself, it was Reggie. I never saw that side of him, though. He was always concerned about others, more so than himself. That is why so many people cared about him and still love him.

Jack "Goose" Givens played at Kentucky from 1974 to 1978 and is the school's third all-time leading scorer with 2,038 points. He scored a career-high 41 points in the National Collegiate Athletic Association Championship game in 1978, leading Kentucky to a 94–88 win over Duke and its fifth national title. His number, 21, was retired by the school, and his jersey hangs in the rafters at Rupp Arena.

Preface

If you came of age in the 1980s, you were subjected to some unfortunate things—pegged jeans, BIG hair, and *Caddyshack 2,* to name a few. Big East basketball was not among them. It wasted little time, following its inception in 1979, in becoming a zeitgeist as much as a basketball conference. Beyond the special players and great teams, the Big East had flair and a New York swagger. ESPN's nightly college basketball tripleheaders propelled the conference *and* the network.

When Pitt entered the Big East in 1982, it was a brave new world for the Panthers' basketball program. A football school quickly went from competitive to contender. Reggie Warford was a big reason for that. As an assistant coach to Roy Chipman, Reggie recruited blue-chip talent to Pitt. When the Panthers went 24–7 and won the Big East regular-season title in 1987–1988, they had five players who averaged double figures in scoring, including Charles Smith and Jerome Lane. All five were recruited by Reggie.

I met Reggie through my cousin Tom Brown, a dentist who seems to know everybody in Pittsburgh. Tom would tell stories about Reggie playing at the University of Kentucky and coaching at Pitt. I hung on every word and finally got to meet Reggie at one of my uncle's annual Fourth of July parties in Greensburg, about thirty miles east of Pittsburgh.

Tom had said that Reggie might give me some basketball pointers. I could not have been more excited. My hopes dimmed when I saw Reggie at the party holding a different kind of court. He oozed charisma, and people wanted to be around him. No way, I thought, will he want to leave to shoot hoops with some kid. But that is exactly what Reggie did. We walked to a nearby basketball court, and Reggie taught me how to shoot and showed me different drills. Not once did he seem anxious to get back to the party. It meant the world to an awestruck junior-high-school kid.

I learned while researching Reggie's incredible story that he had once done something similar for another kid, coincidentally also with the last name "Brown." Stuart Brown was a wayward teenager when Reggie came into his life. A phone call from Reggie eventually led to a lifelong friendship. Today, Dr. Stuart Brown is a world-renowned veterinarian specializing in horses. "People like Reggie Warford have their fingerprints all over who I became," said Dr. Brown, who lives in Lexington. "Reggie Warford continues to this day to have an incredible impact on my life."

I talked with Dr. Brown for almost two hours one night. Of the scores of interviews I conducted for this book, none resonated more than that one. His Reggie stories made me reflect on my early experiences with him. I realized that Reggie had not just been doing my cousin Tom a favor when he took me to the basketball court: the man loved basketball, loved using the game to teach and mentor.

Probably the only things he was more devoted to than basketball were his faith and his family. God, family, and basketball were the foundation of Reggie's life. Those guiding forces are why he touched so many lives. Of those three, though, it can be argued that only his family was fair to Reggie.

I received a phone call from my cousin Tom in February 2019. He suggested writing a book on Reggie with one caveat: there might not be much time to do it. Reggie's health was failing. We met with Reggie a week later. He spun stories about growing up in rural Kentucky and playing at the University of Kentucky for Coach Joe B. Hall. I was mesmerized. That conversation started a journey that was rewarding beyond what I can put into words. Reggie and I became close. His family became my family. They were always as concerned with what was going on in my life as they were about progress on the book.

The bittersweet part about the experience: Reggie's body was shutting down the entire time we worked on the book. Between 2014 and 2019, he had had heart and kidney transplants, and those surgeries only topped a long list of health problems he was battling. It could be humbling to see what they had done to a former world-class athlete.

One time I had to open a small wrapper of chocolate for Reggie because his shaking hands would not allow him to do it. Another time he took a bathroom break while we were in his dining room but could not make it back to the table, and we finished the interview in the living room. That day he told me that simply walking to the nearby kitchen was the equivalent of running a five-kilometer race for many people. One day his daily pain was so intense that he started crying. He thought it was a private moment, but Tyler, the younger of his two sons, saw him. "Boy, I felt like I let him down so much," Reggie said. That was Reggie.

Reggie thinking of others before himself is one of the recurring themes of his life. It runs throughout this book, which covers but is not limited to the barriers he broke at Kentucky, a college coaching career torpedoed by agendas and false accusations, life experiences with Muhammad Ali, Larry Bird, and the Harlem Globetrotters, and health problems that he would not have wished on anyone.

There are so many layers to Reggie's story. The best summation I can give: I have never met anyone who got knocked down by life as much as Reggie Warford and kept getting back up. With a smile.

We worked on the book for almost three years. During our time together, Reggie's breathing became more labored, every step became harder to take. Yet Reggie, through his dignity and courage, remained what he had been since I first met him as a starry-eyed kid: larger than life.

Memes, unlike just about everything else, had a banner year in 2020. One after another offered the laughs that kept us from crying. If you thought your 2020 sucked, Reggie's year would like to hold your beer.

In January, he almost died from septic shock after a respiratory illness landed him in the hospital. Two months later, his younger sister, Velma McKinney, died after a courageous battle with cancer. Her death happened shortly after COVID locked down the country. A heartbroken Reggie had to attend his sister's funeral service virtually. In June, the killing of George Floyd while in police custody stoked Reggie's anger and renewed fears of what could happen to his sons, Grant and Tyler, because of their skin color.

In September, a couple weeks after Reggie celebrated his sixty-sixth birthday, he was given months to live. Right before Christmas, he tested positive for COVID. He ended up in the intensive-care unit. When I texted his wife, Marisa, to ask if there was anything I could do, she wrote back, "Prayers." Countless of those were answered when Reggie recovered from the deadly virus. He returned home in early January.

As 2021 unfolded, Reggie, with Marisa by his side, consistently dealt with grim medical prognoses. By summer, his brother Ronnie and sisters Thelma Freeman and Sharon Greene visited over the Fourth of July so they could be together one last time. Yet as the leaves started to turn colors in October, Reggie was still hanging in there, still defying the odds.

The last chapter of his life did not reveal anything new. It did reinforce that Reggie was nothing if not a fighter. It was something he had done since he was a young boy and then at the University of Kentucky as the second Black scholarship basketball player in school history. History will see him as a pioneer.

Reggie became the first Black basketball player to graduate from Kentucky. He integrated Wildcats basketball. As much credit as he rightfully gets for helping Kentucky win the 1976 National Invitation Tournament Championship, his fingerprints are all over the Wildcats' 1978 national championship, too. If his time at Kentucky had gone sideways, would other Black players such as Wildcats legend Jack

"Goose" Givens, Merion Haskins, Larry Johnson, and James Lee have followed him there?

He would always laugh at my assertion that his Number 15 jersey belonged in the Rupp Arena rafters, with the jerseys of other legends such as Givens. He was the least charitable toward his own legacy than anyone I interviewed for this book. But there needs to be something that immortalizes Reggie. Something major.

Consider this book an argument for that.

1

Strange New World

Different worlds collided when Jimmy Dan Conner and Reggie Warford matched up in Memorial Coliseum, a basketball citadel in a hoops-crazed state. It was a new era of University of Kentucky basketball. Joe B. Hall had taken over as head coach for the legendary Adolph Rupp, the latter having been forced into retirement at the age of seventy after 876 wins and four national championships. Even gods aren't exempt from state retirement laws.

Rupp had left an impossible measuring stick but plenty of talent. The sophomores made up one of the most celebrated recruiting classes in school history. "The Super Kittens," as they had been dubbed, boasted size, speed, and especially pedigree. Four of the seven had won "prep player of the year" honors in their respective states.

Those players, no longer held back by a National Collegiate Athletic Association (NCAA) rule that limited them to playing most of their games for the freshmen squad, would form the nucleus of the next great Kentucky teams. And Conner, Mr. Kentucky Basketball in 1971, might lead them. A 6-foot-4 strapping guard, Conner boasted the skills and matinee looks to become one of the faces of the program. He was the idealized version of a Kentucky basketball player to the boosters and politicians who regularly attended Wildcat practices.

On this day, Hall pitted Conner against a freshman who was a curiosity to many Kentucky basketball fans, an affront to some. Reggie

Warford was a sinewy, lightning-fast guard with a syrupy left-handed jump shot. He was also Black.

The landmark Civil Rights Act had been passed in 1964, but integration had moved at a deliberate pace in the South, stalled by defiance and sometimes by violence. Reggie grew up drinking from "Colored Only"–designated water fountains and sitting in the balcony when he went to the movies. *Guess Who's Coming to Dinner?* was released in 1967, and the seminal movie challenged racial perceptions, even among progressives. It was the first movie that Reggie saw in a theater. He and his friends, relegated to the mezzanine section, were shocked to see Sidney Poitier's character sitting in the back of a taxicab with a white woman even though she was his fiancée. That reaction seems ludicrous now, but that was Reggie's world.

He was just the second Black scholarship basketball player in school history,[1] following Tom Payne, and he would arguably have it harder because of Payne. The big man had starred for only one season before turning pro. A couple months before Reggie left tiny Drakesboro in Muhlenberg County for Lexington, Payne was arrested in Georgia and charged with rape, giving ammunition to those against integrating Kentucky basketball.

None of that mattered to Reggie when he was tasked with guarding Conner in a half-court offense drill. Everything else around him was still so foreign, but Reggie never felt out of place on a basketball court. There, color didn't matter, at least not to Reggie. He simply loved to play, loved to compete.

Shortly after the drill started, Reggie poked the ball away from Conner. The two scrambled after the loose ball, but Conner shielded Reggie from it. After Conner retrieved it, he gave Reggie a hip check. He outweighed Reggie by almost fifty pounds and knocked him off balance. Conner dribbled in and drained a fifteen-foot jump shot. *Welcome to Kentucky basketball, freshman.*

VIPs watching practice clapped with approval. A little later, Reggie again knocked the ball away from Conner. Conner got the ball, dribbled past Reggie, and assisted on a basket. More applause. *Okay,* Reggie told himself, *I get it.* He knocked the ball away a third time but stayed back, thinking it was a smart play. Hall stopped practice and demanded the ball. "Come here!" he barked at Reggie.

Reggie trotted to half court. He thought his coach was going to compliment him on his quick hands. Hall turned to his right and heaved the ball to the end of the court where Kentucky's championship banners were hanging. "Get that damn ball!" Hall shouted. Reggie ran as fast as he could to retrieve it and brought it back to his coach.

Hall turned to his left and heaved the ball to the other end of the gym. Reggie again retrieved it and brought it back to his coach. Hall threw the ball a third time, firing it straight ahead. It bounced through a gym entrance. Reggie stood still as a statue, the blood rising in his cheeks. "I'm not going to get that," Reggie said softly but loudly enough for Hall to hear. He started walking off the court, adding, "You asked me to come here."

Sophomore forward Kevin Grevey intercepted him. "Reggie, he wanted you to run and dive after it," Grevey told him.

"Kevin, all he had to do was say it," Reggie said. "I'd have done anything he said."

A custodian was the only other Black man in the gym that day. He watched the scene from one of the upper levels of Memorial Coliseum. It brought tears to his eyes. "I saw you," he later told Reggie. "You were by yourself."

One basketball game had transcended sports on March 19, 1966, when Texas Western upset Kentucky 71–66 in the NCAA Men's Basketball Championship game. Texas Western had started five Black players against a blue-blood program that had yet to suit up a Black player. The game is hailed as a groundbreaking moment in sports, although the breakthrough was not nearly as dramatic in real time. The NCAA tournament was far from the spectacle that March Madness is today. The title game was played at ten o'clock on a Saturday night and was televised on tape delay in some parts of the country.

The game has been mythologized as a clash of binary forces, but there is plenty of gray, starting with Rupp. That game, because of the stark contrast between the teams involved, cast him as a recalcitrant if not bigoted taskmaster unwilling to embrace change. But Dick Gabriel, who has covered Kentucky sports more for than forty years, said Rupp had considered integrating the program in the early 1960s. Gabriel, who directed a documentary on Rupp, said the legendary coach met with Branch Rickey, the Brooklyn Dodgers owner who signed Jackie Robinson in 1945 to help break Major League Baseball's color line.

Rupp signed the first Black player in school history when he convinced Tom Payne to stay in state. Payne, a 7-foot-1 man among boys at Shawnee High School in Louisville, was one of the most coveted prep players in the country. He was often compared to Lew Alcindor, who led UCLA to three consecutive national championships in the late 1960s.

Rupp wanted a star to break the color line at Kentucky, a player so good that his talent would mitigate the color of his skin to integration opponents. Payne signed with Kentucky in 1969 but did not join the Wildcats until the 1970–1971 season after meeting eligibility requirements. He dominated as a sophomore, averaging double digits in points and rebounds but left Kentucky after just one season, heading for the National Basketball Association (NBA).

When Hall took over for Rupp in 1972, he zeroed in on two Black players, Reggie and 6-foot-6 forward Jerry Thruston, to continue the process that Payne had started. Thruston had won the Mr. Kentucky Basketball Award that year and was a Parade All-American. Recruiting experts Howard Garfinkel and Tom Konchalski of *High School Hoops Illustrated* named Reggie the "sleeper" of the South. Reggie and Thruston promised each other that they would go to Kentucky together after playing in the state All-Star game. "I knew I would have a best friend," Reggie said. "I would go to Kentucky with a brother."

Reggie committed to the Wildcats in May. Hall had sealed the deal by agreeing to speak at Drakesboro High School's boys' basketball banquet. Reggie signed his letter of intent the night of the banquet and called Thruston after he got home. Thruston dropped a bombshell: he was going to Kansas State. "Man, I've had too many calls," Thruston told his incredulous friend, "people telling me they're going to hurt me and calling me all kinds of names."

Reggie told Thruston that he and his family had also gotten some ugly phone calls (they probably would have gotten more, but the Warfords shared a phone line with ten other families, and outside callers often got a busy signal). But as they talked, it became clear that Reggie was not going to change Thruston's mind. He was on his own.

Reggie had at least one thing in common with his fellow freshmen when the Kentucky team convened on October 15, 1972, for the first practice of the season. They all got a metaphorical bucket of ice dumped on them. The Joe B. Hall who had recruited them bore little resemblance to the Joe B. Hall who entered the locker room that day.

"This is horseshit!" he yelled while banging on lockers. "Sit your asses down!" The freshmen, who had been standing around joking with one another, scrambled to find seats. Dave Miller, a 6-foot-7 forward, said in a pronounced country accent, "Ray-gee, I thought he told us he didn't curse." Reggie nodded. Hall had told that to his parents. Hall had also said that Kentucky did not practice on Sundays. That assurance had particularly resonated with his father and may have been the main reason why Reverend Roland Hayes Warford allowed Reggie to go to Kentucky despite his reservations. Now here Reggie was on a Sunday at his first Kentucky practice—and Hall had sworn before they even reached the court.

Reggie and the rest of the freshmen quickly learned there was no shallow end to Kentucky basketball. Coaches yelled at them to follow what the older players were doing. Two lines formed for a footwork and hand-quickness drill in the center court circle. Reggie found himself paired with Steve Lochmueller. A 6-foot-7 sophomore who weighed close to 250 pounds, Lochmueller was a physical specimen and later played for Kentucky's football team. If not for injuries, he might have had a career in the National Football League (NFL). The returning Wildcats knew to avoid Lochmueller in the drill where two players, their elbows tucked inside their legs, tried hitting each other's knees in the confined space. Reggie quickly found out why.

Lochmueller landed a blow that buckled Reggie's knee. Then another. And another. "He. Wore. Me. Out," Reggie said with a laugh. "I had been hit that hard plenty of times before, but I could always hit back."

After the drill, Assistant Coach Dick Parsons told Reggie, "There's a lot of stuff we've got to teach you, son, but the idea is not to get hit, so you need to stay away from Lochmueller."

Reggie's adjustment to Kentucky went far beyond that. He lived in Holmes Hall with the rest of the basketball players, but he was the only Black student who resided there. Other Black athletes, including those from the football team, lived on the other side of campus.

As an eighteen-year-old kid away from home for the first time, Reggie started college in virtual isolation. No one in his dormitory looked like him. No one on his team looked like him. Few in his classrooms looked like him. Even fewer who looked like him lived on campus because many Black students commuted.

It was against this backdrop that Hall erupted at Reggie for not diving after a loose ball.

Hall, for all his bluster, was just trying to make a point. But he did it in front of everyone—and all were white except for the custodian, who was out of sight. Reggie's pride simply would not allow him to accept such treatment, so he walked out of practice. Reggie was still seething when he got to his dorm room. He called home and told his father, with angry tears spilling out of his eyes, that he wanted out. "You don't quit," Roland Warford told him. "If you say you're going to do something, you're going to do something. You're not walking off."

Reggie next called his high school coach. He told Roby Harper to call Austin Peay, to call Western Kentucky, two schools that had heavily recruited Reggie. "Yeah," Harper said, "they said you might be giving me a call." He was referring to the Kentucky basketball coaches, who had already gotten in touch with one of Reggie's mentors. Harper tried to calm him down, but Reggie did not feel much better after they talked.

Shortly after that, there was knocking on Reggie's door. It was Dick Parsons, assistant coach turned peace broker. Reggie tried to hide the fact that he had been crying. "You can't leave, Reggie," said Parsons, who often played good cop to Hall's bad cop. "We're learning about you, and you about us. You don't want to do this. I know you can play." Reggie returned to practice the next day. Nothing was said to him about what had happened. No laps were run, no punishment dispensed. It was like a reset had been hit for Reggie and Kentucky basketball. If only it were that easy.

Jim Andrews was Kentucky's best player when Reggie arrived on campus. A 6-foot-11 center with an array of moves, he averaged 21.5 points per game in 1971–1972 on the way to first-team All Southeastern Conference (SEC) honors. It was a story after a game if he *didn't* score and rebound in double digits. Andrews considered the paint his and wasn't shy about letting his teammates know about it. "Don't bring that in here, little fella," Andrews would say if Reggie drove to the hoop.

Reggie, who also loved to talk trash, clicked with Andrews right away. Andrews looked at Reggie as just another player, something that Reggie never forgot because of Tom Payne. Andrews had played with Payne, and the two had become close despite their fierce battles in practice. Andrews saw Payne as a teammate and friend, but the situation of the larger context was not that simple in the late 1960s. When Kentucky played in the Deep South, the team had to find restaurants and hotels that allowed both white and Black people. Even in Lexington, some restaurants refused to serve them together.

"I go to schools to speak," Andrews said, "and I'm telling [students] these stories, and they're looking at me like I'm some sort of green-eyed monster. They can't believe that really happened." Payne lived it. His size and physicality made him a target of fans when the Wildcats played on the road. So did the color of his skin. "I've been spit on. I've had water thrown on me. I've been called every name in the book," Payne recalled of away games while he was at Kentucky. "Guys would foul me in ways that they weren't supposed to foul me, and the ref would just turn a blind eye to that, and when I fouled them back, they would call those."

Payne did not experience such blatant bigotry at the University of Kentucky itself, but he never felt welcome on campus. He became good friends with Derek Bryant, the first Black baseball player at Kentucky, and the two spent a lot of time in the part of Lexington where Bryant had grown up. If Payne did not have games or practices on weekends, he went home to Louisville. "I didn't have a social life on campus," Payne said. "It wasn't going to happen at that time. They just weren't going to relate to me at that time."

Reggie had similar experiences as a freshman. After one preseason practice in his freshman season, a prominent local booster sidled up to him after Hall left the gym. "I don't know what you think you're doing, boy," he said, "but you'll never play a minute here." Reggie shrugged off the comment, but as in the Hall ball-throwing incident, there was only so much he would abide.

He made a stand before one game by taking a seat during the singing of "My Old Kentucky Home," a school tradition. When the second line of the song came up, "'Tis summer, the darkies are gay," some students shouted, "The darkies!," and pointed at Reggie, laughing. Reggie, standing next to the team doctor, V. A. Jackson, said, "I can't do that." He sat down. Jackson tried to get him to stand, even putting his arms on Reggie's shoulders to try to help him up. Reggie shook his head. "Doc, I can't," he said. "I can't do this."

Boos echoed throughout Memorial Coliseum. His teammates were baffled. Why were their own fans booing before a game? "After the game, they wouldn't let anybody talk to me but the coaches, and everybody wanted to know what happened," Reggie said. He told Hall that he could not represent his race if they were getting called "darkies." "Reggie, it's just a song," Hall said. Not to Reggie, who refused to cede his ground. The incident became a cause célèbre because of something that had happened five years earlier but had become a contentious issue. Greg Page, who had been one of the first two Black football players, along with Nate Northington, to sign with Kentucky, had suffered a neck injury in practice that left him paralyzed. Page died a month later—the night before teammate Nick Northington became the first Black person to play in an SEC football game.

"They wanted to name a building after Greg Page, and white people didn't want a building named after him," Reggie said. "There was enough racial tension, and Jim Crow attitude was on campus, and the Black Student Union and Alpha Phi Alpha and Kappa Alpha Psi, both Black fraternities, were people that I knew. They talked to me because of the racial atmosphere. To them, I was just another person, like they were, feeling discriminated against. But I did not feel discriminated against because where I came from that's the way it was. Black and white people didn't live next to each other."

Maybe he was too young, too naive from his upbringing in the rural part of the state that was all he knew before arriving at Kentucky, but Reggie did not see himself as an agent of change. He *became* an agent of change but may have been the last to recognize that his being at Kentucky was about more than basketball. He simply was not into labels beyond *basketball player*.

But it could never be that simple, and overt racism is not all that Reggie had to deal with that first year. One incident made him wonder if he was the target of a seemingly harmless locker-room prank because of his skin color. Reggie was under a showerhead when a couple of teammates started physically moving him away from it. They moved him three more times, laughing, before Reggie walked out. It was probably just a joke played on an unsuspecting freshman, but Reggie also noticed that it had not been played on any of the other freshmen who were on scholarship. "When I looked around," he said, "I didn't feel like I had any friends."

Reggie wiped the soap off with a towel and dressed. He left the locker room without saying a word. For months, he showered in his dormitory after practice. Sometimes he wondered why he had not listened to those who had thought he was crazy for signing with Kentucky. "The Black people were telling me, 'Man, you're going to go up there and transfer to Western [Kentucky] or somewhere in a year, or you're going to come back home,'" Reggie said. "I didn't see what people told me I would see."

That isolation led to loneliness he had never felt in his life. Making it worse was that Reggie had trouble fitting in even with Lexington's Black community, who usually rooted for Louisville or Western Kentucky because those programs had Black players. "Sometimes it was even tough for me to go into the community," Reggie said, "because it was, 'Why are you there? You sellout. You're an Uncle Tom.'"

One time as Reggie was getting a haircut in the Black section of Lexington, the barber harangued Kentucky. Reggie felt obligated to defend the program, which led to a heated argument. Halfway through the haircut, Reggie got thrown out of the barbershop. He left with what he called a "clown" haircut—one side neatly trimmed, the other a thick Afro. It would have been comical had it not been so symbolic of how caught in the middle Reggie sometimes found himself between the racist white establishment and Black people who saw him as accepting, not challenging, it.

Hall was not oblivious to the challenges Reggie faced. He asked sophomore forward Bob Guyette to room with Reggie. Guyette had grown up in Illinois and had played against Black students. He didn't think twice about Hall's request, and he and Reggie were fine as roommates. Hall also asked a couple of his Black friends in Lexington to serve as mentors to Reggie, including Louis Stout, who had played for Hall at Regis University in Denver in the early 1960s. Stout "loved Joe B. I couldn't understand why," Reggie said. "Back then I couldn't understand why anybody loved Joe B."

Stout was one of the top officials in the state high school athletics governing body. Before meeting Stout, Reggie could remember only his maternal grandfather, Judge Dean, talking to whites on their level. That made Stout a little intimidating to Reggie, as did the fact that he often dressed in a suit. "Back home, I didn't see Black men in suits and ties," Reggie said, "except on Sundays." Stout provided Reggie with a sounding board; his close friendship with Hall made him a de facto line of communication between the two. If Reggie told Stout he had a problem, Hall was going to hear about it.

Vert Taylor also opened his home to Reggie. He, too, was a prominent Black man in Lexington, holding a lofty position in the state prison system, and had a son who was only about five years younger than Reggie. Reggie would go to the Taylors' home for meals and play basketball with Vince Taylor, who later played at Duke and at the professional level. "They were always there to look after me when my parents couldn't," Reggie said. "When things were bleak and lonely and bad, [Vert Taylor] gave me place to come to his house." People such as Louis Stout and Vert Taylor played critical roles in Reggie's acclimation, but they could do only so much.

The hardest part for Reggie his freshman year was the day-to-day loneliness, which he tried to mitigate with music. He taught himself to play piano on the twenty-third floor of the Towers, a dormitory where the football players lived. He had gravitated to the Towers because it may have been the one place on campus where he did not feel like the only Black person. Being there alleviated some of the loneliness, but he did not have many social options. Playing piano helped him pass the hours he was by himself.

Ping-Pong helped, too. Reggie became a whiz at it, and he made his closest friend that year over their epic Ping-Pong matches. Todd Carsteen and Reggie often drew crowds in the basement of Holmes Hall. They played a different kind of game than everyone else, spiking shots, putting wicked spin on the ball, and diving as if every point were life or death.

One other close friend Reggie made that year lived on his dormitory floor. The young man (whose name Reggie did not remember) had a severe case of muscular dystrophy and used a pencil in his mouth to operate a motorized wheelchair. He and Reggie bonded over their love of music. They sang together, and their favorite tune was "Never Been to Spain" by Three Dog Night. Left unsaid between them was how challenging it was for them to make friends. "I'm a young, eighteen-year-old Black athlete playing basketball, and one of my closest friends is a quadriplegic who is not able to go play Ping-Pong and can't go with me to eat," Reggie said. "I would hang out in his room sometimes, and sometimes he would come over to the door and visit with me."

Meeting girls, something most male college freshmen took for granted, was difficult for Reggie. There were so few Black girls on campus that he and a football player at Eastern Kentucky dated the same girl. One weekend, she went out with Reggie; the next weekend she went out with the football player. That was life his freshman year, and it could be distilled in this statement: "If I had a good day," Reggie said, "I had no one to share it with. From that perspective, I was the loneliest basketball player in America. I didn't have anyone that looked like me that I could commiserate with and talk with."

He drew strength from his family, especially his older brothers, Ronnie and Billy, and younger brother, Derrick. "Ronnie, Billy, and Derrick, in their own way, were extremely tough guys, so I wanted to be like them," Reggie said. "Crying about my situation wasn't going to make it any better, and I never wanted to appear weak in front of my older brothers. I wanted to be the type of person that they had shown me that you should be. You didn't need to start stuff, but you didn't let yourself get bullied, you didn't let yourself get talked down to."

That mindset helped Reggie push through the hardest year of his life. It also sustained him after tragedy struck. On January 28, 1973, Billy Warford was killed in a car accident. He was twenty-two. Billy had been a terrific athlete and had served two tours in Vietnam. He had been accepted to the state police academy. To Reggie, Billy had been invincible; it meant everything that Billy was so proud of his younger brother's being at Kentucky. Shortly before Billy's death, Reggie was home for Christmas break, and Billy asked him to be in his wedding. He implored Reggie to do something else for him. "Don't drink. Don't get high. Don't do all that crazy stuff," Billy said. "You've got a chance to make it."

Two weeks later, Reggie returned to his dormitory late on a Saturday night. The dorm phone rang, and it was Ronnie. Reggie was on the phone when Roby Harper burst through the front door. "Don't take that call!" he yelled. Reggie's high school coach had driven three hours to Lexington to give Reggie the devastating news in person but arrived a fraction too late.

Ronnie told Reggie that Billy had been killed earlier that night. Reggie's knees buckled. Harper grabbed him. "Not Billy," Reggie said in disbelief. "Nobody can kill Billy." Harper drove Reggie back to Drakesboro. As soon as Reggie got home, he and Ronnie went to the mortuary. The tragedy still did not seem real to Reggie even after he saw Billy. But then he and Ronnie were shown the car, which the accident had nearly cut in half. They took some comfort that Billy, who had broken his neck, died almost instantly.

Reggie turned to the same coping mechanism that had gotten him through his first semester at Kentucky. He found a pickup basketball game every day he was home, even the day of Billy's funeral. He sang at the service and never forgot how inconsolable his father was. Roland, as tough as any man Reggie knew, did not just cry during the final good-bye to Billy, he wailed. "He sounded like a wounded animal," Reggie said.

Reggie returned to Kentucky, just as Billy would have demanded. His first game back for the freshmen team, he scored 24 points. It was his best game of the season. By the end of the first season, he had played only a total of about fifty minutes in eight varsity games but averaged 16 points per game for the freshmen team and was named MVP of the squad.

Two of the four freshmen who had arrived with Reggie as scholarship players transferred after this first year. The other two would leave after their sophomore season. Reggie thought about transferring until a chance encounter with a sportswriter. He ran into D. G. FitzMaurice of the *Lexington Herald-Leader* one day at Memorial Coliseum. In those days, beat writers traveled with the teams they covered, and FitzMaurice, a New York City native, had taken a liking to Reggie and been protective of him. On one occasion, when the Wildcats had played at the University of Mississippi, FitzMaurice had seen Ku Klux Klan members gathering in the Oxford town square as Kentucky's team bus rolled through it. He quickly changed seats with Reggie, so Reggie had an aisle seat and could not be seen. Reggie was grateful for that. They became friendly, so naturally Reggie stopped to chat when he saw FitzMaurice at Memorial Coliseum. Reggie told him he was not sure if Kentucky was for him. He was considering transferring.

"Yeah, you're right," FitzMaurice said. "You probably should go. Everybody said you couldn't make it. You weren't tough enough." Maybe the New Yorker in FitzMaurice led him to be so blunt. Or maybe he saw something that Reggie did not see in himself. "It was reverse psychology on a naive kid," Reggie said. "I don't like people telling me what I can and can't do."

He was staying at Kentucky. For better and for worse.

2

Roots of Strength

The University of Kentucky stretched out Reggie Warford's world in every way imaginable—athletically, academically, and even socially, as limited as those opportunities were in Lexington. Yet one thing that never changed as Reggie outgrew the small world that had been his youth: Roland Hayes Warford was the undisputed man of the house. Reggie received a stark reminder of that while on a break his freshman year.

Reggie had unusually quick hands and never backed down from a fight. He consistently skirmished with teammates—not over race but over the fact that Reggie, at 6-foot-1 but only 155 pounds, competed against bigger players. His hands and quick propensity to use them once caused longtime Wildcats equipment manager Bill Keightley to observe he should have been a boxer.

During his freshman year, Reggie became enamored with a different hand-to-hand sport.

An ROTC armory offered martial arts classes, and the instructor, Sin The, seemed straight out of a Bruce Lee movie. He was a tenth-degree black belt and could do all the things Reggie had seen on TV and in the movies. Reggie started taking Sin The's classes and returned home feeling sure of himself. Maybe too sure.

Back home, he was sitting at the kitchen table as his father cooked fish, and he said he was getting an education so he could go further than his dad. He said he was going to be smarter than his dad and one day have a better house.

"Son," his father said, "I want all of that good stuff for you."

Reggie should have left it there, but he was eighteen years old and kept talking. Finally, his father said, "Boy, when did you get so smart?" He started standing up, like he was going to put Reggie in his place.

"Dad, you can't do that anymore," Reggie said.

"What do you mean? I can't do what anymore?" he said.

"Dad, I know kung fu," Reggie said.

He jumped up from the table and into a karate stance. Pow! Pow! Pow! Reggie's father hit him three times before he even reacted. "I was rescued by my momma," Reggie said. "He didn't knock me out, but he stunned me. It was like, 'What was I thinking?'"

The lesson Reggie's father gave him that day also reinforced that you did not mess with Roland Hayes Warford. Heck, the existence of his children was proof of that.

Roland met Valencia Dean in Union City, Tennessee, on June 1, 1948. Both were recent high school graduates and, Valencia's father, Judge Dean, had sent her to Union City for college. One day when she went with a date to the movies, Roland was there with some friends, and they started flirting with Valencia. Roland, with a pack of cigarettes rolled up in a sleeve of his white T-shirt, quickly dispensed with any subtleties. He stood up and asked Valencia what she was doing with the young man sitting next to her. Valencia's suitor got the message and left. It was a wise move. Roland had been given the nickname "We" because fighting him was like fighting two people. He was not shy about going after what he wanted.

Roland took Valencia, wearing a dress, home on the handlebars of his bicycle. He said he would return the next day to pick her up. She thought he meant in a car. When Roland arrived on his bicycle, Valencia went back inside and changed into a pair of blue jeans. They got married on June 25, 1948.

Roland was drafted by the army near the end of the Korean War and stationed at Fort Sill Military Base in Oklahoma. After his discharge in 1956, he settled his family in Drakesboro, Kentucky. Valencia had grown up in that rural hamlet, where her father was a community leader and one of the few Black people respected by the white residents.

Roland and Valencia had eight children: Ronnie, Billy, Pamela, Reggie, Derrick, twins Thelma and Velma, and Sharon. The family suffered tragedy when Pamela died as a baby in her crib.

Life was a daily struggle, as it was for many Black families, but the Warfords were resourceful. When Valencia made one of her chicken dinners, all 5-foot-3 of her would grab a live chicken by the neck and make a winding motion until the body slid off. She dropped the headless chicken into a boiling pot of water, removed it after the body expanded, plucked it, and gutted it. She then dipped it back in the hot water before setting it on the table for dinner. A chicken usually produced nine pieces, one for every person in the family. Roland, as the breadwinner, got the biggest piece. The girls were spared the neck because there were too many bones in it. The four boys chose from what was left. "You didn't want to be late for dinner," Reggie said. "If you got the neck, you had to eat it lightly because you didn't want to bite into the bone, and it wasn't very filling."

The Warfords lived off the land and government commodities that included bread, milk, and cheese. Roland hunted rabbits, squirrels, and turtles and often caught fish for dinner. Reggie was so conditioned to hunting that when he arrived at the University of Kentucky, someone had to tell him he could not shoot a rabbit just because he saw one.

The first time Reggie went to a restaurant, he was fourteen years old. They went to a local Bonanza Steakhouse, and Reggie and his younger siblings—Ronnie and Billy were already out of the house—gorged themselves on steak, potatoes, and green beans. "That was a big treat," Reggie said, "so we were all dressed up."

The Warfords did not have an indoor bathroom until Reggie was a freshman in high school. The outhouse fifty feet from the house consisted of a plank of wood with a circle cut in the middle over a six-foot hole that dumped waste into a sewer ditch. The ditch connected to a creek that carried fecal matter away. The Warfords dropped lye down the hole once or twice a week to make sure the hole did not get backed up.

Before the Warfords had an indoor bathroom, they filled a foot tub with boiled water, and the kids bathed in it on the back porch. The children also shared beds. The four brothers slept stacked in opposite directions, so everyone could fit in one bed. It was the same with the three sisters. "It was the way that you bake chicken legs to fit them all on a sheet pan," Ronnie Warford recalled.

Despite such hardships, the children never knew how tight money was, even if apples and oranges were a treat and served only on major holidays. They never went hungry and always lived in a clean house. "We didn't know we were poor because we were so surrounded by love," Thelma Warford said.

They also had a little adventure in their lives. The Warfords lived in a dry county, and Roland made extra money bootlegging. To get the illicit booze, he and others drove two hours west to Fulton County, which straddled Kentucky and Tennessee and sold alcohol in the part that was in Tennessee. Adults with kids piled into several cars for alcohol runs. A decoy car left at the same time and sped in the opposite direction. "They had a Trans-Am or a Firebird, and they would put that on the road with a Black driver, and they'd speed," Reggie recalled. "Nothing folks liked stopping more than a Black guy in a nice car in the South. My brothers and I would be in with a mom and a dad and a bunch of kids, and they'd give us some ice cream. We would be sitting on top of something on our way back, a car full of beer and liquor. I didn't know it was illegal. That's what they did for as long as I can remember."

Ice cream wasn't the only perk of bootlegging for Reggie and his siblings. They worked the card games that their grandfather, Judge Dean, ran. Dean did not stand more than 5-foot-2, but he enjoyed stature in even the white community. He also seemed much bigger because of the pearl-handled .38 revolver he always carried in a back pocket. Dean worked at the Muhlenberg County Courthouse and knew everybody. He also knew a lot of secrets. His card games included local politicians, judges, and law enforcement officials.

Some of the police officers who played in those card games were among those who tried to bust Roland and his cohorts for bootlegging. It was a tacit cat-and-mouse game. If the bootleggers could sneak the alcohol past the police, it was safe. The police would not raid any homes, especially during card games.

Reggie's spending money came from the quarters and dimes he received for serving drinks. The stakes in the card games were considerably higher. "If you were big, you gambled at Judge Dean's place, and tens of thousands of dollars were lost, and properties and houses," Reggie said. "It was a big-time game, and everybody who came was armed." That included his father, who also regularly carried a pearl-handled .38 revolver. Roland did not suffer perceived slights or threats any better than he did fools. He once shot a man and took off part of his scalp. James Dean, Valencia's cousin, had angrily left a card game at Judge Dean's house when Roland refused to lend him money but then returned with a shotgun and started shooting. Roland fired back, and James shouted that he had been hit. Judge Dean soon arrived on the scene. James was loaded into Judge's Cadillac and taken to the hospital. The police were not called. Befitting his first name, Judge adjudicated the matter, and there was nothing to appeal since his word was often the law.

"Nobody was going to cross my grandfather," Reggie said, "and the fact that [James] shot into his grandchildren's house, he's lucky that all they did was get him sewn up and sent back home. Daddy Judge did take my dad's gun for a little bit."

Valencia Warford may not have carried a gun, but she hardly fit the profile of the submissive wife relegated to the kitchen. "She could hammer a nail as well as any man," Reggie said. Valencia showed as much after concluding that two bedrooms were not enough for a family with seven kids. With the help of a family friend, John Morgan, and another worker, Valencia built the frame for an add-on room and installed the electrical wiring. The only thing it needed by the time the kids got home from school that day was the Sheetrock. "That would have taken most normal people two to three days to get done," Reggie said.

How Valencia paid for the new addition is another story that lives in family lore. Every month Roland received a $50 bond for his military service and stashed it in a footlocker. A keepsake from his army days, the footlocker was his bank since he did not trust traditional ones. When Valencia needed money for building supplies, she made an unauthorized withdrawal. Using a tiny screwdriver, she took the back hinges off the footlocker, helped herself to almost $1,000, and screwed the hinges back on. The next time Roland unlocked the box to make a deposit, he started shouting. Valencia came running. "Oh, Roland Hayes," she said, "somebody done robbed you." A couple of weeks later, Valencia told him what really had happened. "I've never seen such a heartbroken man," Reggie said with a laugh. "My mom didn't fear anybody."

Like her husband, Valencia was not to be messed with, as Roland found out one day.

Billy came home from a card game and told his mother that another lady kept trying to sit on Roland's lap. Valencia locked Roland out of the house. He was looking through a small window on the back door when his incensed wife threw a conch shell, which shattered the glass, and he started howling. Valencia quickly gathered the kids and took them to her sister's house. They stayed there for a couple of days before Judge Dean mediated peace.

Any issues that Roland's drinking and gambling caused in the marriage vanished when he underwent a transformation that few could have predicted. It happened after a church revival.

Valencia attended it with her youngest son, Derrick. Reggie waited for them outside. He was dribbling a basketball against a wall when his father came looking for his mother. Reggie said she was inside with Derrick. Two hours later, with Reggie still there dribbling the ball, his father walked out. Roland took a flask of whiskey out of his back pocket and tossed it in the bushes. He took the pack of cigarettes rolled up in the sleeve of his T-shirt and threw it away, too. "From that day until the day he died, I never heard him say a curse word. I never saw him run anybody down," Reggie said. "He started to go to church regularly. It was the first time [religion] made sense to him, that there was a life that superseded anything that he has now. And these things became worth it: be a better husband, be a better father. One day he said that he was called to the ministry."

The man whom Reggie had never seen read anything beyond the sports section of the newspaper immersed himself in the Bible and religious studies. Roland graduated to delivering fiery sermons from the pulpit, and his transformation had a profound effect on his children. "I never had to look past my nest to find good, strong men, starting with my father," said Derrick, the youngest of the four Warford brothers. "We grew up in a very spiritual home."

Sometimes, though, the focus on spirituality was almost too much. Grace before meals felt as if it might go on until the food got cold. "Sometimes we'd be looking at each other like, 'Gosh, please say thank you. God can hear you. You don't have to explain it,'" Reggie said.

One of Roland's sons followed him into the ministry. It may have been the most unlikely one, given Ronnie Warford's disposition as a young man.

Ronnie served two Vietnam tours, and even his officers had a healthy fear of him. They never knew what he was going to do. He was eventually transferred to California to serve the remainder of his army commitment. Something was missing from his life after he received an honorable discharge as a sergeant. He found it with the help of an army friend. The man was deeply religious, and he and Ronnie talked often on the telephone. They eventually met in Milwaukee, where the Warfords had family, and started going to church together. Ronnie went to college at night through the GI Bill. He joined the ministry and eventually earned a doctorate degree. Today, he is Dr. Ronald Warford—a man who embodies many things, especially how a person can change.

Growing up in Drakesboro, Ronnie was a bona fide tough guy. Six-foot-three and sturdy, he could hoist one hundred pounds over his head with either hand. He was agile and fast enough to catch rabbits with his hands. He strengthened those hands by crushing light bulbs and prided himself on being able to take a punch. "He would go to the American Legion, where he knew all these supposedly bad asses were," Reggie said. "He would challenge the ones that hated Black people most because they would be the ones willing to put the most money down. He'd tell them they could hit him anywhere but his face. He said, 'If you double me over, I give you money. If not, then you give me money.' They said he never lost."

Ronnie would also fight at the county fair, where money was offered to those who could stay on their feet in a fight with a boxing professional. Ronnie usually ended up knocking out the pro fighter. "Realistically, I could whip two grown men, and I'm not saying it in a boastful way," Ronnie said. "I just had that kind of physical strength and determination."

The one documented time that Ronnie did not fight—or, at least, fight back—was when he tried to sneak into the house after breaking curfew. His father was waiting for him and gave him a crack on the head with a lead pipe. Ronnie never broke curfew again.

The worst beating Reggie ever took came at the hands of Ronnie. Reggie tried to fight his older brother, and Ronnie clobbered him. It looked like something out of a cartoon, Ronnie slamming Reggie off the ground with the ease of throwing a rubber ball. Reggie could laugh about it later, but right after it he seethed and vowed revenge. One day he retrieved a .410 shotgun that his father kept in his bedroom. He loaded a bullet into it and hid in a hallway closet. Ronnie and his best friend, David Johnson, were in the kitchen cooking pecan pies when Reggie crept out of the closet. He waited as Ronnie came into view. A cousin, who was visiting from Buffalo, saw Reggie aiming the gun and pushed him from behind just as he pulled the trigger. "The shot sails over Ronnie's head," Reggie said. "He ducks and turns around, and it's the scariest thing I'd ever experienced in my life because he said, 'I've got you now.'" Reggie dropped the rifle and tore out the front door. After a lengthy chase, Ronnie finally gave up and went home.

Reggie ended up at the house of family friend John Morgan, who lived a couple of miles away. When he told Morgan he had taken a shot at Ronnie, Morgan looked at him incredulously. "You did *what?*"

Reggie stayed with the Morgans for five months to let things cool off. He finally came home because his father needed him.

Roland had finally been arrested for bootlegging and wanted his children in the courtroom to gain sympathy from the judge (he ended up serving thirty days in prison). Reggie and Ronnie eventually made up. Their brotherly bond brooked no grudges, something Reggie found out during a tense standoff between Black and white residents following an incident at Ditney Hill. Ditney Hill was in the Black section of Drakesboro and an oasis for kids. They played basketball there and rode bikes down the steep hills as a rite of passage. It was one of the few places in Drakesboro they could claim as their own, where they did not face restrictions because of their skin color.

But a white man named Marvin Gitgum decided to make trouble there one day. Gitgum was a Tarzan enthusiast. To Reggie, he was a couple threads short of a loin cloth. Gitgum liked to carry knives and often walked around shirtless in a pair of blue jeans or cutoff jean shorts. "He figured as long as he had his big knife, he could walk through the Black community, and we'd be scared of him," Reggie said.

One day, Reggie and his teenage friends were guarding clothes and other stuff the group had found. Gitgum, who was in his early twenties, started poking around their haul. Stevie Hines, Reggie's best friend, ran to tell the older boys. They started peddling their bikes toward the younger boys. Gitgum took some clothes and started running. They shouted at Reggie to stop him. Reggie grabbed his bow and arrow and fired. The arrow struck Gitgum when he was at the top of the fence. He yelped in pain and dropped the clothes.

A couple days later, he showed up at the field where Black locals gathered on Sundays for baseball, softball, and a community cookout. The field was not far from a large oak tree that had been used in the most recent lynching of a Black man in Muhlenberg County. The weekly outings usually drew close to one hundred people. That did not matter to Gitgum, who had payback on his mind and a long hunting knife strapped to his waist.

He walked past first base, where David Johnson was playing. "Hey, boy, this ain't the jungle," Johnson said. It was on. Johnson grabbed a shovel from a nearby tool shed, and he and Gitgum started circling one another. Ronnie ran in from the outfield to protect Reggie. The scene got more tense after county sheriff Clyde Ferrell pulled up with three others he had deputized. All had shotguns. Parents started getting in front of their children to shield them. Fortunately, Judge Dean and Ferrell were friends, and neither wanted bloodshed. Ferrell finally got Gitgum into the car, and someone led Johnson away.

That stare down may have been an extreme example of a region with frontier-justice sensibilities. But Reggie came of age in a strange, sometimes surreal intersection of guns, religion, sports, family, and race.

Reggie's parents grew up with Jim Crow laws that disenfranchised African Americans. Their children experienced racism that could be cruel and dehumanizing. Ronnie once had a job sweeping sidewalks outside of the county courthouse. Sometimes older men who congregated near the courthouse would spit tobacco juice where Ronnie was working and say, "Clean it up, ni—er." Ronnie held his temper most of the time, but other times the harassment became too much. During a high school basketball game, a man was shouting such vile things at Ronnie that Ronnie jumped into the stands. He needed a police escort to leave the gym.

Most seared into Ronnie's consciousness was the daily racism of his life. If he wanted a hamburger at a burger joint, he had to go to the side of the restaurant to order and eat it. He drank from water fountains that were designated "For Coloreds." He sat in the mezzanine section at the movies because the regular seats were for whites. It was much the same for Reggie and his younger siblings. "Growing up in the little community that we come from, there is a road that separated white town from Black town," Ronnie said. "You were discouraged to be across the road in white town after dark. That is not something they make up on TV. In the late '50s, early '60s, it was very much a defined place of where you could go and where you couldn't go."

Reggie learned that lesson as an eleven-year-old boy. He was in a service station one day, where a couple of locals were standing around talking. Reggie knew everyone and went to the water fountain reserved for whites. It wasn't an act of defiance; he was simply thirsty. As he drank, one of the men yanked him away from the fountain. He dragged Reggie outside to a rusty pipe that shot water into the air. The man forced Reggie to drink the water designated for Black people.

Reggie stomped home, crying in anger. When he got to his house, Billy asked him what was wrong. As Billy listened, it looked like the veins might burst through his thick forearms. He and Reggie returned to the store. Billy grabbed the man who had embarrassed Reggie and threw him to the ground as if tossing a bale of hay. "Don't you ever put your hands on my brother again!" he said. Reggie walked home with a sense of pride. He also thought how lucky the other men in the store were. Had it been Ronnie, they all would have had to answer to him. "Billy only whipped the guy who did it," Reggie said.

Billy and Ronnie made a similar statement after Muhlenberg County schools integrated in 1965. They were in high school at the time and arrived on the first day to a jarring sight. Someone had painted "whites" on one of the windows in the doors at the school's front entrance and "n—ers" on the other. Reggie watched as Ronnie, Billy, David Johnson, Jolly Jernigan, and several others broke down the door with the slur painted on it.

Reggie was only in sixth grade at the time. He could not have known it then, but he would do something similar, if more metaphorically, years later at the University of Kentucky.

3

A Shooting Star

When Reggie Warford unsuccessfully tried karate against his father, it was not the first time he had been humbled by one of his parents. His mother could also lay claim to that.

As a teenager, Reggie and a bunch of kids were racing near the Warford house. Few, if any, could beat Reggie.

Valencia Warford walked outside and asked Reggie if he thought he was fast. Was the sky blue? Of course he was fast. His mother challenged him to a race. Reggie laughed. His father warned, "Boy, you don't want to race your momma." Reggie had never seen his mother run but was already a couple inches taller and had longer legs. Valencia, an apron tied around her waist and wearing kitchen slippers, lined up next to Reggie.

After a starter shouted, "Go!," Valencia matched her son stride for stride. Then she said, "Bye," and beat him by three steps. Reggie fumed, saying he had slipped at the start, but that was his wounded pride talking. "She beat me, and I was trying," Reggie said. "Oh, it took me a long time to live that down."

This lesson in humility also illustrated that Reggie came from a family of great athletes. His grandfather, Judge Dean, had played baseball against touring Negro League teams, including the legendary Homestead Grays from Pittsburgh, and had taught two of his brothers. One of them, Henry, had a pitch known as "Dammit to Hell!"—what frustrated batters usually said after swatting futilely at his forkball. Brother Charlie also mowed down his share of batters despite having only one arm.

Reggie's first cousin, Bob Lanier, starred at St. Bonaventure and was the first overall pick of the 1970 NBA draft. Another cousin, Sharrieffa Barksdale, competed in the 1984 Summer Olympics in the 400-meter hurdles. Her brother, Valderious (Val), played football at the University of Tennessee from 1978 to 1980 and starred at safety. An interesting side note: Reggie and Val Barksdale did not speak for years because they had gone to schools that were fierce rivals (they eventually bridged that grudge).

Maybe the best athlete that Reggie ever saw was a distant cousin. Michelle Johnson was 5-10, wiry, and strong. She could seemingly outrun lightning. "She was so fast that if we had known people could get paid to run for a living, she would have been a world-class sprinter," said Reggie, who was a couple years younger than Johnson. "She was as fast as anybody." Known as Chelle, she delivered one of the greatest sports plays that Reggie ever saw. During a community softball game, Johnson was playing right-center field when a batter hit a mammoth shot. From Reggie's vantage point, it looked like a sure home run; any ball that cleared the field was as good as an automatic home run because of a steep drop-off. "She took off after that ball on a dead run," Reggie recalled. "She jumped up in the air, going down into the ravine. She makes the catch as she's going down and throws it back in the same motion. She was as good as just about any guy I had ever seen play softball. She played ball for as long as I could remember, and she could run. I knew she could outrun me, and I thought I was the fastest thing around. She was a world-class athlete. We knew it; the world just didn't know it."

Johnson, now in her seventies, still occasionally races young people—and wins. She recalls with fondness her days of playing basketball and softball with men, something that underscores how few opportunities there were for young Black girls in rural Kentucky. "If the opportunity would have been available, I believe I could have played [softball] professionally," Johnson said. "I always said if I had been in a different place and different time, I could have made something of myself. I don't regret it. I loved every minute of [my youth]."

To Reggie, the only all-around athlete comparable to Johnson was his brother Ronnie, who had everything, starting with toughness. When Ronnie played catcher in baseball, he often caught without a mask. He could be just as cavalier while at the plate. He sometimes bunted and did not even pause while rounding first, certain he was too fast for the first baseman to throw to second after Ronnie had gotten a base hit.

His blend of size, speed, and skill translated to the basketball court, too. Ronnie developed into such a player that there was talk of him joining his cousin, Bob Lanier, at St. Bonaventure. That opportunity never materialized, but the real what-might-have-been for Ronnie may have involved football. Muhlenberg County had eight high schools at the time, a large number for a rural community, but Drakesboro High School, which the Warfords attended, was not big enough to field a football team. "Ronnie would have been a Hall of Fame safety. He would have been Ronnie Lott or Jack Tatum," Reggie said. "He was 210 pounds, fast, could hit like a ton of bricks. If Ronnie had played football, I think he'd be like Bob Lanier in basketball."

Billy had similar size and athletic traits. He grew to be 6-foot-3 and looked as if he had been sculpted from granite. He had been a terrific point guard, earning all-district honors, before coaches moved him inside since he was the team's best rebounder. Like Ronnie, Billy could also fight. He boxed in the navy and lost just one bout. "I came along as Ronnie and Billy's little brother," Reggie said. "I had some insulation because people were afraid of them."

Derrick, the youngest Warford brother, excelled at baseball and basketball. Baseball was his top sport, and he may have been the best player among his brothers. As a shortstop and second baseman, he had limitless range. He could also hit. While playing in the Pony Leagues, Derrick led a Kentucky All-Star team to a national championship. Reggie was convinced that Derrick could have played at a big-time college program and possibly in the Major Leagues had a couple things broken his way.

Reggie was not the best athlete among his brothers, but he, too, was physically gifted. He was faster than Ronnie and Billy and had excellent hand–eye coordination. Reggie learned to play basketball on Ditney Hill, where he developed the toughness that became every bit his signature as his jump shot. Playing against older kids who included Ronnie and Billy, Reggie had to be tough.

As easily as basketball came to Reggie, he worked at it, too. In high school, the Drakesboro boys' basketball coach Roby Harper became so exasperated with Reggie breaking into the gym to shoot that he finally gave him a key. Harper, who had been a terrific player and often scrimmaged with the team, and Reggie became close. Reggie trusted him because Harper never tried to change Reggie's game, never tried to rein him in despite pervasive stereotypes. "He didn't care that I was Black," Reggie said. "If I had played for a system coach that you could only do it the coach's way, no one would have ever given me a second look."

Though Reggie stood only 6-foot-1, he could dunk while standing directly under the hoop. His quickness allowed him to get where he wanted with the ball, and his leaping ability allowed him to soar above defenders. His teammates nicknamed him "the Sneeze" because he was harder to stop than one.

Reggie could score at will—"I thought when I turned and looked at the basket that I had a chance to make it"—but he was just as happy to set up teammates such as Dale Todd, Ricky Harris, and Earl "Earthquake" Williams. Drakesboro won thirty-three games in Reggie's junior year and earned the moniker "Big Bad Red Machine." It advanced to the regional tournament before losing to powerhouse Owensboro, a school with ten times Drakesboro's enrollment. Williams may have been Drakesboro's best all-around player that season, and Reggie later learned why. "The truth be known, Earl was about twenty," he said with a laugh. "He came in from Mississippi, and nobody knew who he was. Back then they didn't keep real good records for Black folks."

Plenty of people knew who Reggie was, and he blossomed into a star. He scored 50 points through three quarters of one game before

Harper took him out because the score was so one-sided. Harper once said that Reggie could have scored 80 in a game if he had let him. Reggie's exploits were such that Drakesboro games became must-see events, even when the Drakesboro Cardinals were the visiting team. "They said I never played in a gym that wasn't filled," Reggie said. "I like that as much as anything that's ever been said of me."

College coaches were often in those gyms, especially during Reggie's senior season. One of them was a bespectacled man with ruddy cheeks. His name was Joe B. Hall.

Reggie received enough handwritten recruiting letters to fill a shoebox even if, as a naive country kid, he did not entirely understand what was happening. One came from Digger Phelps at Notre Dame, another from Bobby Knight during Knight's first season at Indiana. Knight attended one of Reggie's games and offered him a scholarship afterward. "I'm not giving you anything," Knight told Reggie. "You come up here, you're going to work your ass off. With your speed and quickness, I think you can be one of the best defensive guards in the Big Ten."

Reggie liked Knight but thought of himself rather as a scorer who could also play defense. And he had options closer to home. One was Vanderbilt University. Reggie took an official visit to the Nashville, Tennessee, school while still an underclassman in high school. He was hosted by Commodores forward Perry Wallace, the first Black scholarship basketball player in the SEC.[1] "I liked him very much, and he told me I could handle the academics," Reggie said. "For him, it was all about convincing me I could be something special."

What stood out to Reggie as much as his time spent with Wallace was the city of Nashville. He had never seen buildings so tall or so many lights, which effectively eliminated Vanderbilt from the running. "Nashville was seventy-nine miles away, and it might as well have been in another country," Reggie said.

Western Kentucky and Austin Peay, each within sixty miles of Drakesboro, also recruited Reggie hard. Reggie knew about Western Kentucky since many teachers at his high school had gone there.

He got to know Austin Peay on a different level, one that would be foreign to kids today. In the early 1970s, there were fewer restrictions on recruiting. Austin Peay assistant coach Leonard Hamilton would pick up Reggie and take him to Clarksville, Tennessee. There, Reggie scrimmaged with the Austin Peay players and got to know them. It felt like a perfect fit. He loved Hamilton, who was young, charismatic, and Black. It did not mean anything that Austin Peay was not a brand name. "I didn't know the difference between Division II and Division I schools," Reggie said. "There were a lot of things I didn't know."

His naïveté included the forces at work in his recruitment. "Western Kentucky coach Jim Richards, who was very good friends with Joe B. Hall, said, 'Joe, you've got to get this guy because he's good enough that he'll stay,' " Reggie remembered. Austin Peay coach Lake Kelly was also good friends with Hall. Like Richards, he recognized that Reggie's recruitment was bigger than basketball. So did Hamilton.

"Man," Hamilton said to Reggie one day, "I didn't know Kentucky really wanted you. They're after you pretty hard."

Reggie shrugged.

"Reggie, if they're after you like that, you've got to go," Hamilton said.

One day a short, rotund man in a brown suit visited Drakesboro High School. He looked important, and Reggie knew that someone from Kentucky was coming to watch practice. He thought it might be Adolph Rupp. It wasn't the legendary Wildcats coach, but rather Donald "Quack" Butler. A Kentucky booster, Butler helped recruit for the Kentucky football and basketball teams.

"Tell me," he said to Reggie, "can you play with fifteen white boys?"

"The question is," Reggie answered, "can they play with me?"

That *was* the question, especially with Rupp still the face of Kentucky basketball. Hall led the recruitment of Reggie, but during that period this was no indication that Rupp was retiring anytime soon. When Reggie met Rupp during a recruiting visit, Rupp welcomed him and said that he hoped Reggie would come to Kentucky.

Another of Reggie's Lexington visits illustrated just how different a world the University of Kentucky was to Reggie—and not just because of his skin color. He attended a dinner at Spindletop Hall, a university-owned mansion that preened on a sprawling farm. He had never been in a house with so many rooms—ones that had formal names. "I thought this was how rich folks lived," he said.

The dinner only added to that belief. Servers were dressed in white tuxedos. Reggie was the only Black person in the room eating dinner, not working it. A long buffet table was filled with trays of baked chicken, fried chicken, ham, roast beef, corn, green beans, mashed potatoes, and macaroni and cheese. Reggie gaped at the spread. He remembered his parents telling their children never to waste food by taking more than they could eat. Reggie helped himself to a modest dinner, taking just one piece of chicken, a couple scoops of mashed potatoes, and some green beans. Former Wildcats guard Jim LeMaster asked Reggie if he wanted more chicken. Reggie hesitated and said, "Well, yeah." Even after LeMaster told him to help himself to as much as he wanted, Reggie was not sure what to do. He took two pieces of chicken, rolled them up in napkins, and slid them into the pockets of his sports coat. "Jim put his hand on my shoulder," Reggie recalled. "He said, 'Reggie, put everything on your plate, and if you want more, we'll take it back to your room.' He took it out of my pocket and put it on my plate. It was one of the nicest things anybody's ever done for me. I was that embarrassed, but if you don't know, you don't know."

Reggie did not know what to do when salads were brought to his table. He had never eaten one. The waiter asked each person what kind of salad dressing they wanted. He heard Roger Woods, another recruit, say, "French." That is what Reggie got on his salad.

Roland Warford was as skeptical about the recruiting process as Reggie was naive about it. He did not get caught up in it any more than he had Reggie's growing stature as a basketball player. Even as Reggie blossomed into a star, he was still Reggie at home. Chores, such as mopping floors and cleaning the chicken coop, came before basketball.

"All of that stuff had to get done before I went to games," Reggie said. "The JV game would be going on, and I'd walk in wearing big hair and a jumpsuit, which was usually lavender."

After Kentucky offered Reggie a scholarship, Roland sat Reggie down for a talk. "Coach Hall told us everything's paid for, and it's worth so many thousands of dollars," Reggie recalled. "My dad said, 'Boy, what do you think just happened?' I said, 'Well, they offered me a full scholarship.' Nobody I knew had ever gotten one. He said, 'They're going to give you a scholarship, and you're an athlete? Don't you think you have to be a scholar?' I said, 'Dad, I'm a really good student.' He said, 'Boy, ain't no white man going to give you money to go to school because you can dribble a basketball. What they're going to do is take you up there and put you on one of them work camps in between your schooling.'"

Reggie dismissed the thought because his father had never gone to college—although he did not dare say that out loud. What helped allay his father's concerns was that Roby Harper wanted Reggie to go to Kentucky. Roland and Valencia trusted Harper as much as Reggie did and so allowed their son to sign with the Wildcats.

Right after Reggie graduated from high school, his father asked him what he was going to do. Reggie said he planned to play basketball until it was time to leave for college. "You grown," Roland said. "You got to go."

Reggie left for Lexington shortly after that. His luggage included five shirts, four pairs of pants, and little else. He also had a sports jacket that Harper and family friend Velma Cottrell had bought him. The first person Reggie met after riding to Kentucky with a couple of football players, including future star Sonny Collins, gave him an unforgettable welcome to Lexington. Patty Eyster was waiting for him outside the apartment building that she managed. She was a beguiling sight to a seventeen-year-old kid who had little experience with girls. Eyster wore a denim-blue shirt tied around her waist and blue jean shorts. She was Daisy Duke before Daisy Duke, a complete knockout. With a cigarette in one hand and a glass of bourbon in the other, Eyster intimidated the heck out of Reggie, especially after she started talking.

"I had never heard a woman say those cuss words before," Reggie said laughing.

The language only got saltier when Eyster asked Reggie about his linens. He looked at her blankly. She asked what he planned to sleep on. Reggie shrugged. Eyster called Joe B. Hall.

"Joe, goddammit, this boy done come up here, and he ain't brought shit," she said.

The coarse language masked the soft spot Eyster developed immediately for Reggie.

"Here's this little thing just dropped out of heaven on this corner," she recalled. "I thought, 'Oh, this poor, pitiful little child.'" Eyster became his mother *and* father away from home. Reggie's apartment was close to her office, and she pounded on his door every morning between 7:00 and 7:30 with the equally brusque wake-up call, "Get your ass up." Eyster cooked breakfast every morning, and the prodigious amounts of food both awed and delighted Reggie. She would make a dozen eggs, biscuits, and a pound of bacon. There were also sausage patties, fresh-squeezed orange juice, and sometimes grits. "I never had stuff like that," Reggie said. "Twelve, thirteen, fourteen pieces of bacon? Yeah, I could get into that."

Reggie worked road construction that summer, and white men made up most of the crew. One of its tasks was demolishing a road that was to be replaced by a highway. The older workers told Reggie that since he was so fast, he had to drop the lit dynamite down a hole and then run like hell. They would laugh and high-five one another after every explosion. After a couple of days, Reggie checked in with Hall, and his new coach asked him about work. Reggie told him what he was doing. "What do you mean?" Hall said. "You're handling dynamite?" He immediately made a phone call. The next day at work Reggie received cold stares and a new task. "They hated me until I left," Reggie said of his coworkers. Not that he paid it any mind—he wasn't in Lexington to work on a road crew. He was there to play basketball and go to school.

Kentucky won eighteen regular-season games and the SEC title in Reggie's freshman season. It advanced to the NCAA tournament and in the second round played Austin Peay. The Governors were led by African American freshman guard James "Fly" Williams, a dynamic scorer and New York City playground legend. Williams, whom Reggie had scrimmaged with at Austin Peay, scored 26 points against Kentucky, helping the Governors take the Wildcats to overtime. Kentucky avoided the upset, but Reggie did not play in its 106–100 victory. He watched as Williams hoisted thirty-one shots and played with the freedom that Reggie rarely enjoyed at Kentucky.

Reggie played sparingly in the varsity games. Before one of them, he received a reminder of how different he was from his teammates. Kentucky was playing at Alabama, which had been integrated by former Wildcats basketball player C. M. Newton. The Crimson Tide had a handful of prominent Black players, including Charles Cleveland, Leon Douglas, and Wendell Hudson, the first Black athlete to receive a scholarship in any sport at Alabama. "There were more Black players on Alabama's team than [on] all the other teams in the [Southeastern] Conference combined," Reggie said.

Reggie, stretching near midcourt before tip-off, looked around the arena. A couple of Alabama's Black players teased Reggie about being Kentucky's only player of color. One said, "Come on, man, I know. You're rooting for us, ain't you?" That never occurred to Reggie, but the question reinforced that he stood apart.

He got another reminder after the season at Kentucky's annual banquet. Reggie and Louis Stout and his wife were the only Black people attending the celebration. "There were plenty of [other] Blacks," Reggie said. "They were serving."

Each player had been allotted two tickets for guests. Reggie's parents were unable to attend, so he gave his tickets to a couple of white students he had befriended—white girls. Each was given a corsage and a small photo card of Reggie since they were his guests. One of Reggie's teammates was aghast—not at Reggie having two white girls as guests but at the perception of it. In a vacuum, the teammate's overreaction would have been preposterous, but this was Kentucky in 1973.

"I wasn't like the movie *Blazing Saddles,* walking around, 'Oh, where are [the] white women at?'" Reggie said. "My sisters are Black and beautiful, so I knew that there were very attractive Black women out there. I had some in my family, and others had them in their families."

A day after the banquet, though, Hall pulled Reggie aside during a voluntary workout. He asked Reggie if he had been good to him. A perplexed Reggie said that they were fine. Hall asked if he was dating white girls. "I wasn't dating anybody, but I had been seen in public with people and stuff," Reggie said. "I said, 'What do you want me to do? Just play basketball and then go over to the projects and hang out there at night?' I was always a Black athlete. There was no day that I escaped that where it was just Reggie. It was always in the context of, 'He's our Black guy.'"

Hall stayed committed to bringing more Black players into the program. Reggie hosted a handful of them on recruiting visits, but as his freshman year neared the end, none had signed with Kentucky. The Wildcats remained in the running for Larry Johnson and Merion Haskins. Both, like Reggie, were Kentucky kids from rural backgrounds. Reggie saw them as lifelines as much as future teammates. During one phone conversation with Haskins, Reggie said, "I can't stay by myself. I need you."

4

Staying the Course

Seven years before Tom Payne became the first Black player to sign with Kentucky in 1970, Clem Haskins helped make history in the state of Kentucky. He and Dwight Smith arrived at Western Kentucky University, becoming the first two Black players to suit up for the Hilltoppers. Their success helped pave the way for the integration of basketball programs in the South. Haskins and Smith led the Hilltoppers to a 66–15 record in their three varsity seasons, each scoring more than 1,000 career points.[1]

The two came heartbreakingly close to leading Western Kentucky against Kentucky in the Mideast Regional Final of the 1966 NCAA Men's Basketball Tournament. The Hilltoppers lost 80–79 to Michigan after Cazzie Russell made two free throws following a questionable call near the end of the game. Clem Haskins was taken third in the 1967 NBA draft, two picks after Russell. He enjoyed a solid NBA career followed by a long college coaching career.

Merion Haskins continued the family legacy, developing into an All-State forward in the early 1970s. It seemed like a foregone conclusion that he would follow his older brother to Western Kentucky. University of Kentucky assistant coach Dick Parsons, however, was shocked when he learned that Haskins had not yet signed anywhere by spring of his senior year of high school. They talked at an All-Star game in Sharon, Pennsylvania, north of Pittsburgh. "I was impressed with him," Haskins said of Parsons. "I found him to be a very honest person. He'd tell you the way it was and that I would be looked after as far as the social aspect of everything."

The social and cultural adjustment he would seemingly face at Kentucky did not deter Haskins. The Campbellsville native had grown up in a part of Kentucky that was predominately white. "Some of my best friends were white people," Haskins said. "I didn't know people hated me because of my skin color until someone told me that. As you get older, you become aware of things like that, but at seventeen and eighteen years old, I didn't know. I knew I was different, but my mother and daddy taught us you treat people the way you want to be treated."

Haskins and Larry Johnson met at the same All-Star game where Haskins connected with Parsons. Johnson also made a favorable impression on Haskins. He was long and athletic and a terrific ball handler. With such large hands, he could catch a basketball with one hand, hold it, and then set it on the ground. He and Haskins became friends, and Kentucky offered each of them a scholarship.

Haskins and Johnson visited Kentucky together and met Reggie. They signed with the Wildcats, and Reggie helped them acclimate at Kentucky. "We didn't know what to do or know what to expect, so Reggie made the transition a lot easier," Johnson said. "He looked out for us. He took us under his wing."

The three became such fast friends that Haskins and Johnson took a what's-yours-is-mine approach to one of Reggie's prized possessions. Reggie owned a white Gran Torino with a black-vinyl roof. He allowed Haskins and Johnson to drive it occasionally. Unbeknownst to Reggie, they interpreted his borrowing policy a lot more liberally than he did. Haskins talked Johnson into getting a key made for it, and they drove Reggie's Gran Torino all over the state. Before long, Reggie started to wonder what was going on with his beloved car. He always parked at a restaurant across the street from campus, usually under the same tree, but sometimes he found the car parked elsewhere in the lot. Equally perplexing to Reggie were times when the gas gauge was lower than what he had remembered.

Decades later, *after* their friendship had been cemented, Haskins and Johnson fessed up to Reggie. The three were in a Lexington restaurant when Haskins and Johnson said they had to tell Reggie something. Haskins started laughing so hard that he got up from the table. Johnson finally said, "Reggie, we stole your car." "Dadgummit," Reggie said, laughing, "I knew it!" It was a small price to pay for the friendship and support that Haskins and Johnson provided for Reggie at Kentucky.

Their first season together gave them little to laugh about. Kentucky stumbled through a 13–13 season in 1973–1974, after coming within a game of the Final Four the previous season.

Joe B. Hall came under intense fire. Some fans hung likenesses of the second-year coach in effigy. Reggie did not have much more love for Hall than the teed-off fans. He spent the season all but tethered to the bench, playing in only seven games and for a total of only fourteen minutes, the fewest among the team. "When you're on a team that's not very good, everybody thinks he can play," Reggie said. "I was upset most of the year."

Reggie's lack of minutes had a lot to do with the players ahead of him. Kentucky, while undersized, had returned its top guards from the previous season: Ronnie Lyons (captain), Kevin Grevey, Jimmy Dan Conner, and Mike Flynn. Grevey led Kentucky in scoring in 1973–1974 (21.1 points per game), and Conner (12.0) and Flynn (11.5) also averaged double digits in scoring.

Reggie knew he could play with them, something he felt he consistently showed in practice. But, he said, "being as good as someone is not being better. If you're as good, then it's the coach's decision. I just thought the coaches preferred to play them more than me."

Hall and Reggie were still learning about one another. Sometimes Reggie felt stifled by the structure his coach demanded. One philosophical difference was that Hall believed that how you practiced was how you would play in a game. Reggie saw practice as a time to try different things and see what might work in a game.

That cavalier mentality made it hard for Reggie to gain Hall's trust. Nothing better illustrated the disconnect between the two than a play Reggie made in practice in his sophomore season. Reggie had the ball at the top of the key against Flynn. He froze Flynn with a jab step and had a clear lane to the hoop. Flynn was four inches taller than Reggie, but Reggie negated that advantage by using only his left hand to lay in the ball. He thought it was a clever play, but Hall groused that it was showboat basketball. You did not play showboat basketball at Kentucky. Reggie got so frustrated that he said, "You're telling me Julius Erving couldn't play for this team because he uses one hand?"

The subtext of showboat basketball and Reggie's Dr. J reference was impossible to ignore. "I played like a Black player, and there was a difference between how a Black player played and a white player played most of the time," Reggie said. "They hadn't seen guys hang in the air, double-clutch, and Joe B. hated that kind of stuff. I'm on a team with all white guys, so they weren't going to have them play like me." Hall's preferred player, at least early in Reggie's career, was the buttoned-down one, the fundamentalist who threw every bounce pass with his thumbs down, forming a ninety-degree angle with the floor. Hall forbid his players from dunking, even in practice.

Ironically, Reggie compared most to Grevey, Kentucky's best player. Grevey had such hops that his teammates nicknamed him the "Kangaroo Kid." Like Reggie, he was a southpaw and a deadeye shooter. The finger rolls and floaters that Reggie used were also a part of Grevey's game. The biggest difference between the two was that Grevey showcased his talents in front of packed crowds at Memorial Coliseum, whereas Reggie showcased his on dirt and asphalt courts in Lexington, often in Black sections of the city. The pickup games that Reggie sought out allowed him to play with the unrestrained joy that largely eluded him at Kentucky.

The contrasting fortunes of Reggie and Grevey—and the fact that Grevey, Conner, and Flynn were returning after the 1973–1974 season—left Reggie frustrated about his future at Kentucky. He went to Hall's office one day to tell him he planned to transfer. He never made it there. He was walking in a Memorial Coliseum hallway when he nearly did a double take. "Ham, what are you doing here?" he said to Austin Peay assistant coach Leonard Hamilton. The two started talking: Hamilton said he was interviewing with Hall, and Reggie said he was leaving Kentucky. "No, no, no, just hang on," Hamilton told Reggie. "I'll talk to you." Hamilton did not need to talk to Reggie after Hall hired Hamilton as an assistant coach. "I wasn't going anywhere," Reggie said, "because I knew that Ham respected me."

Hall made another hire after the 1973–1974 season. Reggie was familiar with this coach, too. Lynn Nance had spent three seasons as an assistant coach at the University of Washington from 1968 to 1970, where he also had played. He made a surprise move in 1970, though, joining the FBI as a special agent. He was forced into early retirement after getting wounded in the line of duty and went to work for the NCAA as an investigator.

That is how he and Reggie had met earlier. The previous year Nance had arrived in Lexington to investigate a possible recruiting violation during an official visit taken by Philadelphia guard Richie Laurel. Reggie had hosted Laurel and knew that for a city kid the social options at Kentucky might not be so appealing. He called a girl he knew at nearby Kentucky State, a historically Black university, and he took Laurel there to go dancing and meet girls. The NCAA did not allow prospective recruits to venture more than eighteen miles off campus; Reggie had taken Laurel twenty-three miles off campus. He had no idea he had done anything wrong. He met with Nance, and the latter concluded that it had been an honest mistake. "We got a hand slap, and he got a job. If you were a conspiracy theorist, you'd worry about that," Reggie said laughing.

The additions of Hamilton and Nance were not the only changes Hall made in the wake of a disappointing season. He signed one of the top recruiting classes in the country, one that included two local Black kids, Jack Givens and James Lee.

Givens won Mr. Kentucky Basketball in 1974 after starring at Bryan Station High School in Lexington. Like Givens, Lee stayed home after starring at Henry Clay High School in Lexington. The two gave Kentucky a pair of skilled and athletic forwards. Mike Phillips, 6-foot-10, and Rick Robey, 6-foot-11, also signed with the Wildcats, providing size that the Wildcats desperately needed. The arrival of

Givens, Lee, Phillips, and Robey gave Kentucky a recruiting class that rivaled the "Super Kittens."

Following a .500 season that was unacceptable by Kentucky's standards, the 1974 preseason training program seemed more like boot camp. It started after Labor Day, following a two-week period in which the players eased back into a routine by playing pickup ball. Weight training became such a priority that Kentucky moved from its own weight room in Memorial Coliseum to the one used by the football team. On days the players lifted, they dressed at Memorial Coliseum and then had fifteen minutes to run two miles to the weight room. Sometimes the coaches drove the players to a spot five miles away from campus and dropped them off. To make sure no one loafed, they followed in cars as the players ran back.

By the start of preseason practice in October, the players' bodies looked different. Reggie, who had arrived at Kentucky weighing 155 pounds, gained 20 pounds after hitting the weights and consuming 5,000–6,000 calories a day. The added muscle did not compromise his speed or quickness. He grew to love the weight room. It was there he showed that he was one of the strongest players on the team. He could bench press 265 pounds and squat 400. As he transformed his body, he wondered if maybe he should switch to football even though he had never played it.

His weight-room statistics did include a memorable tackle that provided his teammates with a much-welcomed diversion. It involved Nance, who stood 6-foot-7, weighed 225 pounds, and had extensive self-defense training from his FBI background. One day while Nance was lifting with the team, some of the players were talking about how no one could take Reggie down in karate. Nance gave Reggie a dismissive look. Reggie turned down several Nance challenges before they started circling each other. "He made a fake, and I went in behind him, did a leg sweep, pulled him back, and knocked him on his ass," Reggie said, laughing. "I would have hit him three times before he tried to get up if we would have been in a real fight. He jumped up, nostrils flaring. I knew to stop."

The feisty tone set in the preseason carried over to the season. Practices were ultraphysical, and both new assistant coaches added a different dynamic to drills. Hamilton, a defensive guru, often jumped into the fray to demonstrate what he was teaching. So did Nance.

"Nance didn't have any problems getting out there and throwing elbows with the bigs, and he was always a little bit salty," Reggie said. "When we started to look like men, we started to play like men."

Reggie crushed the preseason program and was in the best shape of his life. Now a junior, he was ready to make his move on the new-look Wildcats.

Then basketball was taken from him.

This upheaval started harmlessly enough. Reggie, a little late getting to class one day, ran up the stairs of White Hall, covering five in single bounds. Near the top, he blacked out. A student behind Reggie caught him. Reggie quickly regained consciousness, but the incident shook him. It was as if someone had turned out the lights on him. He could not ignore it, given his family history.

Reggie's sister Velma had been born with a hole in her heart and was prone to gushing nosebleeds, likely the result of blood vessels bursting. "It was the most awful thing you could ever see coming out of a little kid," Reggie said. Sometimes Valencia Warford feared for her daughter's life. As she tried to stop the nose bleeds, she would recite from Ezekial 6:16: "And when I passed by thee and saw the polluted and dying on blood . . . I say onto thee while thoust was in thy blood. Velma live."

A heart biopsy revealed that Reggie had hypertrophic cardiomy-opathy. In layman's terms, one side of Reggie's heart was enlarged, compromising its ability to pump blood. He was stunned when told the condition could lead to sudden death if not properly managed. He felt worse when doctors told him he could no longer play basketball.

"That was enough to just literally make me sick," he remembered. "Back then, eighteen- and nineteen-year-old athletes didn't just die."

Especially not ones like Reggie. He was *that* guy teammates told to slow down during running drills so he would not make them look bad. Kentucky required every player to pass a conditioning test before the season. They had to run thirteen 220-yard sprints, and guards were required to finish each sprint in less than thirty seconds. Reggie had made that challenge look easy less than a month before the diagnosis shattered his world.

Kentucky assured Reggie and his parents that it would honor his scholarship. Hall kept Reggie close to the team by requiring him to attend practice. But that made him feel even worse, especially when Kevin Grevey would say, "Man, wish you were out here, Reg." It killed Reggie not to be on the court with Grevey and the rest of his teammates. As he was growing up, he had never just sat and watched an entire basketball game on TV. He was not wired that way, which explains why he knew so little about Kentucky's stature before arriving in Lexington. He lived to compete as much as he did to play, a trait that got him summoned to Hall's office early in his Kentucky career.

Reggie had been playing pickup ball in the Black section of Lexington, and some of the players, still wary if not resentful of Reggie for playing for Kentucky, asked if he could jump. One of them jumped up and grabbed the rim, as if making the point that maybe Reggie couldn't jump. Reggie looked around and saw a car nearby. He took a running start and jumped over it: not the hood but the body of the car—something Reggie was not even sure he could do as he pulled his legs up to his chest after jumping off one foot. The other players started hooting and hollering after he cleared the car. He did not make this newfound skill a regular habit, but he used it to win a couple of bets. News of Reggie jumping over cars eventually found their way to Hall. He quickly put an end to it, and Reggie could live with that.

He did not know how to live with Hall and Kentucky telling him he could no longer play basketball because of his heart condition. As much support as he received, including from his mother, who stayed in a Lexington hotel for a couple of weeks after the diagnosis, he was miserable. During one practice, as he watched his teammates, he finally processed what never playing basketball again meant. He could not accept it. If he died playing, he could think of no better way of exiting earth than by draining an outside shot and taking one final breath.

Years later Reggie would acknowledge the foolhardiness of such thinking. But he was young; basketball was his world. No matter what doctors said, he was never going to stop playing. He told Hall that he would sign anything so he could rejoin the team. The school reluctantly conceded to a waiver, but Reggie needed his parents to sign it, too. He convinced his mother, telling her that he would never stop playing basketball, even if that meant playing pick-up ball for the rest of his life. "I might as well get my education while I'm doing it," he told her.

Reggie returned to the team, and no one treated him differently. The screens he ran into at practice were just as physical, the coaches just as demanding, especially Hall. And Hall spared no one after an early-season loss at Indiana. The third-ranked Hoosiers buried the Wildcats 98–74, and Hall fumed about more than the final score.

Near the end of the game, Reggie was at the scorer's table waiting to check into the game. Knight was there, too, still working the referees. An annoyed Hall told Knight, "You can call your boys off." Knight retorted, "You coach your team!" Before returning to their respective benches, Knight gave what he later called a playful slap to the back of Hall's head. Hall went ballistic. So did Nance, who got in a karate stance before someone grabbed him. After the game, the teams did not shake hands, and Hall ordered his players onto the team bus before they showered. As soon as the bus pulled into Memorial Coliseum following a four-hour drive, Hall told the players to hit the floor.

They practiced until classes started. They returned that afternoon for another practice. It was brutal, but it worked. Kentucky beat ninth-ranked North Carolina two days later at Memorial Coliseum. Eleven days later, the Wildcats were so physical in a 22-point win against Washington State that Cougars coach George Raveling called them the "Karate Kats."

"They said we were setting college basketball back because we were too physical," Reggie said.

The Wildcats went 22–5 that season and roared into the NCAA tournament.[2] Two wins sent them to the regional finals—and set up a rematch against top-ranked and undefeated Indiana.

Reggie and his teammates knew something was different the day before the game when Hall ordered them to get taped for practice. They normally had only a walkthrough the day before a game, essentially practice at half speed so the coaches could go through the game plan. Hall wanted no part of that.

Team managers cleared the gym of everyone else, including a TV production crew and announcers. Hall then picked five players to simulate Indiana's motion and screening offense and put his starters on the floor to defend it. The coaches told James Lee to set a hard pick on Bob Guyette. Lee hit Guyette so hard that he split his head open. It was that way for the next two hours. "It was like a M*A*S*H unit, and [Hall] would just put the next guy in," Reggie said. "That is absolutely the roughest practice that's ever been held on a college floor."

The roughness carried over to the game. Guyette, playing with stitches, barreled through a screen on Indiana's first possession. "No pretense of going over it," Reggie said. "He just clotheslined the guy who set it and knocked his butt down." The teams traded blows for forty minutes before Kentucky outlasted Indiana, 92–90, to advance to the Final Four. The game, an instant classic, was one of the best wins in school history. The Wildcats beat Syracuse in a national semifinal game, and only a late rally by UCLA, which had upended Louisville, spoiled a "Bluegrass State" national-title game. The Wildcats did not play their best against the Bruins, losing 92–85. UCLA claimed its tenth national championship under John Wooden, the last one for the legendary coach. Despite the disappointing finish, the season redeemed Hall for the 13–13 record the previous year. But it was another struggle for Reggie.

The heart diagnosis had set him back, and the missed practices never allowed him to make a bid for significant playing time (he played in fourteen games and averaged 3.6 minutes per game). There were two noteworthy moments for Reggie, though. The first came when five Black players were on the floor for the first time in program history. Reggie recognized the significance as he was at the scorer's table, waiting to join Jack Givens, James Lee, Larry Johnson, and Merion Haskins. The second came in the penultimate game of the regular season: Kentucky routed Vanderbilt 109–84, and Reggie made the longest unofficial shot in Memorial Coliseum history.

Reggie, inbounding the ball on Kentucky's baseline with just a couple seconds left in the game, threw a baseball pass to Mike Phillips for an alley-oop. Phillips jumped but pulled his hands away when he saw the ball going into the basket. The fans and Reggie's teammates went nuts. Reggie, forgetting that no time had elapsed, ran sheepishly to the locker room thinking the game was over. "Over the years, if everyone who told me they were at that game was really at that game, that would be twice as many as Memorial Coliseum could hold," Reggie said. "Or it became conflated with, 'Oh, you did that to win the game,' I made a 93-footer that didn't count, and we were up by 20."

Reggie's recollection of the shot is similar to his reaction immediately after it. It almost embarrassed him. He did not want to be remembered for some fluke shot. He wanted to make his mark on Kentucky basketball, to be a reason why the Wildcats won games. That did not happen his junior season, but no matter how much it frustrated him, he never put himself above the team. "The worst thing you can do is complain when you're on a winning team, and I didn't want to do that. I didn't want to be the guy that bitched and complained," Reggie said. "That's stupid, and when guys are playing well, you bide your time until they're not because it's not equal, it's not even, it's not fair. It's subjective, and that's what you sign up for in athletics."

Although Reggie accepted his role, those close to him stewed about it. "I was more angry than Reggie was [about his not playing] because I saw the type of player he was," his brother Derrick said. "It was very difficult watching him sit the bench as long as he did. He seemed to handle it with a lot of dignity and class."

Patty Eyster, who had looked after Reggie from the day he set foot on campus, was good friends with Hall. She told Reggie that she was going to talk to him. "No," Reggie told her, "don't you go get in the middle of me and playing." She held her tongue—"It would have been a Mafia-esque threat because Patty knew everything," Reggie said laughing—and Reggie kept his head held high. Despite his frustration, he always felt he had the respect of his teammates. They saw him every day. They knew how hard he played and how skilled he was. His confidence never wavered; he knew he just needed an opportunity. The question, with one season left in his college basketball career, was if the opportunity would ever come.

"I had on more than one occasion a teammate tell me, 'Man, get the heck out of here and go somewhere and be a star.' But I didn't look at it as being a star," Reggie said. "I wanted to compete and play. And by the time Jack and James got there, I was already there with Larry and Merion. I wasn't going to desert them."

5

Power of Perseverance

Reggie could count on one hand the number of teammates he had *not* tried to fight at Kentucky. The skirmishes had nothing to do with race. Reggie simply never backed down from anybody. In his first three seasons, he often matched up in practice against Jimmy Dan Conner. Conner was 6-foot-4, with long arms, broad shoulders, and an athleticism that even at Kentucky set him apart. Indeed, Conner had been Mr. Kentucky in basketball as a senior in high school and had won the equivalent of that award in football. A tall, strapping quarterback, Conner had almost as many college suitors in football as in basketball. "He was the best athlete that I ever saw at that time," said Kevin Grevey, who was in the "Super Kittens" recruiting class with Conner. "There wasn't anything he couldn't do."

Grevey saw that the first time he played Conner in tennis. Grevey had grown up playing the sport. Conner had never played it, but Grevey had to work to beat him—something he attributed to Conner's physical gifts and ferocious will to win. "Jimmy Dan Conner might have been the nastiest, toughest guy," Grevey said. "And that's who Reggie had to guard."

Conner, Grevey, and the rest of the "Super Kittens" were newly minted alumni when preseason practice started in 1975. The departures of those players provided an opening for Reggie but with no guarantee for regular playing time. Three highly touted guards, Dwane Casey, Truman Claytor, and Pat Foschi, had signed with Kentucky in 1975.

Foschi arrived in Lexington with comparisons to "Pistol" Pete Mar-
avich, underscoring how Reggie, even as a senior, would still have to
fight for minutes.

Reggie did that—literally—in front of the fans who packed into
Memorial Coliseum for the 1975 Blue–White game. Reggie and center
Mike Phillips battled for a rebound, and each player had his hands on
the ball when the 6-foot-11 Phillips yanked it away. Reggie fell backward and landed on his head. It sounded like an egg hitting cement,
and the crowd gasped.

After a couple seconds, Reggie got up and made a beeline toward
Phillips. He jumped on the startled big man's back near midcourt and
started swinging. Phillips tried reaching behind him but to no avail.
Forward James Lee had to pull Reggie off Phillips. As with other fights
with teammates, Reggie forgot this one as quickly as it had started.
"I fought with my own brothers," Reggie said. "That didn't mean I
didn't love you. I love the guys I played with."

The incident reflected the sense of urgency that Reggie took into
his final season. He seemed to be gaining traction in his bid to start
when he suffered a setback. In one practice, Reggie's mouth turned
into an unfortunate landing spot for an elbow belonging to freshman
Bob Fowler, a square-jawed, pogo stick of a forward from Michigan.
Fowler soared for an alley-oop pass, and Reggie looked up right as the
6-foot-5, 230-pounder's elbow crashed into his face. One of Reggie's
front teeth caught in Fowler's arm like a fishhook. The other one bent
back so far that it touched the roof of Reggie's mouth. The team doctor
took it out with a pair of tweezers. Reggie rinsed with peroxide and
lodged a couple of cotton balls into the gaps where the two front teeth
had been. He returned for the final half-hour of practice.

Unfortunately, Reggie needed a root canal and missed the season
opener. He returned for the second game of the season at North
Carolina, with Claytor starting ahead of him. The fourth-ranked Tar
Heels beat the Wildcats 90–77 in a game where Reggie had boos and
racial insults hurled his way.

Near the end of the first half, Reggie was guarding Phil Ford. The
Tar Heels guard tried to get a handoff from Mitch Kupchak and use

the center as a screen. Reggie stuck to Ford like gum. The next thing he knew, Kupchak was on the floor, writhing in pain. As Kupchak was holding his stomach, a referee called Reggie for a technical foul. He still had no idea what had happened. "People are booing and yelling, 'Throw his ass out! Get the ni—er out!' All of this stuff," Reggie recalled. "Joe B. takes me out. He says, 'Get your ass on the bench!' I said, 'I didn't do it! I didn't foul him!' He didn't want to hear it."

Hall could be forgiven for thinking that Reggie had flattened Kupchak. Reggie was a physical player and could make playing against him hell for his own teammates. "Reggie was the only guy I ever saw who could control you with his fingers," Jack "Goose" Givens said. "He would stick them right in the side, and from there he would turn you to where he wanted you to go. It felt like little knives."

Reggie's tenacity—and the fact that center Danny Hall confessed at halftime that he had flattened Kupchak with a "pile driver"—compelled Hall to turn to Reggie after Kentucky's middling 5–3 start for the season. When Kentucky opened SEC play on January 3 at Mississippi State, Reggie made his first career start. "What's funny," he said, "is when I became a starter, everybody was surprised but me."

Not everybody was surprised. "He was a guy who could come in and put 30, 40 points on you, and you wondered, 'What the hell happened?'" Merion Haskins said. "You knew you had to help when you were playing against Reggie because one man could not stay in front of him. This guy was so physically strong." "Reggie was semi-nasty," Dwane Casey said. "It helped me just going against him every day [in practice], the physicality, the speed, the quickness."

Reggie had one of his best-ever practices shortly after becoming a starter. He could not miss and kept shooting and shooting and shooting. Hall summoned Reggie to his office afterward. Reggie, still riding high, did not expect the talk that his coach gave him. "Reggie, we're here to win basketball games, and basketball is a war," Hall said, drawing out the last word so it was two syllables. "Son, to win the war you've got to have cannons, not popguns. Shit, you're a popgun. Phillips and Givens are cannons. Get the damn ball to my cannons, son."

Reggie got the message, but he also proved to be more than a popgun. He consistently scored in double figures after becoming a starter. He also emerged as the Wildcats' unquestioned leader. Givens, the team captain, left no doubt about that while speaking at a Kentucky basketball luncheon. "This is our captain," he said of Reggie. "How he goes, we go."

Reggie joined Givens as a captain, and from that point forward the team belonged to "Old Man." Reggie's teammates had given him that nickname because of his bow-legged walk, which looked like it belonged to a senior citizen. The moniker fit in another, more endearing way. Reggie had been through so much at Kentucky. The wisdom he had acquired dovetailed with off-the-chart basketball smarts. Younger players looked up to him, in particular Black players who had followed him to Kentucky. "He knew everybody, and everybody knew Reggie. If you wanted to meet a girl, you had to hang around Reggie to get to know all the girls. They really loved Reggie," Casey said with a laugh. "He was just popular. Everyone wanted to be around Reggie."

By the time Reggie was a senior in 1975, there were seven Black players on scholarship, giving the Kentucky team a completely different look than when he had gotten there. Reggie was different, too. He enjoyed a comfort level he had not had his first couple of years in Lexington. He hung out with teammates, and one of his favorite activities was singing while Phillips played the acoustic guitar. "That was the Kentucky I didn't walk into, but over time things changed," Reggie said. "It was a different atmosphere. And it's not like those guys from the first years were enemies, but they didn't know me, and I didn't know them. As we got to know each other, it was better."

Nothing illustrated how much Kentucky basketball had changed than when the team voted to see the movie *Superfly* during Reggie's senior season, which was still being shown at theaters years after its release. Hall often took the team to movies before games, especially on the road, so they could get away from basketball and bond. In Reggie's first three years, he sat through white-centric movies that had white action heroes such as Jan-Michael Vincent and marginalized Black people. "They were murdered, they were beat up by bullies. Even when they were in the right, they were still wrong," Reggie said. "You got tired of it after a while."

Things changed with the vote to attend *Superfly*, which had primarily Black main characters. It was symbolic of the stature Reggie had achieved when he finally got into a position to lead the Wildcats. "One of the things I liked about Reggie is he didn't say, 'Man, I did it this way. This is the way I would do it if I were you,' He would say, 'Here's what could make you better. Look, why don't you try this?'" Givens said. "That kind of made guys relax a little bit and not feel like he was telling them what to do. The way he carried himself, that demanded respect from the young guys, and guys would listen to him. Down the stretch that season, Reggie just flat took over and became the man."

Unfortunately for the Wildcats, it looked like the season was going nowhere after a February 14 loss at Vanderbilt. The defeat dropped Kentucky, which had opened the season as the sixth-ranked team in the country, to 10–10. All the remaining games would be against conference opponents, and the SEC was loaded with talent. Tennessee had Bernard King, who won three consecutive SEC Player of the Year Awards, and Ernie Grunfeld, who joined King in winning Conference Player of the Year when they were seniors. Even with this talent, the Volunteers did not win the conference in the 1975–1976 season. Alabama captured the title behind Leon Douglas, the first four-time All-SEC player in school history. The 6-foot-10, 230-pound center averaged 20.6 points and 12.4 rebounds per game as a senior. Reggie King, who later won back-to-back SEC Player of the Year awards, led a supporting cast that also helped the Crimson Tide to a 15–3 conference record.

For Kentucky, the preseason favorite to win the SEC, disaster struck early in conference play. In a win over Georgia, junior forward Rick Robey suffered a season-ending knee injury. The loss of Robey and the strength of the SEC had Kentucky staring down the barrel of a losing season with just six games remaining; the program had not had such a season since 1926–1927.

That situation made Reggie the perfect person to lead the Wildcats. He had battled for everything he had gotten and was not about to blink now. The Wildcats reeled off four wins in a row, averaging a little more than 90 points per game, to stave off the threat of a losing season. Alabama visited Memorial Coliseum in the penultimate game of the season, and the Wildcats avenged an earlier 13-point loss to the Crimson Tide. Reggie scored 12 points in a 90–85 win, including one of his most memorable Kentucky baskets. At the end of the first half, he hung in the air, as if suspended, before shooting a floater in the lane. The ball went over Douglas's outstretched arms and into the basket. It was one of the highlights from the Wildcats' victory over the sixth-ranked Crimson Tide.

That win set up a huge regular-season finale against Mississippi State. With Kentucky set to move into Rupp Arena the following season, no one wanted to be remembered for losing the last game at Memorial Coliseum.

With just a little more than a minute left in the game, Mississippi State held a seven-point lead, which probably felt like double digits with no three-point shot or shot clock. One of Mississippi State's players was so sure of a win that he broadcast it—literally. Bulldogs guard Joe Dean Jr. grabbed the Mississippi State play-by-play announcer's microphone and yelled, "Mom, we just beat Kentucky! We just beat Kentucky!"

He said it loud enough for the Wildcats to hear, and the boast galvanized them. They were not going out like this. Reggie let Bulldogs guard Ray White beat him off the dribble while Kentucky was in a full-court press. Larry Johnson stepped up, momentarily stopping White. Reggie flew in from behind, snatching the ball from White. A photographer captured the stunned look on White's face as Reggie, who looked like a motorcyclist leaning forward to keep up with the speed of the bike, stole the ball. "You can look at the picture and tell what just happened by the look on his face," Reggie said. "To me, it's my best basketball picture."

Reggie's steal set up a basket that trimmed Mississippi State's lead to five points. The Bulldogs could not put away the game at the free-throw line. Kentucky tied it at the end of regulation, and the teams went back and forth in overtime. A short Jack Givens jump shot delivered a 94–93 win, and pandemonium broke out at Memorial Coliseum. "The fans were excited because we had such a Kentucky-style comeback," Reggie said. "When you bleed blue and white, like the Big Blue Nation does, that's the type of thing Kentucky is expected to do, and we did it."

There is an ironic postscript to the final game at Memorial Coliseum. Joe Dean Jr., the son and namesake of legendary SEC announcer Joe Dean, later became an assistant coach at Kentucky, which made it impossible for him to live down the false Mississippi State win he had crowed about over the radio.

Despite its strong finish, Kentucky, at 16–10, did not receive an invitation to the NCAA tournament. The National Invitation Tournament (NIT) extended a bid, though, but it was soundly rejected in a team vote. Players thought the NIT was beneath Kentucky (or they were already looking ahead to spring break). Reggie was the only player who voted to play in the NIT. In the end, that was enough for the man with veto power. Hall wanted the Wildcats to play in the NIT for Reggie, the only senior on the team. He accepted the invitation.

That left "Old Man" with one last chapter to author in his star-crossed Kentucky career.

In the spring of 1976, the NCAA Men's Basketball Tournament had far from the bloated field that it does today. It took only thirty-two teams, and only a handful of those were champions from non–power conferences. That left some very good teams, even ranked ones, for the NIT. Kentucky, despite the program's blue-blood status, entered the tournament under the radar. Four of the twelve teams that played in the NIT received first-round byes. Kentucky was not among them, despite ending the season on a six-game winning streak.

Dick Gabriel, a junior at Kentucky, covered the basketball team for the student newspaper. He and three others were dispatched to New York City for the NIT, where all games were played at Madison

Square Garden. They packed only enough clothes for a couple days, figuring Kentucky would make an early exit.

Kentucky beat Niagara 67–61 in the first round and then outlasted Kansas State 81–78 in the quarterfinals. The Wildcats met Providence, which had upset Louisville in the quarterfinals, for the chance to play for the NIT title. Givens scored 20 of Kentucky's first 30 points, finishing with 36 points. The Wildcats needed every one of them—and a Larry Johnson basket at the buzzer—to beat the Friars 79–78. By then, Gabriel and his fellow reporters were out of clean clothes. "We had to go to a laundromat," Gabriel said.

Reggie had more pressing concerns. He had pulled a rib muscle against Providence and experienced such stabbing sensations when making sudden movements that he could not practice the day before the NIT Championship game. And his playing status was not the only thing on his mind as Kentucky prepared for Charlotte and star forward Cedric "Cornbread" Maxwell. Reggie received word that his teenage sister, Velma, had been flown by helicopter to the University of Kentucky Medical Center. Born with a hole in her heart, she needed to have a pacemaker installed. Hall gave Reggie the option of flying back to Lexington on a private plane to be with her. Reggie would not hear of leaving his teammates.

He might have had second thoughts after what happened the day before the final game of his career. That afternoon the team was walking back to its hotel after lunch at the famed Toots Shor's Restaurant. They passed women handing out business cards advertising dates. It was obvious to Reggie that they were call girls. Bob Fowler and Truman Claytor made plans to contact them anyway. Reggie laughed and told them they were getting played, but they were freshmen in a big city. "We're only going to be in New York one time," Fowler told Reggie. Such thinking was why Hall had Fowler room with Reggie that season. Fowler had a wild side, and Hall hoped Reggie would help rein him in. It worked for most of the season.

After the final team meeting of the season, Fowler dressed up in his Kentucky blazer, the same one players had worn on the flight from

Lexington to New York City. Reggie figured Fowler and Claytor would quickly learn they were getting hustled and return to their rooms. No harm, no foul. But he later heard a knock on his door. It was Hall making a curfew check.

Reggie called out that he was in his room. But the lock turned, and Hall walked into the room. Hall pulled out the pillows that Fowler had stuffed into the bed and Reggie did what he could to cover for his teammate. He said he didn't know where Fowler was. Hall took off his shoes and got into the empty bed. Reggie didn't know what to do but go to sleep. He woke up when he heard a key in the door lock. Fowler entered the room and asked Reggie who was in his bed. "This is Papa Bear," Hall said.

Fowler and Claytor did not get sent home, but their flouting of team rules set an ominous tone. Many of their teammates were angry at them for creating a distraction. They knew they would have to play well to beat Charlotte. The 49ers were on a roll behind Maxwell, and the NIT title game had been billed as the biggest in school history. Governor James Holshouser of North Carolina flew to New York City for it.

The opening tip went to Larry Johnson, and he threw a pass to Reggie on the right wing. Reggie took three dribbles and shot from 17 feet out. The ball hit nothing but net. Before the game, Reggie had told Hall to pull him if he missed his first shot. That meant he was too injured to play, and Reggie, who got a muscle-relaxer shot right before the game, did not want to hurt the team. His opening shot rendered that worry moot, but he spent most of the first half watching his teammates, anyway.

He made a floater in the lane to give the Wildcats a 13–10 lead less than five minutes into the game but was called for a charge after the shot. He headed to the bench with his third foul. Dwane Casey replaced Reggie and gave Kentucky a huge lift. He scored three quick baskets, including a top-of-the-key jump shot that gave Kentucky a 17–10 lead.

The Wildcats' advantage was short-lived. As Kentucky fouls piled up, Maxwell dominated, just as the future Boston Celtics star had the entire tournament. He scored 13 of Charlotte's first 25 points and 17 in the first half. Givens and center Mike Phillips joined Reggie in picking up three fouls, forcing Hall to rely on a short bench. It did not look as if this would be Kentucky's night, especially after a tip-in by Merion Haskins at the end of the half was waved off. Haskins's basket had clearly happened before the buzzer, but no amount of arguing by Hall could change the call. Kentucky went into halftime trailing 37–34.

Givens picked up his fourth foul a minute into the second half. Phillips joined him on the bench after being whistled for *his* fourth foul. Reggie helped keep Kentucky close. He made a pair of jump shots, including a twenty-footer with a hand in his face, to trim Charlotte's lead to 47–43. But Kentucky's foul problems persisted. James Lee was called for his fourth with just less than thirteen minutes to play, forcing Hall to sit his starting front line and do something he probably loathed: give significant minutes to Fowler.

Fowler sparked Kentucky with his energy and leaping ability. He made a layup off a nice feed from Reggie after Charlotte had built a seven-point lead. Givens made back-to-back jump shots to cut Charlotte's advantage to 57–55. A Fowler free throw reduced it to a one-point lead at 59–58, setting up the defining sequence of the game.

Charlotte forward Melvin Watkins tried a hand-off to guard Bob Ball near the top of the key. Reggie knocked the ball away from Watkins and scooped it up. He had so much speed as he raced to the other end that he almost had to bend back, as if he were doing the limbo, to make a left-handed layup.

Kentucky had its first lead of the second half, 61–60, with three-and-a-half minutes to play. After the teams traded points, Reggie made another huge basket. It came at a little more than a minute to play and with Kentucky down 63–62. Reggie drilled a twenty-foot jump shot—his last basket in a Kentucky uniform—and Maxwell was called for his fifth foul while jockeying for paint position with Phillips. Since the foul was on the floor, Phillips went to the foul line for a one-and-one opportunity. The sophomore calmly made both free throws to give Kentucky a 66–63 lead.

Phillips sealed the win with less than ten seconds left by rebounding a missed Larry Johnson free throw, when Kentucky was leading by just one point. Phillips made the putback and was fouled. Reggie jumped into his arms and yelled, "That's great, baby! That's great!" Phillips made the free throw, and Kentucky won 71–67.

The Wildcats finished the season with ten consecutive wins, becoming the first Kentucky team since 1946 to win the NIT (in that earlier season, the Ralph Beard–led Wildcats had won the NCAA tournament *and* the NIT).

Johnson played a terrific second half, scoring 10 points, taking a key charge, and running the offense with his masterful ball handling. Givens, Phillips, and Lee had their moments, too. Fowler stepped up when the Wildcats needed it while playing with one of the smallest lineups that anyone could remember.

But Reggie had led the Wildcats—just as he had done since becoming a full-time starter. He scored 10 of his 14 points in the second half. His steal and score might have been rivaled only by the twenty-footer he drained near the end of the game. Maxwell, who had scored more than 100 points in the course of the NIT, was awarded the game MVP, but that vote had been taken at halftime after Maxwell had dominated the first twenty minutes. The Wildcats knew who the real MVP was, and Givens gave Reggie the game ball in the victorious locker room.

More than forty years later, Haskins did not hesitate to answer when asked if Kentucky would have won the NIT without Reggie. "No," Haskins said. He paused and doubled down. "Hell, no. There was no way we could have won it without him. He was just the glue," for the season as much as for the final game of his career at hallowed Madison Square Garden. "Reggie just showed so much leadership. He showed you can sit for three years, and when you're asked to play, you're ready," Haskins said. "He had prepared himself for that moment."

No one was happier for Reggie than Kevin Grevey. Grevey, a first-round draft pick of the Washington Bullets in 1975, was in his rookie NBA season and could not attend the NIT title game. He would not have been able to follow it, either, had fate not intervened. The night of the game Grevey was scheduled to appear at a Bullets promotional event, but he got hopelessly lost on his way there. He finally called the team's general manager, who told him not to worry about it and just go home.

Grevey pulled into an empty parking lot and listened as legendary Kentucky announcer Cawood Ledford called the second half of the game. "It was better than watching it because Cawood was an amazing announcer who could paint a beautiful picture on air," Grevey said. "I knew the guys, they're my brothers, and I wanted them to win so bad, and Reggie was having such a good game. I was so thrilled for him."

When Kentucky won, Grevey was so excited that it felt as if he had played in the game. After he got home, he started calling former teammates so they could bask in the win. What still resonates with Grevey is how Kentucky had won. "Reggie worked so hard for that moment, and you never know if the moment's going to come, but you've got to believe that it is, or you just keep pushing that rock up that hill and hope that there's a reward at the top," Grevey said. "Maybe Reggie didn't have a lot of opportunities, but that says a lot about a person and a player that can persevere, keep grinding, and be ready when that opportunity presents itself. Boy, was he ever prepared, and he succeeded. What a great way to finish."

Time did wonders for Reggie's relationship with Joe B. Hall. It led him to love the man and the coach, something he once had never thought possible. The older Reggie got, the smarter Joe B. Hall got. That's how it is with many players who play for demanding coaches. But Reggie's experience was so different from that of his teammates. He was the first Black basketball player to live on campus. He was the first Black player to play four years at Kentucky. He was the first Black player to graduate from Kentucky, earning a degree in arts and sciences.

Adjusting to a big school as a freshman is hard for most people. Imagine doing it with the pressure of playing basketball at a basketball mecca *and* breaking new racial ground at a place where such ground had barely started to thaw. Reggie never blinked. Because of that, no one will ever know what would have happened had he left

Kentucky early on. The African American players Merion Haskins and Larry Johnson followed him to Kentucky. Then came Jack Givens and James Lee. They were followed by Truman Claytor and Dwane Casey. Two seasons after Reggie graduated, Givens led Kentucky to its fifth national championship. Givens, Lee, and Claytor started that season, combining to average 36.9 points per game, almost 44 percent of Kentucky's scoring.

"It was inevitable that changes would be made and the program would evolve just simply because every other program in the country did," said Givens, a Lexington native. "But people in my community and the neighborhood I grew up in and the church I grew up in, the high school I went to, it certainly would have caused people of color to say, 'Hey, man, you mean you're going to go get involved in that stuff? Look at what Reggie just went through. They're not ready to change.' The other thing that could have happened, Reggie could have stayed and been one of those guys in the locker room who was very disruptive from within. Sometimes that's even worse. But he wasn't. He did his job. He did it the best he could, and it made us appreciate that."

Even after Reggie grew close to Hall, he wondered how much the coach appreciated his playing ability. "I bet it was twenty years after I had graduated, we were walking in Memorial Coliseum, and he gives me a hug, I give him a hug," Reggie said. "He finally just dropped the player–coach thing and said, 'What do you think about your experience at Kentucky?' I said, 'Coach, overall it was a good experience. I met some great guys that are going to be my friends for life. I love every one of them, but I wish I could have done better.' He said, 'Why? What do you think you could have done?'"

That was the one question Reggie had hoped Hall would not ask. "In my ignorance and stupidity, I gave him a truthful answer," Reggie said. "I said, 'Coach, you had a lot of great players. I don't know that I would have been a great player, but I would have been the best shooter you ever had, and you never took advantage of that.' He said, 'Is that what you think?' I said, 'Oh, that's what I know.' That's how confident I was. I just remember when there were times that the basket looked so big, but I remembered that I was a popgun and not a cannon, and so I got the ball to my cannons."

But Reggie also recognized one of basketball's immutable facts: only five can play at one time, something that is magnified in uber-competitive programs like Kentucky, and there is only one ball. There were misunderstandings between Reggie and Hall, including the ball-throwing incident during Reggie's freshman season. But as Reggie learned, Hall was tough on all his players. He was a coach of his generation, a time when there was a fine line between motivating a player and embarrassing him. Every player was a candidate for Hall's wrath.

Kentucky used a multitude of drills to build toughness. Some involved coaches whacking players with pads. Joe B., being Joe B., would swing so hard that sometimes his glasses ended up on the side of his head. At one practice, he hit Bob Guyette while the forward was going up for a rebound, and Guyette fell sideways and landed on his chin. "That is horseshit!" Hall yelled. "Guyette, by God, you started, stumbled, farted, fumbled, and you failed! You failed at basketball!" Guyette was a future Rhodes Scholar, and Reggie knew him to be a truly nice guy. But at that moment teammates had to restrain Guyette, with blood pouring from his chin, from going after Hall. After berating Guyette, Hall told team managers to wipe the blood off the floor so they could resume practice.

Practices were brutal, and during close games Hall would tell his players that they would win because no one had worked harder than them. As talented as the 1974–1975 team was, Grevey remembers a bigger reason why it advanced to the championship game of the NCAA Men's Basketball Tournament. "I played ten years in the NBA, and there was never a more physically intimidating, tough bunch of guys as that [Kentucky] team," he said. "Coach Hall built it that way, and that's how you won."

Hall could be as huggable as a cactus, but the prickly side bonded Reggie and his teammates to Hall for life. It gave them something to laugh about every time they got together. Joe B. stories were one reason why he grew to love Hall. Another was the perspective Reggie gained after he himself went into coaching. He saw from that side of the curtain how coaches had to think about the big picture and not just about basketball. Where Reggie did not understand why giving his basketball banquet tickets to two white girls caused such a stir, Hall had to answer to boosters and powerful people who were aghast at the thought of a Black man dating white women in 1973.

Reggie left Kentucky as a champion, a hero to many, and with a degree. He started a process that, in hindsight, looks inexorable, and he endured struggles that made it easier for those who followed him.

Reggie never looked at his history that way. Nothing better illustrates his humble attitude than what happened when Kentucky won the national championship in 1978. Reggie had been in St. Louis for the Final Four and hung out with the team. The day of the game, he hugged each player and told them Kentucky would beat Duke that night. Then he drove back to Ames, Iowa, where he bought some nonalcoholic champagne and a couple of sandwiches. He watched the game by himself.

It was not nerves that caused Reggie to do this; he was sure Kentucky would beat Duke. He simply did not want to be there after the Wildcats beat the Blue Devils 94–88 behind Jack Givens's 41 points. "I was really popular then, and I didn't want to be around to diminish anything from my teammates," Reggie said. "I've never thought about it as far as getting any credit for what they accomplished. I thought, 'These are my guys, and these are my teammates. I predicted that they would be national champions, and this is the culmination of that, and I'm so proud of them.'"

6

A Coach Is Born

A couple days after Reggie graduated in May 1976, Joe. B Hall called him to his office. He had gotten Reggie an assistant manager job at a Lexington K-Mart. His first day, Reggie was handed a clipboard and told to walk around and get to know people. He wasn't quite sure what his job was other than to be Reggie Warford, co-captain of Kentucky's NIT Championship team.

Shortly after Reggie's entry into the workforce, though, Lynn Nance called him. The former Kentucky assistant coach had recently accepted the head job at Iowa State. He was in Lexington and wanted to meet. Over lunch, Nance said he was looking for an assistant to help him implement the triangle offense. Nance had learned the triangle when he played for Tex Winter at the University of Washington, almost twenty-five years before Winters's offense was made famous by Michael Jordan and the dynastic Chicago Bulls. Nance needed someone who could help teach the triangle and recruit the caliber of players that Iowa State needed to compete in the Big Eight.

"Well," Reggie asked, "who are you going to hire?"

"I was hoping you," Nance said.

Nance offered him a job with a $13,900 annual salary. In those days, it seemed like a lot of money to a twenty-one-year-old, even if Reggie had not been on his current job long enough to know what K-Mart was paying him.

Reggie accepted, becoming the youngest assistant coach at a major college program, and flew to Iowa the following day. He spent the first couple nights sleeping on the floor of a fraternity house before renting an apartment from legendary Iowa State wrestling coach Harold "Hank" Nichols.

Reggie's younger brother, Derrick, joined him in Ames after graduating from Paducah Junior College in Kentucky. Derrick had helped the Kentucky school to the National Junior College Athletic Association Tournament Championship before transferring. At Iowa State, Derrick could live with Reggie and go to school free since Reggie worked for the university. Reggie thought Derrick, an excellent defender and natural floor general, could help the Cyclones. He became sure of it after watching Derrick practice with Iowa State.

Derrick settled in and became popular with his new teammates. One day Reggie arrived home early from a recruiting trip and found Derrick and a friend smoking marijuana. Reggie, who did not drink or smoke, went ballistic. Angry words gave way to shoving. The fight stopped just short of the brothers throwing punches. Nance allowed Reggie to handle the matter, and Reggie kicked Derrick off the team. "Derrick had the unfortunate luck to have an anal-retentive brother who was a coach," Reggie said. "Half the people in America, maybe more, were smoking weed in the '70s. Any other coach would have let him go, made him run, or made him do some other stuff. That's one thing in life I'd like to go back and change."

Reggie's actions do not look nearly as draconian when viewed in context. He was younger than some of Iowa State's players. If he did not come down hard on his brother, it might give license to the others to test him. Derrick did not let the misstep derail him. He joined the ROTC, graduated from Iowa State, and entered the air force as an officer. He and Reggie put the incident behind them and stayed close.

Even without Derrick, a Warford played regularly with the Cyclones. Reggie practiced with the team, and it did not take long for Nance to recognize that he had a serious problem: his best player was also one of his coaches.

Iowa State had gone 3–24 in 1975–1976, the worst record in school history. Progress came in increments under Nance. Led by Bob Fowler, who had transferred from Kentucky, Iowa State went 14–13 in 1977–1978, and the Cyclones finished third in the Big Eight with a 9–5 conference record. Reggie spent so much time on the road that he bought a second car just for recruiting trips. He was like Leonard Hamilton at Kentucky—a young, charismatic coach who could connect with players, in particular Black ones.

One lesson Reggie learned from Hamilton was never to let a potential problem get to the head coach. That helps explain his over-reaction to Derrick. Reggie may have had to grow into that part of the job, but teaching basketball came naturally to him. "We didn't have Michael Jordan at Iowa State," Reggie said, "but the tenets of the triangle offense are really good, and I could teach that better than anyone. I knew the potential for all the ways you could add to the offense and improve it."

One of Reggie's most memorable coaching moments in Ames also taught him a valuable lesson. He drew up a play that led to the winning basket in an upset of Kansas State, a top-ten team led by future NBA star Rolando Blackmon. In a postgame interview with reporters, Reggie talked about how Iowa State had baited Kansas State into double-teaming a Cyclones player, leaving another one wide open to make the game-winning shot. His words were more a product of jubilation than braggadocio, but Kansas State coach Jack Hartman was not happy. He later called Reggie a neophyte. "I wasn't a neophyte; I was a damn neophyte," Reggie recalled with a laugh.

The two teams met in the first round of the Big Eight Tournament, and Kansas State clobbered Iowa State. Afterward, Hartman mused that Reggie must not have watched enough film to figure out the Wildcats for the rematch. A chastened Reggie apologized to Hartman.[1] The veteran coach appreciated the gesture and said, "Reggie, you have a chance to be a really good coach. Don't let everyone know what you're thinking all the time."

As much as Reggie took to coaching and grew into it, he also played basketball every opportunity he got. And he could still ball, as the Iowa State players could attest—and Nance could lament. One day a friend approached Reggie about suiting up in an Amateur Athletic Union (AAU) showcase that featured several former University of Iowa stars. That invitation eventually led Reggie to Boston—and the most memorable H-O-R-S-E game of his life.

Nothing was more symbolic of Reggie putting Lexington in his rear-view mirror than what he did with his beloved white Gran Torino Elite. After he accepted Nance's job offer, Nance said a car would be waiting for him in Iowa. Reggie parked his Gran Torino at Blue Grass Airport and never returned for it. Ever. It may still be sitting there.

He didn't put Kentucky basketball behind him, though. He returned to Lexington when his schedule allowed and continued to help the basketball program. He mentored some of the younger Black players, including Lavon Williams. A Parade All-American and Mr. Basketball in Colorado, Williams played sparingly his first two seasons at Kentucky and struggled to adjust. "Kentucky was one of those places [where] if the players were asked to run through a brick wall, they would say, 'OK,'" Reggie said. "Lavon would have been one of the first players to ask why."

Who better to bridge the gap between a dogmatic coach and a pensive player with an independent streak than Reggie? "A lot of things I experienced didn't really sit well with me, and Reggie would kind of talk me off a cliff," Williams said. "That was some tough shit we went through, and I would never, ever want my kid or anyone else's to go through it. Reggie had a tougher road to hoe than most people, and he kept a lot of tension down that people didn't realize [was there] and was kind of the man behind the scenes. He mentored me through the program."

Reggie's best mentoring in Lexington did not involve a Wildcats player but rather a teenage boy. During one of Reggie's Lexington visits, Stuart Brown asked him if he would talk to Brown's son and namesake. Young Stuart Brown was in junior high school and struggling. His parents were divorcing, and Stuart had recently transferred from a small private school to a large public one. He was angry about his parents' divorce but had trouble talking about it. He had yet to make any good friends at his new school and felt lost.

One night Stuart got a phone call from Reggie. He perked up when he heard the name. He had watched Reggie play at Memorial Coliseum and was awestruck that a Kentucky basketball player was calling him. "He must have talked to me for two hours about what was going on with me, why I felt like I felt," Brown recalled. "It was somebody who cared enough in a young person's life to reach out to them and help them kind of get their bearings."

When Reggie returned to Lexington, he would take young Stuart out for a meal or to a Kentucky basketball game. He also provided one of the biggest thrills of Stuart's life. Stuart played basketball in a church league and told Reggie his team had made it to the finals of the season-ending tournament. Reggie told Stuart and a teammate to meet him. And to bring a basketball.

"I'll never forget this," Brown recalled. "He walks us over to Memorial Coliseum and finds Kentucky equipment manager Bill Keightley, who was 'Mr. Wildcat.' He asks him to turn on all of the lights in Memorial. Reggie takes us out there and starts working on our shots, and he's teaching me free-throw technique." Joe B. Hall walked into the gym. Surprised to see Reggie, he asked what they were doing. "We're trying to win the Versailles Church League finals tomorrow night, Coach," Reggie said. It was a defining moment in the lifelong friendship that the younger Stuart Brown and Reggie developed. What started with a phone conversation Brown now looks back upon as a lifeline. "I could have really gone astray if it wasn't for Reggie Warford," said Brown, who ended up playing several sports in high school and excelling academically. "I always knew that he had my back. I never had doubt that he was going to be there. It wouldn't be like he blew into town and [say,] 'Oh, I didn't have time to call you.' He always called."

The summer before Brown started veterinary school, he and his mom were eating breakfast one morning. She was reading the *Lexington Herald-Leader* and came across a quiz about how well parents know their children. She started asking him the questions. One asked who his childhood hero was. "That's an easy one," Brown said. "It's Reggie Warford."

Ev Cochrane knew everything about basketball in the state of Iowa. He even wrote a book about it. His general-manager skills, however, were lacking—at least for an AAU showcase for which he assembled a team. He recruited Reggie to play against a team led by former Iowa stars Scott Thompson and Bruce "Sky" King. But he added a caveat: "We have this one guy that played at Iowa State a long time ago that's 6–8 and you," Cochrane said. Yet what looked like a hopeless endeavor almost changed Reggie's life. He played two of the best games of his life, scoring almost 100 points. No one could guard him, and the competition was good enough that a few NBA scouts attended the games.

Shortly after that, Reggie received a phone call from former Kentucky teammate Rick Robey. Going into his second season with the Boston Celtics, Robey was on the other line with a team scout, who invited Reggie to a preseason camp that preceded the arrival of veteran players.

Reggie arrived in Boston with little fanfare—and was known to many as "Reggie Warfield." "They spelled my name wrong in the Boston papers because [NFL wide receiver] Paul Warfield was really big during that time," Reggie said.

Reggie played well enough to earn an invitation to training camp. There, he competed against the likes of Larry Bird, Dave Cowens, Cedric "Cornbread" Maxwell, and Nate "Tiny" Archibald. He loved the competition. He also felt comfortable around the players—with one notable exception. One day a group of them were in a hot tub, including Bird, Cowens, Robey, and M. L. Carr. They were joking around when Bird looked at Cowens. "Larry said, 'Dave, do you know what I like about you?' Dave said, 'No, what, Larry?' Larry said, 'Not a motherf—ing thing,'" Reggie recalled. "Everybody sort of laughed nervously, like I did. They might have gone out and had drinks together that night for all I know."

Reggie found himself in Bird's crosshairs on his most memorable day with the Celtics. It started when Bird challenged him to a game of H-O-R-S-E. The two matched each other shot for shot, even bank-ing in three-pointers from the wings. The game lasted so long that it delayed the start of a scrimmage. With legendary general manager Red Auerbach and Coach Bill Fitch watching from a golf cart at the other end of Boston Garden, Reggie finally won the game. "I banked in a couple from the top of the key," Reggie recalled. "Bird made one, and then he missed the other."

In the scrimmage, Bird, who hated to lose, exacted some revenge when he and M. L. Carr trapped Reggie on the sidelines after Reggie had picked up his dribble. "Bird and Carr beat the hell out of me," Reggie said. "I thought about getting my elbows out, parallel to the floor, and trying to get through them, but it was the most physical double-team I was ever in."

He committed a turnover, but there was another play in the scrim-mage that he later wanted back even more. With Cowens in the high post, Reggie got a lesson from the crafty Archibald. "He was dribbling, and he turns his back to me and gets real low. I knew that if I got up on him, he was going to hook me and go around," Reggie said. "As Archibald backed into me, he bounced it between his legs *and* my legs, which I didn't see. He turned around and didn't [seem to] have the ball." Reggie was so surprised that he stood up for a split second. Archibald zipped past him, and Cowens fed him for an easy layup. It was a textbook give-and-go with a Globetrotteresque flair to it. "Nobody had ever made a play like that on me," Reggie said. "I gave him every reason to make me look bad. I can still see it as plain as day."

Reggie did not make the team, but the Celtics tried to convince him to play in the Eastern Basketball Association (a forerunner to the Continental Basketball Association), so they could monitor his progress. Reggie declined and so never knew if he might have been the beneficiary of an injury that necessitated the Celtics adding a guard to their roster. They signed Gerald Henderson, who helped the team win two NBA titles during a successful career.

After getting released by the Celtics, Reggie was on the same flight to Chicago as Fitch. He asked the veteran coach if he was good enough to play in the NBA. Fitch said the main thing holding Reggie back was the twenty-four-second shot clock. "I was a little bit too safe with the ball," Reggie said. "I was strong enough. I was quick enough. I could shoot it well enough. But the Celtics didn't need Archibald Lite. He was just better."

Reggie declined the Celtics' offer to play in the Eastern Basketball Association because he had a stable job at Iowa State. His thinking might have been different had he been able to see into the future—and not just because of the injury that provided an opening for Henderson.

The 1979–1980 season at Iowa State turned into a chaotic one. A whirlwind romance led to Lynn Nance divorcing his wife and marrying Kentucky women's basketball coach Debbie Yow. He resigned from Iowa State in the second half of the season, and Reggie and Rick Samuels were co-coaches the rest of the way. Reggie knew his Ames days were numbered, though, after Iowa State embarked on a coaching search. In a what-if footnote, the school hired Johnny Orr away from the University of Michigan, picking him over a young head coach at Army by the name of Mike Krzyzewski.

Reggie did not inquire about staying at Iowa State or even getting another coaching job. He had become disillusioned by the drama that defined his final season in Ames. Also, he looked at the college basketball landscape and saw only a couple of Black head coaches. If he stayed in coaching, he wanted a chance to be a head coach at a major-college program. Concluding that he might never get that opportunity, he decided to go to law school at the University of Kentucky.

One lazy Sunday afternoon, Reggie was in his Ames apartment watching Julius "Dr. J" Erving and the Philadelphia 76ers when Dr. Roy Chipman called. The University of Pittsburgh was going to introduce Chipman as its new head basketball coach the next day, and he wanted Reggie to join his staff.

Reggie was surprised, to say the least. He had never met the man. He had been recommended to Chipman by Will Rackley, who was set to succeed Chipman at Lafayette University. Rackley gave Reggie a glowing recommendation based on how persistent Chipman was over the phone. Reggie agreed to go to Pittsburgh the next day only because it was a free trip. "I just thought I'll go to the city, have a couple of good meals, come back to Iowa, and drive down to Lexington," Reggie said. "I went to Pittsburgh with no intentions of taking the job."

He attended Chipman's introductory news conference and made an immediate impression on Sandy Myslinski, the wife of Pitt athletic director Casimir "Cas" Myslinski. Reggie was young and charismatic, the kind of coach, Sandy Myslinski told him, that could help pull Pitt basketball out of the shadow of the football program. "It was funny," Reggie said, "because she thought Roy was the hayseed and I was the sophisticated city guy and that he was going to need my help."

Reggie heard enough that day to shelve his law school plans. He knew almost nothing about Pittsburgh—including the Steelers, who were three months removed from winning their fourth Super Bowl in six seasons.

During one of Reggie's first days on the job, he went to Fitzgerald Field House to watch the Panther players in some pickup games. They were playing against a team of Steelers, including star running back Franco Harris. The teams split the first two games; Reggie intervened before the third. He wanted to see different combinations of his new players, but the Steelers players balked at the intrusion. They were the Steelers, and this was the way they did things.

Reggie had never heard of Harris or the "Immaculate Reception." It probably would not have mattered if he had. To Reggie, this was Pitt's gym. He told the Steelers that they were there as a courtesy. The conversation soon got heated enough that Reggie thought it might get physical. "Franco was bouncing the ball hard," Reggie said. "Even my own players thought I was the bad guy. They were like, 'Coach you're crazy. Those guys will put you in a trash can.'"

Steelers cornerback Dwayne Woodruff, who knew Reggie through his wife, Joy Woodruff, helped defuse the confrontation, and Reggie eventually became good friends with Harris.[2] They often played pickup ball together, laughing at how they met. "After I got to know Franco," Reggie said, "he was as good a person as advertised."

Reggie also came as advertised. At Iowa State, he had connected with players but also drew the line between coach and friend. That approach served him well when Pitt's star player became one of Reggie's responsibilities. Sam Clancy was a gifted power forward. His size and speed later led to a ten-year career in the NFL even though he never played football at Pitt. He averaged a double-double in points and rebounds in 1978–1979, and his size and strength were a problem for Panthers' opponents. Clancy's fleeting interest in class, though, became Reggie's problem.

Reggie countered it by driving Clancy to campus and walking him to his classes. That worked until Clancy had a friend wait outside one of the classroom buildings until Reggie drove away. The friend would tell Clancy when the coast was clear, and he would split. Clancy and a couple other players missed enough class that it got back to Chipman. He put Reggie in charge of disciplining them, and Reggie channeled his inner Joe B. Hall. While he was at Kentucky, he and his teammates would shudder when they heard Hall shout, "Get a wall!" That meant running the steps at Memorial Coliseum and touching the wall at the top of every row. Reggie decided to make a point by reprising this punishment—with a catch. Instead of making players run the steps at Fitzgerald Field House, he summoned them to Pitt Stadium. At six o'clock in the morning.

If the truant players thought that was over the top, imagine their reaction when they saw Reggie. He wore fatigues, complete with a belt and a .22 pistol sidearm. The costume, meant as a joke, got their attention. They ran every step in Pitt Stadium and got the message.

Pitt won the Eastern 8 Conference in Chipman's first two seasons, making the NCAA Men's Basketball Tournament in consecutive years for the first time since the late 1950s. Then a seismic change occurred. Pitt joined the Big East in the spring of 1982, right as the esteemed basketball conference was entering its heyday.

Pitt would have to recruit better to compete in the Big East, and Reggie became the point man in that endeavor. He emerged as a top-notch recruiter and helped Pitt land players it once had little hopes of getting. Those blue-chip recruits formed the nucleus of teams that created basketball buzz in a football-crazy city.

It all started with Curtis Aiken. But before this blue-chip guard signed with Pitt, he almost cost Reggie his job.

7

Recruiting-Trail Tales

Recruiting was a lot like shooting a basketball to Reggie. It came easily to him, but he also worked at it. Just as he loved nothing more than spending hours launching jump shots in empty gyms, he embraced long drives on solitary roads. He loved the challenge of identifying difference makers and trying to convince them to come to his school.

Reggie could spin recruiting stories for days, and few entertain more than his courtship of the enigmatic Chuckie White.

White was a cousin of former Boston Celtics standout JoJo White, with the game to live up to the family name. As an assistant coach at Iowa State, Reggie could not keep his eyes off the 6-foot-4 White the first time he saw the St. Louis–area star play. As White effortlessly drained shots and dunked on overmatched opponents, Reggie knew he had found a difference maker for an Iowa State program that had won three games the previous season.

"I go see him and establish a pretty good relationship, but he's a little strange," Reggie said. "As I start talking to him, I figure out he was stranger than I thought." The biggest indication that White was, well, different could be seen during pregame warm-ups. He dribbled an imaginary ball to the basket and finished with a pantomimed layup or dunk. Reggie didn't know what to make of it. His bigger problem was what his boss might think of it. At an All-Star game they were scouting, Reggie told Nance to overlook what he saw from White before the opening tip.

73

"What do you mean?" Nance asked. "He doesn't warm up?"

"Oh, he warms up," Reggie said. "You've just got to see."

The first time White got the ball in the layup line, he flipped it to the player behind him. He air-dribbled to the basket before exploding for a two-handed dunk. As White was high-fiving his teammates, Nance looked at Reggie. White put on absolute show before tipoff—without a ball. He imaginary-dribbled behind his back and dazzled with an array of dunks. "The people there had seen him enough to know that he was a little odd," Reggie said, "and they were going absolutely crazy."

Whatever misgivings Nance had about White because of that display evaporated after the game started. The first time White got the ball, he drove baseline and finished with a reverse dunk. His pregame routine, although unconventional, was no act from a poseur. This kid could really play. "He had 30 points that night, and there were two eventual NBA players in that group," Reggie said.

White signed with Iowa State, and Reggie soon learned that his idiosyncrasies extended off the court. White called Reggie one day to say he wasn't coming to Ames. He planned to get a job instead. Reggie was incredulous. "Chuckie, you have a chance to be like your cousin JoJo. You are an elite player," Reggie said. "You are walking into a situation where you can be one of the top-two players in our program. What are you thinking?"

White said he did not want to come to Iowa State for a reason that had nothing to do with basketball or the school. He owned several pairs of expensive alligator shoes and was worried someone would steal them. Reggie assured him that nobody would touch his shoes, but White would not budge. Finally, Reggie promised to personally look after the shoes. That was good enough for White. Now, he told Reggie, he could get rid of the box. *Box? What box?* White told Reggie that he kept a box with a snake in it to protect the shoes.

"Chuckie," Reggie said, "when you want your shoes, how are you going to get them?"

After a long pause, White said, "Coach, I hadn't thought that far yet."

White enrolled in school and excelled in the preseason. But after an exhibition game, White told Reggie that he wanted to move to Nebraska. Reggie was flabbergasted. After White said he planned to marry a girl he had met at school, Reggie asked if he had gotten her pregnant. White assured him that he hadn't; he simply wanted to get married. With some quick thinking, Reggie said there was a married player on the team and that White could still get married without giving up basketball. White agreed to stay in school. The more Reggie saw him in practice, the more convinced he was that he was watching a future NBA player. Reggie could not wait to unleash him on the Big Eight.

"The day before one of our games I got a note: 'Dear Coach, gone to Nebraska. Thanks for everything.' Never heard another word from him, and I don't know if anyone else did either," Reggie said. "From the day he left campus, I don't know whether he went north, south, east, or west. It was absolutely the worst time I ever had as a coach because he was so valuable, and we didn't bring in anyone who was able to do close to what he could do. . . . I have no idea what happened to Chuckie or the alligator shoes."

In 1983 at Pitt, Reggie found himself in a similar situation as he had been at Iowa State. He needed to find better players for Pitt to compete in an elite conference. The season before Pitt joined the Big East, Georgetown had come within a basket of winning the NCAA Men's Basketball Tournament. A jump shot made by a North Carolina freshman named Michael Jordan denied the Hoyas their first national championship. They won that elusive title two years later behind center Patrick Ewing and a swarming, suffocating defense.

Only a monumental upset by Big East brethren Villanova in the 1985 title game kept Georgetown from winning back-to-back national championships. That year St. John's joined Villanova and Georgetown in the Final Four, cementing the Big East's status as the top basketball conference in the country.

That is the landscape Pitt navigated, and Reggie knew he had to find "catch-up" players for the Panthers to compete in the Big East after leaving the Atlantic 10. He and Chipman zeroed in on Curtis Aiken, who was from Buffalo, New York, and guard Dwayne "Pearl" Washington from New York City. Washington had already established himself as a playground legend with his otherworldly passing ability. But there were questions about whether he could shoot well enough to become a premier guard in the Big East.

Reggie went hard after Aiken, and the two connected instantly. "He was one of those guys where I felt like I was talking to my brother," Aiken said. "There was nothing phony about him. He was a straight shooter. Everything was personal with him, which I liked."

Pitt emerged as a serious contender, if not the leader, for Aiken. But during the 1983 Big East Tournament, he verbally committed to the University of Kansas. Chipman was livid and called Reggie to his hotel room. He told Reggie it wasn't working out, that he was making a change. Reggie was to return to Pittsburgh immediately, and they would talk when he returned from the Big East Tournament (the Panthers had already lost, but the coaches stayed for the rest of the tournament).

With nothing to lose, Reggie called Aiken. What follows is the conversation that gave Reggie's Pitt coaching career a stay of execution:

"I just want to tell you, it wasn't you," Aiken said.

"What do you mean it wasn't me?"

"Well, one of the other coaches tried to get me to commit over the phone, and after I kept telling him no, he started cussing."

"Well, shoot," Reggie said. "Do you like Pittsburgh?"

"Man, I love Pitt. I wanted to play in the Big East. My brother will get a chance to see me play in Pittsburgh. He won't be able to come to Kansas very much."

"Curt, let me ask you something: Will you give me a chance to recruit you if I come to Buffalo to see you?"

"Yeah."

Reggie took the news to Chipman, including the part about someone else sabotaging the recruitment of Aiken. When he asked if he could go to Buffalo, Chipman asked for how long. "Until he signs," Reggie said. He stayed there a week, reiterating to Aiken that he had NBA potential. He also stressed that he could help him in other ways. He could not give Aiken money, but he could connect him with boosters and other Pitt alumni who provided opportunities outside of basketball, including internships and work programs in careers that interested him.

That was the model Reggie sold Chipman on to upgrade recruiting. "We needed work and jobs programs so that players could get money legally and want to come to Pitt," Reggie said. "I wanted Pitt to be the best opportunity to further careers after graduation."

Aiken signed with Pitt, and Reggie kept his job. The next year, with Reggie as the point man, Pitt landed highly touted swingman Demetreus Gore from Detroit. Right before Gore committed, Charles Smith, a forward from Connecticut, visited Pitt. Reggie got Aiken and Smith together and, leaving them alone, went to the O, a famous hot-dog joint on campus. Reggie was simply following the recruiting variation of Newton's first law of motion: a body in motion stays in motion unless interrupted by an outside force.

"People say, 'How did you get Charlie? How did you get Charlie?'" Reggie said. "Curtis got in my car, and Charlie was in there, and they were comparing Curtis to Tony Dorsett. Curt could draw great talent like Dorsett drew great talent, and that's what we were thinking. I let Curt talk to Charlie. I already had a pretty good feel that we were going to get Demetreus Gore. Demetreus and Charlie had played in an All-Star game. I said, 'Charlie, Demetreus doesn't compete with you. He just makes you better.' Both Curtis Aiken and Demetreus Gore helped persuade Charlie to come here."

After surviving the near firing, Reggie became Pitt's top recruiter and Chipman's most indispensable assistant coach. He landed another celebrated recruit following the arrivals of Aiken, Gore, and Smith.

Before LeBron James, Jerome Lane was *the* legend at St. Vincent–St. Mary High School in Akron, Ohio. Lane was in some ways a template for James: a tall guard who combined good rebounding with exquisite passing skills. "I had seen him play in AAU, and he was the best point guard I had seen," Reggie said. Reggie's mind raced with the possibilities of putting Lane on the same floor as Aiken, Smith, and

Gore. Lane had made it clear that he did not intend to sign during the early-signing period in November. That did not deter Reggie. He wanted to get Lane on campus to experience the atmosphere at Fitzgerald Field House. The arrivals of Smith and Gore had created a stir, and Reggie persuaded Lane to visit for the 1984–1985 season opener.

Pitt stormed to a big lead against overmatched St. Francis (also a Pennsylvania school), dazzling the crowd with its slick passing. After St. Francis called a timeout, Reggie told Chipman, "I'm going to get Jerome." Leaving the bench, Reggie went a few rows back and sat down. He watched the game with his arm around Lane. "All of those guys can play. You're the last piece!" Reggie told him. "Wouldn't you like to be a part of this? Isn't this a place where you could see yourself, man? You've got to come to Pitt. We're a family."

Finally, Reggie asked, "You want to come here?" Lane said, "Yeah, Coach."

Reggie angled for more than a verbal commitment. No way did he want Lane going through his senior season unsigned, giving other schools a chance to flip his commitment. They called Lane's coach, and Lane convinced him that he wanted to go to Pitt. He signed with the Panthers before leaving Pittsburgh.

A year later Reggie was just as relentless while trying to add another coveted piece to the core group he had been instrumental in assembling. Rod Brookin, a small forward from outside of Harrisburg, Pennsylvania, had given the Panthers a verbal commitment before his senior season, but Reggie sensed he was wavering. He went to see Brookin play and visited him after the game. The two sat on the couch at Brookin's grandmother's house watching TV and chatting. Reggie drew out his stay, knowing the other coaches waiting to visit Brookin could not do so until he left. At around two o'clock in the morning, Reggie started nodding off. When Brookin mentioned how late it was, Reggie said, "I'm not leaving until you come to Pitt, man." Reggie took off his shoes and told Brookin they would split the couch.

"Coach, you crazy," Brookin said.

"Rod, I'm not leaving, man," Reggie said. "We need you. We've got Curtis. We've got Charlie. We've got Jerome."

Brookin signed with Pitt, but Reggie never got to coach him, nor did he reap the full fruits of his recruiting labor. Chipman stepped down after the 1985–1986 season, and Pitt hired Paul Evans away from Navy. Reggie was not retained, but his fingerprints were all over the 1986–1987 Pitt team that broke through in the Big East. The Panthers finished second in the conference with a 12–4 record. They won twenty-five games and advanced to the second round of the NCAA Men's Basketball Tournament before losing to Oklahoma. Five players averaged double figures in scoring that season: Smith, Lane, Aiken, Gore, and Brookin—all recruited by Reggie. Lane led the country with 13.5 rebounds per game. He dominated as a power forward, though Reggie always maintained that Lane did not play his best position at Pitt. "He should have been a point guard," Reggie said. "I know he could rebound, but no one's ever going to know what a great ball handler he was because Evans saw Jerome's length and stuck him under the basket for the rest of his career."

In Reggie's six seasons at Pitt, the Panthers went to the NCAA tournament three times. The recruiting classes that Pitt signed provided the foundation for a program that ascended to the top of the Big East less than a decade after joining the conference. To Reggie, the biggest what-could-have-been at Pitt was how good the Panthers might have been had he landed the recruit who would go on to become one of the more decorated players in Kentucky history.

Long before Kenny "Sky" Walker blossomed into an All-American and two-time SEC Player of the Year, he was a springy forward from Roberta, Georgia, a small town with about a thousand residents. Reggie found out about Walker through Charles Harris, who had played for Reggie at Iowa State. Harris, who was from Macon, Georgia, called Reggie, saying there was a player Pitt had to see. He cautioned Reggie that Walker, although 6-foot-8, was only about 185 pounds. "Man, he'll get killed in the Big East," Reggie said.

Harris said Walker had a forty-one-inch vertical leap, which was enough to get Reggie to Georgia. Reggie fell in love while watching Walker play and arranged for him to visit Pitt. When he returned to Pittsburgh, he told a skeptical Chipman that Walker could play with anyone in the country. "Chipman went down there to see Kenny play, and he almost lost his mind," Reggie remembered. "He said, 'We've got to get him.'"

Reggie was not worried about Kentucky as a rival recruiter. The Wildcats were all in on Billy Thompson, the number one high school player in the country. Thompson and Walker played the same position, so Reggie didn't think his own alma mater would make a serious run at Walker.

Wildcats assistant coach Leonard Hamilton recruited parts of Georgia, though, and Walker was in his territory. He did not show much more than cursory interest in Walker since Kentucky had a good chance of landing Thompson. However, Louisville coach Denny Crum was constructing a pipeline from Camden High School in New Jersey, across the Delaware River from Philadelphia, to Kentucky's archrival: Thompson followed high school teammate Milt Wagner to Louisville, leading Hamilton to set his sights on Walker.

Hamilton employed a master stroke when he used Reggie against Reggie. He told Walker to look at the guy recruiting him at Pitt and what going to Kentucky had done for him. Reggie was furious, even though he considered Hamilton a good friend. He got a sinking feeling when he called Walker, knowing Kentucky was in hot pursuit of him. Walker talked with a distant tone that Reggie had never heard. When Walker told him that the Big East played "bully ball," Reggie knew he was headed to Kentucky. It was a crushing blow. Walker ended up scoring more than 3,000 points at Kentucky and became the fifth overall pick of the 1986 NBA draft.

"I would have had Kenny 'Sky' Walker, Charlie Smith, Demetreus Gore, Curtis Aiken, Jerome Lane at the same flippin' time," Reggie said. "That's how close I was. I get chills thinking about it."

The most rewarding recruiting experience of Reggie's coaching career came while he was at Pitt, but it had nothing to do with signing a player.

In October 1983, Reggie traveled to Kentucky with Roy Chipman. They were staying in Lexington and visiting a high school player the next day. Reggie was driving on Maxwell Street, a thoroughfare that cuts through Lexington. Chipman started telling a corny joke, and Reggie felt obligated to feign interest. When he glanced to his right at Chipman, he saw a house engulfed in flames. He stopped immediately, and they jumped out of the car and ran to it.

An elderly man and woman were inside. Each was unconscious. Reggie and Chipman took a running start and slammed into the door. The impact left Chipman with a sprained shoulder, and the door remained closed. Reggie jumped and kicked it open. Fire from a kerosene stove that had exploded roared out at him. Undeterred, Reggie ran into the house, picked up the woman, and carried her to safety. He returned and carried the man out. He went back a third time, but, fortunately, no one else was in the house.

Reggie and Chipman stayed at the scene until the firefighters and paramedics arrived. When they got back to the car, Chipman said, "Warford, you are amazing! You saved those people's lives!"

Reggie did not think it was a big deal. He and Chipman resumed work the next day, and he flew to Maryland to visit another recruit. He was watching ESPN in his hotel room when he learned that his cover had been blown. Chipman had told Pitt's sports information department what had happened, and the news spread quickly. "Chipman made me look really heroic," Reggie said. "When you see yourself on *SportsCenter* as an assistant coach, you've [usually] been fired, been killed; it's usually not a good thing. I just happened to be there and tried to do a good thing and it worked out."

Reggie's life-saving actions garnered attention from all over the country. John Thompson and Mike Krzyzewski took Reggie to breakfast one morning at a prep basketball tournament where college coaches were scouting. The U.S. Basketball Writers Association gave him its annual Most Courageous Award. He was a guest on *The Jim Rome Show*. Coors invited him to its Denver plant for a tour and offered him a free case of beer every month for the rest of his life. He did not drink, so he politely declined the offer.

Reggie received a plaque from President Ronald Reagan, and Governor John Y. Brown of Kentucky awarded him the state's Medal of Valor. Reggie, with his mother and a niece also in attendance, received the medal during a ceremony in the governor's office. "We're fond of anyone who used to play University of Kentucky basketball," Brown said during the presentation. "But we're especially proud of you, Reggie, now that you've come home and demonstrated the true character and the courage that you exemplify as an individual."

A year later, another recruiting trip took a fortuitous turn, leading Reggie to the love of his life.

8

Fall from Grace

In August 1985, Chipman sent Reggie to Philadelphia to see Hank Gathers and Bo Kimble. Reggie did not think Pitt had a chance with these high school teammates, but he had just come out of a long-term relationship, and Chipman wanted him to get out of the office for his own good.

Reggie flew to Philadelphia and watched Gathers and Kimble in a summer-league game. He returned to Philadelphia International Airport in time for a red-eye flight back to Pittsburgh. While he was in the ticket line, two men flirted with a leggy blonde who had recently graduated from Villanova University. Reggie could tell she wanted nothing to do with them. He finally told the men, "She's with me."

It would have been love at first sight in the movies but for one nettlesome detail: Marisa Bolinski was not interested in *any* of them, including Reggie. She was on her way to visit her boyfriend, a medical school student doing his residency in Pittsburgh, and wore a ring with a noticeable rock. Although she was not engaged, the ring usually proved effective in warding off guys.

But as Marisa would find out, Reggie was not most guys. Reggie flew so frequently that he was on a first-name basis with many of the U.S. Air staff members. After the flight to Pittsburgh was delayed, he asked Marisa if he could buy her a drink. She turned him down. Twice. She finally relented after the flight was further delayed.

Marisa and Reggie talked and found common ground: each was a recruiter. Marisa did hers for Thomas Jefferson University Hospital, Reggie for a major-college basketball program. They interviewed each other to see who was better at it. They shared some laughs and said their goodbyes when boarding finally started for their flight.

Reggie had played enough basketball to know when to go back-door, and he had a manager surreptitiously switch Marisa's seat. When she got to her new seat, it was next to Reggie. The two continued to talk, but Marisa thought that was the end of it after the plane landed in Pittsburgh. "I never expected to see him again," she remembered.

Reggie and Marisa had exchanged business cards, and a couple weeks later he flew to Philadelphia on a recruiting trip. He showed up at her workplace with a bouquet of flowers. Marisa, a bit flummoxed, did not know what to do when he asked her out. One of her colleagues, smitten with Reggie, said, "I'll go!" Marisa finally agreed to dinner.

Marisa found Reggie attractive and was drawn to his confident demeanor. They kissed that night, but she tried talking him out of pursuing her. She told him she was too young to get seriously involved, that she would end up breaking his heart. Plus, she was involved with another man. She even wrote that to him later in a letter.

One day she called Reggie and said she was coming to Pittsburgh. Did he want to have lunch? Reggie told her that he only wanted to see her if she was coming to Pittsburgh to see him.

The morning Marisa arrived in Pittsburgh, she drove to Reggie's house in Blackridge just east of the city. When he got to the door, she dropped a small suitcase inside. "I'll be back in an hour," she said. She returned after breaking up with her boyfriend.

Marisa is not sure when she fell in love with Reggie. It was probably between the time he sang "First Time Ever I Saw Your Face" to her and quoted Shakespeare when she visited him at the Big East Tournament in New York City. "He had a lot of culture for a jock," Marisa said, "and I thought that was pretty cool."

Not that everything in the relationship was happy ever after. Reggie and Marisa dated for five years because Reggie was hesitant to get married. Heart disease ran in his family, and he told Marisa that he did not expect to live past fifty. Their roles reversed then: Marisa chased after Reggie as their relationship evolved.

After they married in 1990, neither knew that they would go through hell and back together. Adversity would bring them closer rather than drive them apart. For Marisa, the tough times could never eclipse the one thing that connected her to Reggie for better and for worse. He made her want to be a better person.

Pitt started preseason basketball practice in October 1985 with high hopes. The Panthers had come off a season in which they went a respectable 8–8 in the Big East and made the NCAA tournament. They returned a strong nucleus in guard Curtis Aiken, swingman Demetreus Gore, and power forward Charles Smith. Joining them was highly touted freshman Jerome Lane, who had the body and athleticism to bang in the Big East. Pitt also had a bench with experienced veterans.

If Pitt looked ready to take another step, the same held true of Reggie. He was thirty-one years old and widely hailed as one of the top young talents in coaching. Roy Chipman had promoted Reggie to associate head coach, giving him significant input in the team's offense. He felt Reggie was ready to lead his own Division I program.

Against this blooming backdrop, in late October Reggie received phone call from Patty Eyster, a close friend going back to his Kentucky playing days. "Honey, have you seen the paper?" said Eyster, who still lived in Lexington. "They've got you in there looking like Al Capone." Reggie had been singled out in a wide-ranging *Lexington Herald-Leader* exposé that detailed payoffs and cheating in big-time college basketball, particularly at Kentucky. One of the stories claimed Reggie had offered money to Steve Miller to sign with Pitt. The same story alleged that he had facilitated a $10,000 offer from a booster to Doug West to sign with Pitt. Reggie was incredulous when he saw the story. How in the heck had Steve Miller landed him in the series written by investigative reporters Jeffrey Marx and Michael York?

Miller was in his second year at Western Kentucky when the story broke and not remotely near Reggie's radar. Reggie had recruited Miller, who was from Lexington, but he wasn't sure Miller was a program-elevating player, so the recruitment never got out of neutral. Reggie tried to sell Miller on playing Big East games in front of his father, who lived in Boston. He did not know that there were hard feelings between Miller's father and his mother, who were divorced. She was angered by Reggie's pitch, which pretty much ended Pitt's chances. Miller never even visited the school.

However, Miller told reporter Michael York that Reggie had said there were benefits if he signed with Pitt. It was something Reggie told every player he recruited and had nothing to do with payola. But the combination of two aggressive reporters and a college kid who was not media savvy resulted in the twisting of the story. The one the *Lexington Herald-Leader* printed claimed Reggie had offered to split money from the raise he would get if Miller signed with Pitt. Reggie could not believe it.

The Doug West allegations were just as preposterous to him. West, from Altoona High School in central Pennsylvania, became close with Reggie after Pitt started recruiting the small forward. Their relationship evolved into that of older and younger brothers. West even stayed at Reggie's house a couple times during unofficial visits to Pitt. Reggie was so stunned when West signed with Villanova that he wondered if money or benefits had swayed West to spurn Pitt. In the *Herald-Leader* story, West said that an Altoona-based dentist, Dr. Joe Haller, had offered him $10,000 to sign with Pitt—and that Reggie knew about it.

Reggie would not have recognized Haller if they passed on the street. He knew that Haller had called Chipman, a friend of his, to tell him about West. But Reggie vehemently denied knowing any-thing about a $10,000 offer. Before the story ran, he told York to double-check with people close to West about the claim. That is how sure he was that the claim was not true. As for Miller, had Reggie told him there would be benefits if he went to Pitt? Absolutely. Reggie told York as much during interviews.

Reggie had pitched both Pittsburgh's status as one of the top corporate headquarters in the country—thus the job and internship opportunities that would be available to Miller—and the benefits of playing in the Big East, which offered top competition and maximum exposure to large media markets. Reggie laughed at the notion that he offered Miller money. Miller was in the same class as Charles Smith and Demetreus Gore, two of the most celebrated recruits in Pitt history. Why would Reggie have offered money to a kid he was not sure would move the needle for Pitt basketball but not to Smith and Gore?

Reggie had reason to feel as betrayed by Marx and York as he did by Miller and West. He had had extensive contact with these reporters before their exposé. He had talked to York at least three times on the telephone. He had met with Marx in Lexington when he had returned for a roast for his friend, the longtime *Herald-Leader* sportswriter D. G. FitzMaurice.

Reggie did not know that when he first started talking to York and Marx, they weren't just digging for dirt on Kentucky; they were excavating for it. They approached him under the guise of doing a story on recruiting in college basketball, never mentioning that they were trying to expose its dark underbelly. "They were after Kentucky and Joe B. Hall," Reggie said. "The way to get more people to read your paper was to have sensational stuff."

Marx and York's exposé was a reporting tour de force. Fifteen former Kentucky players went on record, saying they had received $100 handshakes, money, and other benefits from boosters. Some had been disgruntled about their Kentucky experience, but others had become All-Americans. Joe B. Hall denied knowing anything about such benefits, yet Kentucky was cast in the harshest light among the programs cited in the report. Marx and York later won a Pulitzer Prize for investigative reporting.

It is beyond ironic that Reggie got caught in the *Herald-Leader*'s dragnet. He had told Marx and York that he did not know of any cheating while he was at Kentucky, that he had never received impermissible benefits. Maybe he had been naive, but he had worked during the summers, which was allowed by the NCAA. The only paid speech he ever gave was on the day of his graduation, a couple of months after he had led Kentucky to the NIT Championship. He had received $500 for talking to a YMCA group.

What most hurt Reggie was that Marx and York impugned his integrity and assassinated his character by labeling him a cheater. "I always believed that you never had to cheat and give money to players," Reggie said. "I operated from the idea that you gave them opportunities or revealed opportunities and taught them how to take advantage of them. You put a person in a job that they can intern in from the time they get with you until the time they leave, so by the time they leave, they're ready to do something. That's what I tried to do."

Reggie had other reasons for never offering money to recruits. In addition to his infamous parsimonious ways—Roy Chipman always joked that Reggie was too cheap to buy someone a cup of coffee—he never wanted someone to have something that could be held over him. On a more personal level, he said, "My dad wouldn't have stood for that, or my mother."

An exposé that became the talk of college basketball said otherwise. Trying to counter the allegations was no easier than trying to put toothpaste back in a tube. They eventually became so overwhelming that at one point Reggie put a loaded semiautomatic pistol in his mouth and pulled the trigger.

Initially, it had looked like the storm might pass. A couple days after the *Lexington Herald-Leader* series ran, Steve Miller retracted his statement about Reggie. Pitt's athletic director Edward Bozik talked to players Reggie had recruited. Following an investigation, Pitt concluded that Reggie had done nothing wrong. The NCAA eventually cleared Reggie, too, after its own investigation.

Reggie had to deal with another shock to the system during the 1985–1986 season. After a 74–63 loss at West Virginia on December 14, Chipman submitted his immediate resignation, citing family reasons. Pitt talked Chipman into finishing the season, and the Panthers reeled off four consecutive victories, including an 80–76 win over eleventh-ranked Georgetown in their Big East opener. But Pitt struggled the rest of the way. The Panthers lost five consecutive games in February, dooming their chances of returning to the NCAA tournament. They finished the season with a disappointing 15–14 record following a first-round loss to Southwest Missouri State in the NIT.

After Chipman's resignation became official, Reggie thought he had the inside track to the head-coaching job. Chipman cautioned him, however, that the *Herald-Leader* series was too fresh for Pitt to seriously consider him. John Blanton, an associate athletic director in charge of finances, told Reggie that Pitt might think he was too young for the job and might be leery because he was single. Reggie and Blanton, who was Black, were close, and Blanton was always straight with Reggie.

Reggie thought it a little silly that not being married might work against him. He was in a committed relationship with Marisa Bolinski, his future wife. More importantly, most of the returning players wanted him to become Pitt's next coach. He was convinced their voices had been heard after he met with Bozik. "He led me to believe and led John Blanton to believe that I was going to get the job," Reggie recalled. Reggie was so convinced of it that he drove to Kentucky to give his parents the good news. He told them that he expected to be introduced as Pitt's next head coach the following week. After the NCAA Men's Basketball Tournament slapped its usual March grip on the nation, Navy upset Syracuse in the Sweet Sixteen. Navy's riveting run, fueled by dynamic center David Robinson, ended in the regional finals with a loss to Duke. By then, the Midshipmen's coach Paul Evans had emerged as a hot coaching prospect. Reggie was at his parents' house, watching TV, when ESPN college basketball analyst Dick Vitale offered his take on the Pitt job. "There goes Dicky V, 'Oh Pittsburgh! This is the guy you need! Paul Evans! A disciplinarian! [Pitt's] got great players with Charles Smith and Demetreus Gore! They need discipline! Pittsburgh, if you're smart, pick up Paul Evans!'" Reggie said. "I was like, 'I've got to go back to Pittsburgh now.'"

He drove through the night and arrived early Monday morning. "I called John Blanton, who told me what was going on," Reggie remembered. "He said, 'Paul Evans is on campus. They're putting a package together for him.' I said, 'Bozik told me that I would be the

coach.' He said, 'Reggie, he called the board [of trustees] together.'"
Evans accepted the job, and Reggie knew he would be seen as a threat
by an incoming coach because he was so close with the players. Evans
did not even interview Reggie before assembling his new staff.

Reggie soon found himself on the outside looking in at college
basketball. Coaches sympathized with him, but more than a few said
they couldn't hire Reggie because of the *Lexington Herald-Leader* allegations. Maryland coach Bob Wade and Reggie were friends dating back
to Wade's coaching days at famed Dunbar High School in Baltimore.
Reggie had recruited Dunbar players such as Reggie Williams and Sam
Cassell. He did not get either player but earned Wade's respect. Wade
"talked to all kinds of coaches, telling them that I got a raw deal,"
Reggie said. "He went out of his way to try to help me." Unfortunately
for Reggie, Wade did not have an opening on his staff, nor did other
coaches who supported Reggie.

Because he now could do nothing in basketball, he opened a high-
end clothing store in Pittsburgh with a couple of business partners.
He enjoyed it, especially after he sold Pittsburgh Steelers wide receiver
Louis Lipps a $14,000 fur coat. But selling clothes was not his passion.
He yearned to coach and continued to pursue it, but the *Lexington
Herald-Leader* had made him radioactive.

During a visit with Patty Eyster in Lexington, Reggie showed
her some of the job rejection letters he had received. They were not
just form letters. Many said they would have loved to hire Reggie but
could not because of the allegations that would follow him to his new
job. Eyster was furious at what the *Herald-Leader* story had wrought.
"You need to sue their ass," she told Reggie.

Valencia Warford had always been fiercely protective of her son Reggie.
During a game at Memorial Coliseum in Reggie's senior season, he
took a charge. As he was on the ground, Georgia forward Jacky Dorsey,
who had been whistled for the foul, stepped on his head. Reggie
jumped up, and James Lee grabbed him before he could go after
Dorsey, a future NBA player. Valencia, from the stands, yelled loud
enough for Reggie to hear, "Don't you hurt my baby!"

The two had a special relationship; even after he became a rising star in the college coaching ranks, he called his mother every other day to talk or just to see if she needed anything. This concern for his mother endeared him as much as anything to Marisa while they were dating. "I've heard the saying if you want to know how a man's going to treat his wife, see how he treats his mom," Marisa said. "Reggie treated her with the utmost respect."

When Reggie was weathering a kind of hurt he had never experienced, Valencia read him Bible verses over the phone. One that resonated with both was Psalm 37: "When others despise you and speak ill of you . . . ." She often called at the exact time Reggie needed to hear her voice.

Valencia gave strength to Reggie as her own health was failing. At age forty-three, she had had open heart surgery. By November 1987, almost fifteen years later, her heart was in such bad condition that she was told she only had a couple of months to live. As her life neared its end, she could proudly look at her children and see the job that she and Reverend Roland Hayes had done as parents. All six living Warford children had college degrees or graduation certificates in their chosen profession. Four of them, including Reggie, eventually earned advanced degrees. All the children were religious and hard-working, living embodiments of what their parents had instilled in them.

It had not been easy. Money had been tight in a household with seven children. The Warfords had received government commodities, but what they had usually wasn't enough, even after Roland got a stable job with the Tennessee Valley Authority following years of pouring concrete. Sometimes they needed items from nearby Folger's Market but did not have the money to pay for it.[1] "This man [at the market] let us charge food," said Thelma Freeman, one of Reggie's younger sisters. "They did it for us because Daddy's name speaks for itself." That always stuck with Thelma, and the memory of it is still powerful enough to bring her to tears. Reverend Roland Hayes Warford always paid his debts, always preached that not doing so would have maligned his name. He instilled in his children that their name was who they were and never to let anyone slander it.

This lesson, more than anything, put Reggie at odds with the *Lexington Herald-Leader*. He would have accepted the newspaper printing a retraction to the article that had sullied his name, but it refused, so he initiated a lawsuit. The attorney that Reggie hired sat on the lawsuit for almost a year, and when the *Herald-Leader* dug in, he advised Reggie that he did not have a case.

A mutual friend then led Reggie to Larry Roberts. A former University of Kentucky tennis player who was a partner in a Lexington-based law firm, Roberts thought Reggie had a strong libel case against the *Herald-Leader*. But the one-year statute of limitations had expired. Roberts would have had an easier time getting a gun into a courtroom than Reggie's lawsuit. He explored their options, striking gold when he talked with a professor at the University of Kentucky Law School. The professor said the *Herald-Leader* might have provided an opening when it commissioned a reprint of the exposé in January 1986. Touted as a model for newspapers to investigate major college programs, the reprint had been distributed to college presidents and athletic directors across the country and news agencies. The reprint, however, did not include Miller's retraction that Reggie had offered him money to sign with Pitt. With this information in hand, Roberts filed a lawsuit in December 1986, a month before the statute of limitations on the reprint expired.

Despite getting his opportunity in court, Reggie struggled like never before. The *Herald-Leader* story had deeply wounded him. It made him question how others saw him. "He got to a point where he needed someone to endorse almost everything he said," Marisa remembered. "He was so insecure."

Even if he won the lawsuit, he did not know if he could ever get his good name back. That thought sent him into a spiral that he later realized was a deep depression. "I would sit on the couch at nine o'clock in the morning, and it would be four-thirty or five o'clock before I moved," he said. "I hadn't really watched TV. I had sat on the arm of a couch for almost eight hours and not moved. That happened so many times. There's nothing worse than feeling like you need to be doing something, and you don't know where to start. You can't fully appreciate how disconcerting it is to realize that you have no worth."

That lack of a sense of self-worth pushed Reggie to the brink. One day in his Penn Hills home, just east of Pittsburgh, he put a .380 Llama in his mouth and pulled the trigger. When he opened his eyes, the gun was still in his mouth, but he realized that the bullet had not fired because one of the two safeties on the gun was still engaged. He dropped the gun and started shivering.

A couple of weeks later, Valencia Warford died at the age of fifty-six. Reggie drove to Kentucky, going immediately to his father's study to listen to some of his old sermons. He found a cassette tape his mother had left for her son. "Hi, this is Valencia, your mother," she said on the tape. Tears rolled down Reggie's face as his mother told her children to love one another and stay close. More than a thousand people packed into Church of God and Christ in Mayfield, Kentucky, for the funeral. Reggie and Velma sang solos, and Reggie played "Yes Lord" on the piano.

Reggie returned to Pittsburgh with a heavy heart and adrift. There, he encountered more setbacks. A manager at his store had allowed friends to take clothes without paying for them, so Reggie had no choice but to shutter the store that had been his primary source of income. He missed two mortgage payments, and his house was repossessed. It became clear to him that it was time to go back to Kentucky. Roberts needed help with the lawsuit, and Reggie was eager to immerse himself in the fight for his name.

He left Pittsburgh with no money, no house, and no job prospects in coaching. Things would get worse before they got better.

9

Rise and Redemption

A thirty-three-year-old Reggie Warford returned to Lexington in April 1987 as the player who had led Kentucky to the 1976 NIT Championship and the man who had received the state's Medal of Valor in 1983 after rescuing two people from their burning home. Yet he could not have felt more removed from such triumph and heroism. He was broke. He also was broken, even if he tried to mask it. "I didn't walk around with my chin dragging on the ground," Reggie said. "I wanted to project that I was OK."

What Reggie did *not* do showed how far he was from OK. He refrained from calling former teammates in Lexington, such as Jimmy Dan Conner, Mike Flynn, and Jerry Hale. Surely, they would have helped him. He also refused to ask for help from his closest friends, including Jack "Goose" Givens, a living Lexington legend. For five months, Reggie lived out of his car and often ate from dollar menus at fast-food restaurants. His suits were folded neatly in the trunk of his car. The rest of his clothes were spread across the backseat. Some nights he parked across from Memorial Coliseum and slept there. "Other times I would sleep outside of my friends' houses," Reggie said, "and early in the morning I would call them and [say], 'Hey, man, I just got into town. Can I come over and get a shower real quick?' I dressed in a suit seven out of ten times. I was poor and destitute, but at least I looked good."

The biggest challenge Larry Roberts, his lawyer, and Reggie faced with the lawsuit was money. The *Lexington Herald-Leader* could afford a drawn-out court case. Expenses for Roberts's firm piled up quickly. It weighed on Reggie that he could not help financially, but he could barely afford his own meager expenses. He became so desperate that he applied for a minimum-wage job at a Lexington laundromat. "They said I was overqualified," Reggie said. "When you're not eating, you're not overqualified."

He eventually found work as a salesman at a car dealership in Lexington and received a break from an unlikely source. One day actor/comedian Jim Varney wanted to buy a Lincoln. Someone told him that Reggie had played basketball for Kentucky. Varney, a Lexington native, chatted him up and then proceeded to take the opposite approach of most buyers. Instead of casting a wary eye at the extras offered with the car, he told Reggie to load up the Lincoln with every accessory. Reggie made close to $2,000 on the sale. "Mr. Varney had no idea what that money meant to me at that time," Reggie said.

It allowed him to rent an efficiency apartment and get his suits dry-cleaned. Still, money problems were the one constant in the two years that Reggie lived in Lexington. After he got into an accident that totaled his car and put him in the hospital, he was told it would cost $2,000 every day he stayed there, so, with no health insurance, he limped out. A cousin working at a different car dealership leased Reggie a used car, which he drove until it got repossessed following a missed payment. After that, he rode a bicycle around Lexington.

When Roberts needed help with the case, Reggie pedaled six miles to his office. Sometimes, as he listened to his Walkman radio while on his bike, talk-show hosts made jokes about him. Motorists drove by Reggie pointing and laughing. Reggie wondered what he did to deserve such schadenfreude.

Before Reggie's lawsuit got to court, he thought he would be getting the break he had sought since leaving Pitt. In the spring of 1988, Dwane Casey, Reggie's former Kentucky teammate and a Kentucky assistant coach, emerged as the frontrunner for the head coaching job at the University of New Orleans. Casey talked to Reggie about joining his staff. "Dwane said, 'Man, f—k all of them, motherf—ers. We're going to go to [New Orleans] and turn that s—t around and show them what we can do,'" Reggie remembered.

Shortly after that, the two were in Pittsburgh for the Roundball Classic. The annual All-Star game attracted top high school seniors and college coaches from all over the country. Casey's next stop was New Orleans to sign the contract that would make him the Privateers' next men's basketball coach. Reggie was with Casey when the latter received a phone call that abruptly changed both their lives.

The *Los Angeles Daily News* was running a story that Casey had mailed money to a California prep star Kentucky was recruiting. The money had allegedly been found in a FedEx package opened by one of its employees and linked to Casey. Reggie could see the color draining from Casey's face with the telephone pressed to his ear. Casey called officials at New Orleans and insisted there was no truth to the story. He pleaded with them to let the situation play out, but to no avail. The job went to Tim Floyd, who later parlayed his success at New Orleans to the head job at Iowa State and later with the Chicago Bulls.

After the *Daily News* story, Casey found himself in the same situation as Reggie. Each saw their college coaching careers irreparably damaged by allegations of cheating. Casey would eventually sue multiple entities for the story, which proved to be false, and win a huge settlement. He said to hell with US college basketball and went to Japan to coach professionally. Casey revived his career overseas. He eventually broke into the NBA and became head coach of the Toronto Raptors in 2011. After a seven-season stint there, he took over as head coach for the Detroit Pistons.

Before any of that, Casey and Reggie had found themselves linked for the wrong reason. One day Reggie was listening to a Lexington sports talk show and heard something that made him laugh in spite of himself. It was a joke that Dwane Casey and Reggie Warford had gone into a hardware store and paid $6.99 for nails and $10,000 for a hammer. "I still think it's funny as heck," Reggie said.

That was one of the few things Reggie found funny during that time. One indignity or slight seemed to follow another. The worst happened during his short stint as a limousine driver after he picked up an entourage from the *Lexington Herald-Leader*. The group included Jeffrey Marx and Michael York, the reporters who had written that Reggie had offered money to Steve Miller. They drank champagne in the backseat as Reggie, in a chauffeur uniform that included a hat, drove them to the Lexington Hyatt-Regency for a celebration. "I heard they asked for me specifically," Reggie said. "They waited until I jumped out of the car and opened the door for all of them. They threw quarters in the air as a tip. They were just laughing at me." Reggie found a new job within a week.

Larry Roberts believed so strongly in Reggie's case that he climbed out on a limb for it. The firm where he was a partner decided that the case was too much of a risk, even after sinking significant money into it, so Roberts left the firm and went out on his own. He felt he had truth on his side but faced a cadre of lawyers paid handsomely to prove otherwise.

Roberts thought he got a huge break during discovery, when both sides are required to turn over relevant if exculpatory evidence to the other. All the interviews Marx and York had taped fell under discovery, including a York interview with Steve Miller that was at the crux of the lawsuit.

As Roberts listened, he could not believe his good fortune. To him, it clearly showed that Reggie had never offered Miller money to sign with Pitt. Reggie, too, had a eureka moment after poring over transcripts of the interviews that pertained to him. One between Reggie and York in which Reggie felt he had successfully refuted any claim that he had done anything improper while recruiting Miller was not included in the tape transcripts turned over by the *Herald-Leader*. Reggie had a terrific memory, and when he did not see in the transcripts what he had told York about Miller's claim, he was convinced the tape had been doctored.

"I [had] told them [York and Marx], 'This didn't happen, this didn't, this didn't happen,'" Reggie said. "Once they eliminated that part of the tape, all they had was their word against my word, and their word would win because they were newspaper guys." He knew the tape could not help him if it had indeed been doctored, but he had another idea. If he could get the phone bill with the call, he could bust the *Herald-Leader*. Reggie felt like a detective as he tracked down a copy of the bill from the phone company. After he finally secured it, the length of the billed phone call did not match the length of the corresponding interview that had been turned over in discovery.

Roberts hammered home that point by having an employee from the phone company testify that customers are not charged after a phone call is completed. The jubilation from that courtroom victory was fleeting, however.

The opposing side petitioned for a directed verdict, contending that Roberts had not met the burden of proof required of the claimant since Reggie had been a public figure when the story was published. Judge James Keller granted the petition, giving himself discretion to rule on it in place of a jury. Before the ruling, Reggie and Roberts felt good about their position. Roberts argued that since Roy Chipman was the head coach at Pitt, he was considered the spokesman for the men's basketball program. He was the public figure, Roberts contended, not Reggie.

What happened before the trial started also made Roberts and Reggie feel as if they would be in good standing with the judge. One night Reggie saw two men attacking a young woman at his apartment complex. He fought them off, and it turned out that the victim was Keller's daughter. Knowing that Reggie's good deed might compromise the appearance of impartiality, Keller offered to recuse himself. Neither side objected to his continuing to hear the case, but Roberts probably wished he had taken Keller up on the offer.

Roberts said he was led to believe that Keller would rule Reggie a private figure, which would have opened the door to damages if the newspaper were found guilty of libel, even of negligence. Right before Keller issued his ruling, though, he told Roberts that he had changed his mind and considered Reggie a public figure. Roberts said he never got a reason for Keller's reversal in thinking.

The decision torpedoed Reggie's case because it is close to impossible for a public figure to win a libel suit. Even if malice is proven, punitive damages are severely limited. It looked as if the fight that had consumed almost four years of Reggie's life was over.

The trial lasted four days, after which Keller ruled for the *Herald-Leader* in a direct verdict. Roberts tried to cheer up Reggie by taking him to play golf. Reggie made two pars and a birdie on the first three holes. While they were on the fourth tee box, Roberts joked, "You're not playing like someone who just lost a million dollars." Reggie topped his tee shot. He made double bogey and then another. They stopped playing.

Roberts appealed the circuit court decision to the state Supreme Court. To Reggie, it seemed like a lost cause. He despaired that he would never get his good name back. One night he started driving to the house of John Carroll. The editor of the *Lexington Herald-Leader,* Carroll had also been named in the lawsuit. Reggie's opinion of the man only hardened after their paths crossed during depositions and the trial. Reggie saw Carroll as a pompous man who had ruined his life.

After the verdict in the *Herald-Leader*'s favor, Reggie resolved to shoot Carroll. "I had lost myself," he remembered. "I thought the only way for me to reclaim my manhood was to hurt the person who had set out to hurt me. Knowing something is wrong and still going ahead and doing it takes a lot. But when I left my apartment that evening with my pistol, I didn't have anything else to lose."

Reggie stopped at a service station near Carroll's house. While filling his car with gas, he ran into the chief justice of the state Supreme Court, where Reggie's case was to be heard in appeal, and the judge offered encouragement. "Son, you hang in there," he said.

That encounter did not deter Reggie. What changed the course of a handful of lives was when Reggie, still at the service station, saw one of Carroll's two daughters emerge from a car at their house. The sight pulled him back from the brink. "If his little girl hadn't gotten out of the car, I don't know what I would have done," Reggie said.

"I wanted to hurt him but didn't want to hurt his kids. I was still a compassionate person. The problem was I felt like no one really understood all the stuff that was going on." Reggie went home. And after that near-tragic night, he started to win.

The state Supreme Court reversed Keller in a unanimous decision on all eleven issues Roberts had appealed. It also wrote a scathing rebuke of Keller's ruling. The *Herald-Leader* appealed the decision, and the case went to the U.S. Supreme Court. After the Court upheld the state court's decision by a 4–3 vote, the *Herald-Leader* approached Roberts about a settlement. Reggie flatly rejected it. He wanted to make the *Herald-Leader* pay completely for what it had done to him. If it had just been about winning or losing, Roberts would have backed Reggie, but there were other considerations.

If they did not settle, Roberts would have to try the case again, this time in front of a new jury. It could drag out for another year and a half. Juries could be unpredictable, and nothing was guaranteed. Even assuming they won, a jury would decide how much money would be awarded to Reggie, which could vary wildly. "For a guy that had nothing, he couldn't pass it up," Roberts said. "It was too good a deal."

The settlement money would pay all debts incurred during the case, including almost $90,000 to Roberts's former law firm and the personal ones Reggie had accumulated. There would be enough left for Reggie to move on with his life. With too many variables involved, Roberts advised Reggie to accept the settlement, albeit reluctantly: Reggie had a pregnant wife back in Pittsburgh; it was time to go home to her.

Reggie wanted to proceed, despite Roberts's advice. "For him, it was always about integrity," Marisa said. "What they said about him was so not who he was. I remember being on my hands and knees one night just praying this would be settled because it was just getting to the point where it was so uncertain." Marisa's angst finally convinced Reggie to settle. One of the first people he called was Dwane Casey, who had won a multi-million-dollar settlement following the debunked allegations that had derailed his college coaching career. "Reg," Casey said when he learned that his friend was going to settle, "if you can live with it, that's a good thing."

The night before Reggie signed the settlement at the *Herald-Leader's* attorneys' office, Casey called his personal tailor in Lexington. The tailor opened his store after hours, and Reggie sorted through a bunch of different outfits before settling on a double-breasted olive-colored suit. He looked good leaving the attorneys' offices but still wanted to ride off into the proverbial sunset. He needed his car to cooperate. At the time, he was driving a cream-colored Audi with almost 150,000 miles on it. It was not the most reliable in terms of starting. How would it look if the car conked out after his triumph over the *Herald-Leader?* Reggie said a short prayer and pumped the gas pedal with bated breath. The car revved to life. "I put that bad boy in drive," Reggie said, "waved in the rearview mirror, and drove to Pittsburgh to be with my bride."

Almost thirty years later, Larry Roberts still has mixed feelings about the lawsuit's coda.

He and Reggie had stared down an opponent with exponentially more resources—and a big lead because the burden of proof in libel cases is weighted heavily in defendants' favor. Still, Roberts felt a bit hollow after the settlement. It did not represent total victory, something he felt his client deserved. "It's unbelievable the pain and angst that Reggie went through just trying to survive," Roberts said. "He never heard from these two idiots who wrote that newspaper article, and they should have called him and apologized. [*Lexington Herald-Leader* editor] John Carroll wasn't about to apologize. It's awful, and I'll say it until the day I die because they didn't treat him right. It was the most satisfying and one of the most disappointing cases that I've ever had. We went after them, and we gored them. They know it, and they didn't like it. I'd like to get those guys in court tomorrow." Reggie's family and friends would probably pay for courtroom seats if that happened.

Stuart Brown was in veterinarian school as the lawsuit played out. Reggie had mentored him, and Brown never doubted that the allegations made against Reggie had as much truth to them as Santa Claus. "Here's a guy who can't help but do it the right way. That's just his innate nature," Brown said. "The sad thing is just how callous the media can be and have such little journalistic responsibility to take chances on things that ruin people's lives. I knew how devastating that had to be, knowing Reggie like I did. It's just so gut-wrenching to have your life's work trounced like that."

One of the ironies of the whole saga is that the *Herald-Leader* pursued its exposé to ostensibly bring about honesty—and change—in major college basketball, yet, to Reggie, the newspaper torpedoed its own credibility by printing false allegations against him. "They won a Pulitzer, but they lost any moral authority because of what they did to win it," Reggie said. "They knew what was on that tape, and they knew it was doctored. And they got up on the stand and lied. I don't begrudge a person doing their job. I didn't begrudge them writing a story if they wanted to write a story about college athletics. But when they changed the whole last part of that tape and they cut that out, that was dishonest. I know what happened. I know what they did."

The *Herald-Leader* settlement pulled Reggie out of financial hardship, but one thing it did not do: open doors that had been closed for far too long.

10

Long Road Back

In October 1991, the *Basketball Times* published "The Vindication of Reggie Warford." It was a massive roundball version of *War and Peace,* apropos since Reggie had just settled his lawsuit after five years of fighting to restore his good name.

If the settlement Reggie won from the *Lexington Herald-Leader* went a long way toward his quest for vindication, *Basketball Times* founder Larry Donald's story put an exclamation point on it. It quoted former Pitt head coach Roy Chipman, who recalled a conversation with one of the authors of the Steve Miller story. How, Chipman had asked, could the newspaper have gone after Reggie the way it had? According to the *Basketball Times,* Chipman said the reporter responded, "Because Reggie Warford is a liar. He is lying to us about Kentucky, so we can write about him whatever we want." That conversation bolstered Larry Roberts's claim that the *Herald-Leader* had committed "tremendous malice" by running specious claims because Reggie had not given them the dirt that they coveted on Kentucky basketball.

The *Basketball Times* article also took aim at allegations made about Reggie in *Raw Recruits,* published in January 1991. The book quoted Reggie as saying, "These things happen," when Doug West purportedly told him about a booster offering him $10,000 to sign with Pitt. Donald, through telephone records, showed that the conversation in question took place *before* West said the booster offered him money. In other words, it could not have taken place.

Donald closed his story on Reggie with this:

> It's been a long time since anyone in college basketball has thought of this man. Embarrassingly so.
>
> The weeks, months and years ahead will tell us if that's to change, a circumstance worth keeping in public view if the sport is to redeem itself in all of this.
>
> See, it may well have been a newspaper story which began the troubled times for Reggie Warford, but it is the insecure and suspicious nature of college basketball which has kept him out of the game. Warford needs today exactly what he needed in 1986 . . . some coach with the courage not destroyed by whispers to give him a chance.
>
> Only then will this story, long in duration and filled with an unimaginable number of twists and turns, have the sole element it now lacks.
>
> A happy ending.

Larry Roberts knew a truly happy ending might never happen— ironically because of the case he built against the *Herald-Leader*. Roberts had gotten depositions from a slew of head college basketball coaches who said Reggie's reputation had been too tarnished to hire him, even though they believed he had done nothing wrong. "The coaches told me, 'If I took Reggie, then Duke would say [to potential recruits], "Look, you're being recruited by a guy who's under investigation by the NCAA,"'" Roberts remembered. "Nobody was going to take him. I got a representative from every conference to affirm that to show that he was blacklisted."

Reggie heard as much from head coaches who reached out to him. One was Stanford head coach Mike Montgomery. Another was Kentucky head coach Eddie Sutton, who succeeded Joe B. Hall in 1985. Sutton had given a deposition, saying he would have hired Reggie in a minute but could not because of the *Herald-Leader* story. He had also testified at the trial. "Mike Montgomery wrote a beautiful letter, made a phone call, gave me encouragement," Reggie said. "Eddie Sutton was a stand-up guy. He said, 'Reggie, I can't hire you. Let me tell you why.' He was extremely straightforward and honest. He said, 'Not everybody could undergo the type of scrutiny that you've undergone. I know I wouldn't want to go through that.'"

Reggie heard from more head coaches after the *Basketball Times* story, but none had openings on their staff. So he started working full-time at Shuman Juvenile Detention Center in Pittsburgh. He was a counselor for three years, then got a job as a drug-and-alcohol therapist at a Pittsburgh medical center. During that time, he approached his younger brother Derrick about starting a business. Reggie was now well versed in security and private investigations. He saw a need for security in everything from visiting nurses who made house calls in high-risk neighborhoods to schools that also were in potentially dangerous areas.

He found the perfect person with whom to partner. Derrick had distinguished himself during an air force career that sent him all over the world. He had worked in intelligence and counterintelligence for the US Air Force Office of Special Investigations. He had provided security detail for heads of state and become friendly with President George H. W. Bush. He had aided in the capture of the Panamanian dictator Manuel Noriega.

Derrick was finishing his air force career in 1992 when Reggie asked him to go into business. Reggie fronted the money to get it started; Derrick provided his expertise. Reggie rented half a floor in a Pittsburgh office building, where he and Derrick launched R&D Security. They worked in private security and often collaborated with Pittsburgh police, even in keeping the peace among rival gang factions. On one occasion, Derrick arrived at a tense scene involving gang members. He tried to de-escalate the situation but soon became embroiled in it. Amid an argument that could have taken a bad turn, Reggie pulled up. "He gets out of the car," Derrick recalled, "and this guy says, 'Hey, Reg! What's going on? Long time no see!'" Reggie's presence lowered the temperature immediately. A gang member who had given Derrick a hard time apologized. He didn't know that Derrick and Reggie were brothers. "He said, 'I know I'm a bad person, but your brother's a good person, and we would never hurt Reggie,'" Derrick said.

R&D Security thrived, growing to more than one hundred employees. Still, Reggie was ready to walk away from it—or at least sell his half to Derrick—after a chance encounter with Roy Chipman in 1995. Duquesne University was making a coaching change and had reached out to Chipman. He was confident he would get the job and asked Reggie if he would return to coaching with him. "Let's ride," Reggie told him.

The job intrigued Reggie for a couple of reasons. Duquesne had some basketball history with players such as Norm Nixon and Chuck Cooper. In 1954, Cooper was the first Black player drafted by an NBA team. Cooper had played high school basketball in Kentucky and drawn the attention of Wildcats coach Adolph Rupp. According to Dick Gabriel's documentary *Adolph Rupp: Myth, Legend and Fact* (2006), Rupp told Cooper that he could not sign him because of Jim Crow laws. He called other coaches on Cooper's behalf, though, including Duquesne's Chick Davies. Davies signed Cooper, who led the Dukes to three consecutive top-ten rankings. Duquesne was far removed from those glory days and the Nixon and B. B. Flenory years that followed. But Reggie thought he could help reinvigorate the program. He could sell the city of Pittsburgh to recruits, as he had done while at Pitt. Reggie also felt confident that he could find good players who had been overlooked.

Chipman told Reggie that he planned to coach for a few years before turning over the program to him. But then one night Reggie got a phone call from Chipman around eleven. He was calling from UPMC Presbyterian Hospital in Pittsburgh. "I'm in trouble," Chipman told Reggie. Reggie threw on some clothes and raced to the hospital. Chipman said he had been diagnosed with an aggressive form of cancer. A nominal Christian, he told Reggie that he worried that if he prayed now, it would look as if he were only doing so because he was sick. "This is your lucky day," Reggie said, "because that's not a prerequisite for why you need to learn to pray. Being in trouble or being in distress is when God expects you to call. You can do a lot of it on your own, but He needs to carry you a little bit. You need to express that Jesus Christ is your Lord and Savior and that you believe in Him." Reggie gave Chipman some Bible verses, and they prayed together. They hugged before Reggie left.

A year later Chipman went into hospice. When Reggie visited him, Chipman did not weigh much more than 110 pounds. He was so frail he wore a North Carolina T-shirt that belonged to his wife. Reggie joked that Chipman had worn the shirt because he knew Reggie did not like North Carolina. He kissed Chipman on the forehead, and they laughed. They talked about old times, and Reggie asked Chipman if he was right with everybody. "I'm really glad you're here," Chipman told Reggie. "I'll want you to speak when the time comes."

Chipman died in August 1997 at the age of fifty-six. Reggie delivered one of the eulogies at his funeral. Before Chipman passed, he had told Reggie, "You need to coach. That's what you were born to do." Around that time, Long Beach State head coach Wayne Morgan called Reggie and asked him to join his staff. The job offer came with a catch, though: it paid a dollar a year.

One night before leaving R&D Security, Reggie called Marisa to say he would be home soon. Four hours later, Marisa called. *Where are you?* Reggie did not know. On his way home, he had seen a school gym and cars in the parking lot. He had stopped and wandered into a game between elementary-age kids. Reggie did not know any of the pint-size players or parents, but he sat down anyway—and watched several games with rapt attention, as if his beloved Kentucky Wildcats were playing.

Only the phone call from his anxious wife jolted Reggie out of his trance. Basketball, no matter the level, had that effect on him. There was something about the bouncing of the ball and the squeaking of shoes on a wooden floor that drew him to the sounds, as if the Pied Piper in high tops were playing.

Morgan tapped into this effect when he reached out to Reggie. The two went back to their Big East days when Morgan was an assistant coach at Syracuse and Reggie an assistant coach at Pitt. They had been rivals but also became friends because of mutual respect. Morgan told Reggie that he questioned the loyalty of some of the coaches on his Long Beach State staff and needed someone he could trust.

With a full staff and limited resources, Morgan could not afford to pay another assistant. Reggie listened to Morgan's dollar-a-year pitch and said, "Well, you got me at the right time."

R&D Security was established enough that Reggie could take a leave. The major drawback of the job: he and Marisa would have to make their marriage a bicoastal one. They had two young sons, Grant and Tyler, and Marisa had a good job as a human-resources professional in Pittsburgh. Knowing how unstable coaching could be, they decided that Marisa should stay in Pittsburgh with the kids.

Reggie had another reason for putting some distance between himself and Marisa. Shortly before the Long Beach State offer, he had bought life insurance because during a physical doctors detected cell clusters they feared were cancerous. A biopsy ruled out cancer, but it hardly provided good news. Reggie was diagnosed with sarcoidosis, an autoimmune disease that attacks organs—in his case, it was his liver—and mimics cancer. Reggie did well with treatment, but he had a bad feeling. He wanted to give Marisa an opportunity for a fresh start if things took a bad turn. "I thought that I was doing her a favor," Reggie said, "that if I went out west and something happened to me while I out there, it would make it easier for her to move on."

Marisa would have none of that talk, but she looked at the opportunity as a chance for Reggie to follow his heart, even if it took him thousands of miles away from her. She and the boys flew to California every couple of weeks to visit. Reggie returned to Pittsburgh when his schedule permitted. He talked to Grant and Tyler on the phone almost every night. He loved being a father and felt blessed by his two sons, especially since Tyler had been a miracle baby. Several prenatal tests had showed a disproportionately high probability of serious issues. Reggie and Marisa leaned on their faith and rejoiced when Tyler was born healthy in 1993. The first time Reggie scooped up his second son, he danced while singing "You Are the Sunshine of My Life" by Stevie Wonder.

But the longer Reggie and Marisa lived apart, the more such happy times receded into the background. After two years, their marriage reached a tipping point. Following a four-day visit, Marisa drove Reggie to Pittsburgh International Airport. As they parted, Reggie went to kiss his wife, but Marisa turned her head. The flight back to California gave him plenty of time to think. Reggie loved California and felt Long Beach State was on the rise. He was also drawing a decent salary, having become a full-time member of Morgan's staff after one season. Reggie did not want to leave. He also did not want to lose his marriage. "I knew at the end of the year I was going to have to come home, or we were going to separate," he said.

Reggie hatched a plan to save his marriage and keep his job, though Marisa may have resisted had she known about it. He looked at houses in the Long Beach area, finding one with four bedrooms and a spacious patio and swimming pool. He bought the house and surprised Marisa and the boys with it when they visited. Marisa was slightly alarmed, but Reggie assured her that with his salary the mortgage payments were manageable. When Grant and Tyler saw the pool, they took off their shirts and dived in. "The next day we went to Disneyland, and it was over," Reggie said. "Marisa loved it. When she is in California, her skin has a glow, her hair is lighter. She was just a California girl, and everyone could see it."

Marisa became immersed in the community, and she and Reggie loved it. They had Black, Asian, biracial, and white neighbors. They lived seven blocks from Calvin Broadus Jr., a rising rap star now famously known as Snoop Dogg. "We had the most integrated neighborhood in America," Reggie said. "It was like the United Nations and had some of the best schools."

Long Beach State went 24–6 in Reggie's third season and made the NCAA Men's Basketball Tournament. Life was good, especially for Grant and Tyler. They were Long Beach State's ballboys and went to all the practices and games. The experience was great, with one notable exception. When Tyler was six, he was playing a video game, while Reggie and Marisa were in the next room. They heard a tiny voice say, "I hate this f—ing game!" Reggie, who did not curse, was aghast. He asked Tyler what he had said. When the boy repeated himself, Reggie said, "Tyler, do you know what that means?" "No," Tyler said, "but the players say it all the time." Reggie had a talk with the players, some of whom had to keep from laughing after hearing the story.

One day Marisa received a call from a casting agency saying that someone there had seen Grant and Tyler on TV during a Long Beach State game. Marisa followed up, and the two started modeling and acting. Tyler became one of the models for Target, appearing on cardboard cutouts across the country. He shot a commercial with Pamela Anderson and got to hold her hand. Grant modeled for Tommy Hilfiger and worked with Shia LeBeouf. Grant was a stand-in and Tyler an extra in the movie *Time Machine* in 2002. Two scenes where Grant stood in for an actor as a body double were used in the movie.[1]

"If I had been able to stay there and coach there, I don't think we ever would have moved," Reggie said. Alas, it was not meant to be. Following the 2001–2002 season, Iowa State hired Morgan as its head coach. Reggie had enjoyed the years he had spent in Ames as an assistant coach, but he did not want to move his family there. The Warfords moved back to Pittsburgh after five sun-kissed years in California, and Reggie returned to his security company. He had been back less than year when he got a call about coaching for an iconic basketball team.

While growing up in Kentucky, Reggie had idolized Cassius Clay. He had emulated the loquacious Louisville boxer, talking in rhymes and oozing swagger. When Reggie was in sixth grade, schoolmate Denise Harris started calling him "Cassius Clay." It was not a compliment. The two were in the same class, and Denise could be every bit as feisty as Reggie. They stayed close friends through adulthood, Reggie always treasuring her friendship because he felt she never saw color with him. Indeed, when she called him "Cassius," it was not a Black or white thing; it was a Reggie thing. He *always* seemed to talk. "Cassius, why don't you shut up?" Denise would tell Reggie. "You're not as good as you think you are."

Reggie's infatuation with Clay morphed into adulation as the latter transcended sports. Clay became Muhammad Ali after converting to Islam and refusing to fight in Vietnam. His stand as a conscientious objector cost him his heavyweight title and four years of his boxing prime, but it went a long way toward making him arguably the most famous person on the planet by the mid-1990s.

It was during that time that Reggie got to play the piano with his hero. He was in Lexington on a consulting job for Dick's Sporting Goods, which was trying to break into grassroots basketball. Reggie got a call from the father of Jaron Brown, a young basketball player who was already making a name for himself.

The elder Brown, a Lexington police officer, was part of Ali's security detail. They were going to be passing through the Hyatt-Regency, and Brown asked Reggie if he wanted to meet "the Greatest." That was like asking Reggie if he wanted a lifetime supply of free ice cream. Reggie was seated on the bench of a grand piano when Ali entered the Hyatt-Regency. Brown called him over and introduced him to Ali.

"Pleased to meet you, Champ," Reggie said. "I'm Reggie Warford."

Ali threw a few air jabs. Reggie put up his hands in mock surrender.

"No," he said laughing, "you're too good. I don't want a piece of that."

Reggie told Ali that he had gone to the University of Kentucky and had met him in the press box during a Wildcats football game. They talked for a few minutes, then went to the piano. The two sat on opposite ends of the bench, and Ali started tapping the keys. Reggie soon figured out he was playing "Lean on Me" by Bill Withers. Reggie joined in, and their impromptu jam session was something he never forgot. "He was very nice," Reggie said. "That's the most famous person I ever met."

Some of Reggie's friends told him there was an undeniable "Forrest Gump" quality to his life due to his surreal experiences. It makes perfect sense, then, that after Reggie returned to Pittsburgh from California, the Harlem Globetrotters beckoned. Head coach Rod Baker called Reggie about a vacancy on his staff. "I needed someone that I knew well, someone that I felt like I could trust," Baker remembered later. "Reggie stood out. I don't know how easy it was for him to say yes, but it was easy for me to ask him." The Globetrotters have both show and competitive teams and play a year-round schedule. It is a grind, Baker told Reggie, and not for everyone, but Reggie could not pass up the opportunity.

He was not disappointed, experiencing an intoxicating combination of exquisite skill and nonstop entertainment. Globetrotter games were both sport and spectacle. Players on the show team had to master more than one hundred tricks and were subject to fines if they messed up even in practice. If they were not breaking furniture or lamps, they were told, they were not practicing enough. That was the Globetrotter Way.

It was serious behind the scenes, but there was plenty of laughter, too. One time the joke was on Reggie as he coached against the show team. He had a distinct bow-legged gait—his Kentucky teammates had nicknamed him "Old Man" because of it—and one of the showmen imitated it behind Reggie, the unwitting straight man. "For twenty-five minutes people are falling down laughing, and I don't know what's going on. It got to be so funny that nobody could play," Reggie said. "I'm trying to coach and got mad at Rod because we're supposed to be buddies. I said, 'I hate you, but it's funny as heck.'"

Despite such comedy, the competitive team played against top-caliber competition. Before a game at Michigan State, the Globetrotters added the school's most famous alumni, Earvin "Magic" Johnson, to their team. "Every positive adjective you can say about him as a player is true," Reggie said. "We wanted to simplify some of the offense, so I got this board out, and I'm going to show Magic all the things on the board. Magic looks up at me and says, 'Wait a minute. Who catches it when I go here?' I said, 'Shooting guard.' He said, 'Who catches when I go there?' I said, 'Power forward or shooter.' He said, 'OK, driver, shooter. That's all I need to know.' Michigan State had a couple of future pros. We rocked them. Went into Syracuse and beat them too."

Charles "Tex" Harrison, a legendary player and assistant coach with the Globetrotters, told Reggie he was one of the best coaches he had ever seen. But the Globetrotters were a lifestyle, and Harrison did not think Reggie would sacrifice his family life for the franchise.

A philosophical difference ended Reggie's only season with the Globetrotters. During a meeting, Globetrotters founder Mannie Jackson asked what Reggie thought of center Ron Rollerson. Reggie liked Rollerson, who was 6-foot-11 and enough of a wide-body that his former Temple teammates had nicknamed him "Steamboat." Reggie thought Rollerson was a future NBA player. "I said, 'He's got great hands. Good footwork. Can rebound. He's got the girth. I think he's a next-level player,'" Reggie recalled. "[Jackson] slammed his hand down on the table and said, 'Motherf—er! What do you mean next-level player? This is the highest level!'"

Reggie started to stand when Baker alertly grabbed his wrists under the table. "As soon as [Reggie] said it, I knew something bad was going to happen because of the mindset of ownership," Baker said. "Ownership was made up of former Trotters who had grown up in that environment and then got themselves into position to own it. For them, that's the mountaintop, the epitome of basketball. Trotters want to entertain. The NBA entertains but in a totally different way."

The situation was quickly defused, but a little later Reggie got a knock on his hotel room door. He had been with the organization long enough to know what that meant: a bus ticket and a final paycheck. He met with Jackson the next morning, and the two parted amicably. "They are a great, gifting organization," Reggie said. "When I was there, they gave away about $10 million. That's a heck of a thing for Mannie Jackson to do. He was a remarkable guy, except for the tirade against me."

The memories Reggie had of his Globetrotters experience were priceless. "It's another one of those Forrest Gump things," he said, "because Reggie Warford should have [had] nothing to do with the Globetrotters." He paused and grinned. "But I've got pictures with them."

Reggie was an assistant coach at Pitt when he pulled off a Globetrot-teresque sleight of hand. Only he had done it with his health, not a basketball.

Reggie had dealt with heart issues ever since they almost ended his playing career at the University of Kentucky. Just as in Lexington, he refused to let them slow him down. He played regularly against his players at Iowa State and Pitt. He found pickup games whenever he could in the Pittsburgh area, sometimes with friends such as Franco Harris, Dwayne Woodruff, and other Pittsburgh Steelers. He took up racquetball and became a top-flight player.

What confounded a Pitt doctor was how Reggie could seemingly run all day despite having an enlarged heart. During a check-up in 1983, the doctor cranked up a treadmill to its highest speed. Reggie ran on it for thirty minutes. "He said I was in the best shape he had ever seen a person be," Reggie said. "He called people in to watch because he said people wouldn't believe what I did on the treadmill."

Unfortunately, Reggie could not outrun his heart problems. He managed his condition as best he could. He kept himself in fantastic shape, did not drink or smoke, and took medication. There were some scares that led to trips to the hospital. During one of them, a cardiologist gave Reggie his business card and said Reggie would need him one day.

In 2006, shortly after his Globetrotters stint ended, Reggie was hospitalized with major blockage in his heart. He underwent quintuple-bypass surgery. He was in the intensive-care unit at Jefferson Hospital in Pittsburgh when his status nearly took a fatal turn. As he was talking to doctors, he started falling backward. A nurse ran into the room and yelled, "Code!" Doctors and nurses moved frantically to neutralize a blood clot. Doctors cut open Reggie's chest right there since there was no time to get him to the operating room.

A nurse called Marisa and asked if she could get back to the hos-pital right away. Marisa, who was driving, gripped the steering wheel. "Is he dead?" she asked. Reggie survived, but it had been close. And his heart problems were far from over.

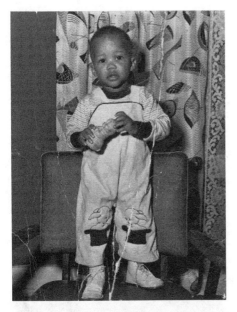

Reginald Garfield Warford was born on September 15, 1954, in Greenville, Kentucky. He grew up in nearby Drakesboro, where he excelled in sports and academics and eventually became a highly recruited basketball star.

Reggie credited his parents, Rev. Roland Hayes and Valencia Dean Warford, for raising him and his siblings the right way through love, faith, and perseverance.

This was a familiar sight when Reggie was growing up. Here he and younger brother Derrick (*left*) received trophies at an athletic banquet in 1969. (Courtesy of Glenda Harper)

Reggie and Coach Joe B. Hall, shown here after Reggie had signed with the University of Kentucky at his high school team's basketball banquet, did not always see eye to eye when he played for the Wildcats. They became extremely close, however, after his playing days were over, enjoying a father–son relationship. (Courtesy of Glenda Harper)

Reggie with Joe B. Hall (*left*), who was then an assistant to Adolph Rupp, and Reggie's high school coach, Robie Harper, after he signed his letter of intent with Kentucky. Harper gave Reggie the freedom to play his game and was like a second father to him. (Courtesy of Glenda Harper)

Reggie in his official Wildcat picture his freshman year, and there is a story behind what he called a "clown haircut." A barber stopped in the middle of the cut after he and Reggie argued because the man bashed the Kentucky basketball program. (Courtesy of University of Kentucky Sports Information Department)

Reggie, shown in the 1972–1973 Kentucky men's basketball team photo, was the first Black scholarship player in program history. It was a trying first year, but Reggie stayed the course and became a starter his senior season. (Courtesy of University of Kentucky Sports Information Department)

Reggie, seated second from the right in the 1974–1975 Kentucky men's basketball team photo, realized the significance of the moment when he was one of five Black players who took the floor together in a game that season for the first time in program history. (Courtesy of University of Kentucky Sports Information Department)

Reggie, seated second from the left in the 1975–1976 Kentucky men's basketball team photo, emerged as a starter and leader of the Wildcats that season, proving that his perseverance had paid off. He helped lead Kentucky to the 1976 NIT Championship. (Courtesy of University of Kentucky Sports Information Department)

Reggie, here in a game against the University of Florida in 1976, could always get to the hoop as well as shoot from the outside. (Courtesy of University of Kentucky Sports Information Department)

Reggie, shown here at Mississippi State, became a co-captain during the 1975–1976 season after Jack "Goose" Givens insisted that Reggie share the designation with him. (Courtesy of University of Kentucky Sports Information Department)

Reggie saved his best for last at Kentucky, emerging as a starter and team leader in his senior year after three frustrating seasons spent mostly on the bench. (Courtesy of University of Kentucky Sports Information Department)

Reggie steals the ball from Mississippi State's Ray White in 1976 to help key a frantic Kentucky rally in the final game at Memorial Coliseum. The Wildcats erased what looked like an insurmountable Mississippi State lead in the final minute to send the game into overtime, where they won 94–93. (Courtesy of University of Kentucky Sports Information Department)

Reggie always had a sweet-shooting stroke—and the confidence he could make any shot. (Courtesy of University of Kentucky Sports Information Department)

Reggie's first coaching job was at Iowa State, and he stayed there from 1976 to 1980 under former Kentucky assistant coach Lynn Nance. Reggie was the youngest Division I men's basketball coach at the time. (Courtesy of Iowa State Sports Information Department)

Reggie and the Iowa State men's basketball team enjoyed the privilege of meeting Governor Robert D. Ray during the 1976–1977 season, Reggie's first one in Ames. (Courtesy of Iowa State Sports Information Department)

Reggie coached at Pitt from 1980 to 1986, becoming the top assistant to head coach Roy Chipman and the Panthers' best recruiter. (Courtesy of Pitt Athletics)

Reggie, while coaching at Pitt, talks with Panthers forward Chip Watkins. Reggie recruited Watkins to Pitt along with many others, including stars such as Curtis Aiken, Charles Smith, Demetreus Gore, and Jerome Lane. (Courtesy of Pitt Athletics)

(*right*) Reggie and Marisa were married on May 26, 1990, after having a long courtship and overcoming adversity that only brought them closer.

(*below*) Patty Eyster with Reggie at his wedding on May 26, 1990. She had become a second mother to him after he arrived at Kentucky the summer before his freshman year, and they remained extremely close. Behind them are groomsmen (*from left*) Dwane Casey, James Lee, Wayne Morgan, Jack "Goose" Givens, Derrick Warford, and Jeff Bolinski.

Reggie, with his son Grant and his father, Reverend Roland Hayes, after Drakes-boro named a street after him in 1992.

Few things gave Reggie more pleasure than spending time with his sons, Grant (*left*) and Tyler (Tiger), and exposing them to music at a young age.

Reggie, Marisa, Grant (*left*), and Tiger were always a close-knit family and cherished the time they spent together.

Reggie and Marisa enjoyed a family trip to Hawaii in 2000 when Long Beach State men's basketball team played there in a holiday tournament. Reggie spent three seasons as an assistant coach at Long Beach State under good friend Wayne Morgan and helped the team make the NCAA Men's Basketball Tournament his final season there.

Grant Warford was signed by
Osbrink Kids Model when the
Warfords lived in California.
He and Tiger were discovered
while serving as ball boys for
the Long Beach men's basketball team.

Tiger Warford was also signed
by Osbrink Kids Model
when the Warfords lived in
California.

Reggie and Marisa gave new meaning to running it back to May 26, 1990. They did not just renew their vows on their tenth wedding anniversary but got married again in Las Vegas.

Reggie with Velma Cottrell (*left*) and Glenda Harper in Drakesboro in 2003, two friends who always stood with him. (Courtesy of Glenda Harper)

The Warford family. *Standing from left*: Derrick, Thelma, Velma, and Reggie; *seated from left*: Sharon, Revered Hayes, and Ronnie. Missing from the photo and dearly missed was the family matriarch, Valencia Dean, who passed away in 1987.

Brothers Reggie, Ronnie, and Derrick Warford were as close as could be. A fourth Warford brother, Billy, was killed in a car accident when Reggie was a freshman at Kentucky.

Reggie's smile and warm personality drew people to him. He never lost them, even while suffering on a daily basis in the later stages of his life.

The Muhlenberg High School Mustangs had reason to celebrate after winning a boys' basketball regional championship in 2010. Tiger is in the front row holding the trophy given to the team.

The Warford family outside of the house Reggie rented for him, father-in-law Beau Bolinski, Grant, and Tiger after returning to Muhlenberg County in 2009 to coach the boys' basketball team after the two county high schools there merged. Marisa stayed behind in Pittsburgh because of her job but visited as often as she could.

Grant Warford punctuated a win that made history in Reggie's first season as head coach of Muhlenberg High School in 2009–2010. The victory, as signaled by Tiger in the background, sent the Mustangs to the state playoffs, the first time a team from Muhlenberg County had qualified for that prestigious tournament.

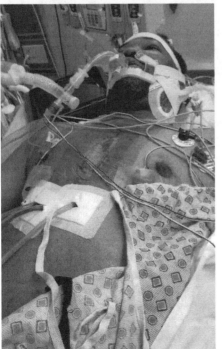

(*above*) Candy and Bob Holland (*left*) and Vita and John Fontana (*right*) helped celebrate Marisa's birthday at a surprise party set up by Reggie. The two couples are dear family friends who helped Reggie and Marisa when they needed it most.

(*left*) Reggie underwent successful heart transplant surgery in November 2014 but then experienced life-threatening complications. Marisa received a 3:00 a.m. phone call to return to the hospital—in case she had to say goodbye.

Grant and Tiger flank their grandfather, Maurice "Beau" Bolinski, who became a second father to them after he came to live with the Warfords in Pittsburgh before Tiger was born. Beau passed away on November 6, 2022, at the age of eighty-six.

Reggie acknowledges fans at a Kentucky game against Florida on February 6, 2016. The Wildcats made it a happy homecoming for Reggie, beating the Gators 80–61 behind freshman guard Jamal Murray's 35 points. (Courtesy of University of Kentucky Sports Information Department)

Reggie with Marisa, Grant, and Dr. Stuart Brown at the American Heart Association Ball in Lexington in 2016. Reggie befriended Brown when the latter was struggling as a teenager, and Brown, now a world-renowned veterinarian, says Reggie played a big part in shaping him.

Reggie, Marisa, and Grant attended the American Heart Association Ball in Lexington in 2016. The event raised hundreds of thousands of dollars in part because Reggie's former Kentucky teammates and others made large donations in honor of him.

Reggie and Kentucky men's basketball coach John Calipari, shown here at the American Heart Association Ball in Lexington in 2016, coached for a season together at Pitt in the early 1980s. Calipari never forgot Reggie's smile and the help he gave a young coach.

Shelley Trondle gave the gift of life when she donated a kidney to Reggie in 2017. The Warford family is forever grateful for her selfless act and the extra time it gave them with Reggie.

Lavon Williams, Freddie Cowan, Reggie, Jack "Goose" Givens, and Larry Roberts, with (*standing*) Dr. Stuart Brown and Larry Roberts. Reggie and Roberts, an attorney, teamed up to win a large settlement from the *Lexington Herald-Leader* after Reggie sued the newspaper for libel.

Former Kentucky players Lavon Williams (*left*) and Freddie Cowan flank former Wildcats coach Joe B. Hall and Reggie during a Lexington visit by Reggie. Williams never played with Reggie at Kentucky but credits him for paving the way for Black players who followed him and for mentoring Williams while he played for the Wildcats.

Denise Harris, Karen Walters, Marisa, Grant, and Matt Allison with Reggie at a Kentucky men's basketball game in October 2019. Harris and Walters were Reggie's close friends dating back to elementary school.

John Calipari, with Reggie and Marisa at the Kentucky men's basketball offices, stayed in regular contact with Reggie as his health deteriorated and often said a prayer for him while attending Mass.

Reggie signs the basketball wall in the Kentucky men's basketball offices during a visit he and Marisa made to Lexington in 2019 for a Wildcats game. He left an indelible mark on the program as a pioneer among other things.

Reggie and Marisa in the Kentucky men's basketball offices in 2019. Reggie loved returning to the University of Kentucky, and after his health faltered, former teammates often planned reunions and other get-togethers based on his ability to travel there from Pittsburgh.

Reggie lived for times like the Kentucky men's basketball alumni weekend in October 2019. Here he is with (*from left*) Jack "Goose" Givens, Lavon Williams, Marion Haskins, Jim Andrews, and Larry Johnson.

Former Kentucky coach Joe B. Hall, with Reggie and Marisa, said he would have "walked ten miles" to see Reggie inducted into the KHSAA Hall of Fame in April 2019.

Marisa, Tiger, Grant, and
Reggie shed tears of joy the
night Reggie was inducted into
the KHSAA Hall of Fame in
Lexington.

Marisa, Tiger, and Grant
always had Reggie's back,
something that inspired him to
keep fighting as he dealt with
unimaginable health issues.

Reggie and the Honorable Tom Piccione, a retired judge, became fast friends after meeting while each was waiting for a heart transplant. After receiving his own transplant, Piccione helped Reggie stay the course when he wanted to give up.

Reggie did not drink, but he always had reason to make a toast with Marisa, the love of his life. Here they are celebrating their thirtieth wedding anniversary on May 26, 2020.

Marisa, Tiger, Grant, and
Beau Bolinski always wrapped
Reggie in love. "Pop Beau,"
as Reggie, Grant, and Tiger
called him, said Reggie was his
best friend.

Reggie loved music in all
forms, and playing piano gave
him a sense of peace, especially
as his health deteriorated.

Reggie and Tiger, the younger of his two sons, grew particularly close before Reggie passed. Tiger always appreciated the life lessons and wisdom Reggie gave him when they talked.

THE WHITE HOUSE
WASHINGTON

October 11, 1983

Dear Mr. Warford:

I was pleased to learn from a recent article in the Pittsburgh Post-Gazette about your courageous rescue of a man and woman from their burning home.

The best among us, those who instinctively choose the selfless and noble course, often do not stop to weigh the cost when they come to another's aid. This is a fitting description of your bravery, and I am proud to commend your fine deed.

God bless you.

Sincerely,

Ronald Reagan

Mr. Reggie Warford
University of Pittsburgh
  Basketball Office
Post Office Box 7436
Pittsburgh, Pennsylvania 15213

Word of Reggie's heroics in saving an elderly couple from a burning house traveled across the country and even reached the White House. President Ronald Reagan sent a letter to Reggie commending him for his quick action and bravery.

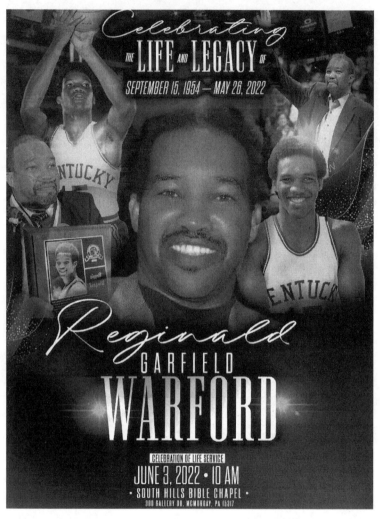

Celebrating
THE **LIFE** AND **LEGACY** OF
SEPTEMBER 15, 1954 — MAY 26, 2022

Reginald
GARFIELD
WARFORD

CELEBRATION OF LIFE SERVICE
JUNE 3, 2022 • 10 AM
• SOUTH HILLS BIBLE CHAPEL •
300 GALLERY DR. MCMURRAY, PA 15317

(*above and opposite*) The front and back cover of the programs given at the Celebration of Life ceremony in Pittsburgh after Reggie passed away on March 26, 2022, provided a montage of his life. Those pictures were brought to life during a final goodbye that lasted more than two hours by different speakers. Marisa was never prouder than when Grant and Tiger spoke jointly about what their father had meant to them. (Courtesy of Darvel McKinney)

THE **CELEBRATION** OF **LIFE** OF

REGINALD *Warford*

SEPTEMBER 15, 1954 — MAY 26, 2022

FORMER UK WILDCATS **PALLBEARERS**

• JACK "GOOSE" GIVENS • LAVON WILLIAMS • JERRY HALE
• FREDDIE COWAN • LARRY JOHNSON • JIM ANDREWS • DERRICK HORD

INTERMENT WILL FOLLOW IN QUEEN OF HEAVEN CEMETERY, MCMURRAY

Reggie received the Kentucky Medal of Valor from Governor John Y. Brown after saving two people from their burning home in 1983. Reggie was driving through Lexington when he saw a house engulfed in flames—and did not hesitate to act.

11

Homecoming to Remember

Bob Holland was looking for size as he drafted fourth-grade players for a Bethel Park youth basketball travel team. He zeroed in on Tyler Warford. It wasn't the name that got Holland's attention but rather the measurement next to it: the kid had requested an extra-large uniform. Holland, who had never seen Tyler, figured he had to be tall.

Unfortunately for Holland, Tyler did not provide the expected height; he just wanted a baggy uniform. Fortunately for Holland, Tyler could play. He and Holland's son, Brian, eventually formed the nucleus of a Pittsburgh-area travel team that played together for years.

If Holland did not know much about Tyler, he knew even less about Tyler's father. Reggie watched practice when his schedule allowed, but he never injected his opinions. Holland had no idea Reggie had played at Kentucky and coached at Pitt.

After one practice, Reggie approached Holland. He told him that Brian had an exceptional feel for the game. Holland thanked him but wondered if Reggie was trying to score points with him. One of the other fathers said, "Well, if Reggie says that about Brian, then he does." Holland replied, "So what? What does Reggie know?" Holland always laughs when recalling how he discovered the *real* Reggie Warford. Reggie became his assistant coach. After a year, Holland's wife told him he consulted with Reggie so much during games that they should switch positions. Holland happily obliged, and his coaching days with Reggie were some of the happiest of his life. It was the same with Reggie.

Reggie had countless stories from coaching in the Big East and in some of college basketball's most hallowed venues, but one of his favorite coaching stories centered on the game-winning shot that Brian Holland made for a middle-school AAU team in a game that stretched into five overtimes. With his team down by two points and four seconds left to play, Reggie ran Holland off multiple screens to get him an open look at the basket. Holland drained a three-pointer at the buzzer to set off a wild celebration. Reggie and Bob Holland hugged as if they had just won a national championship.

Years later, players from those teams talked about how much that time meant to them—and how much they had loved playing for Reggie. Recalling when he first heard that, Reggie choked up. "Don't get no better than that," he said in a whisper. "Don't get no better than that."

Nor did it get better than coaching his sons. Grant and Tyler Warford developed into top-notch players, though with different games. Tyler, the younger of the two, was built like his father, sleek and speedy. He also had his father's feisty disposition, something he had shown as a toddler. One time Reggie's first cousin, former NBA great Bob Lanier, visited him in Pittsburgh. Tyler, then four years old, looked up at the 6-foot-11 Lanier and said, "I'm not afraid of you!" Any wonder why Tyler's nickname is "Tiger"? Grant grew to be 6-foot-5, 230 pounds, with the body and hands of a tight end. The only thing that held him back were unfortunate injuries that hampered him as early as junior high school.

Reggie coached Grant and Tiger when they were a junior and freshman at Bishop Canevin, a small Catholic school in suburban Pittsburgh. Tiger led the team in scoring, and some of the parents complained to the school's athletic director, but Reggie never played favorites with his sons. In making a conscious effort not to do so, he may have been too critical of them. He told the athletic director that Tiger was the team's leading scorer because he was the team's best scorer. It took one game for the athletic director to see that Reggie was not trying to make his son a star at the expense of the team.

While coaching at Bishop Canevin, Reggie's father got sick. Reverend Roland Hayes Warford had done so much to shape Reggie as a strong, God-fearing man, and Reggie wanted to be there when his father needed him most. Also around that time, he received a phone call from Dale Todd. The two had starred together at Drakesboro High School in the early 1970s. But Muhlenberg County had changed dramatically since the early 1970s when there had been eight county high schools. By the early 2000s, there were only two high schools, and Todd called Reggie because they were merging. He was the superintendent of the new school and tasked with, among other things, making basketball work. That may have been the top priority to many in a basketball-crazed county, and he offered Reggie the boys' basketball head coaching job. To Todd, Reggie was the ideal coach to bridge programs that had been fierce rivals. Reggie was still a big name in Muhlenberg County. He even had a street named after him in Drakesboro.

After accepting the job and returning home, Reggie didn't take long to see that he would have plenty of talent to build a winning program. All he had to do was make sure the players did not kill each other first.

Grant Warford, starting a new school as a senior, was understandably nervous on the first day of school. As soon as Grant entered Muhlenberg High School, a fight broke out between two male students. "They were swinging fists and had to be broken up by two security guards," Grant said. "That was what I walked into."

Tiger, a sophomore, felt as if he had been dropped into a foreign country. "I woke up, and I was on a horse farm," he said of the house where he lived with his father, brother, and maternal grandfather. "I drove to school, and I passed cows." In his short life, Tiger had lived only in Bethel Park, just outside of Pittsburgh, and in southern California. It took time for him to get used to those cows—and to seeing fellow students driving with deer strapped to their trucks and walking around school with hunting knives.

Nobody struggled more with the Kentucky relocation than Marisa. She had been against it because she could not leave her job. After Reggie accepted the position, Marisa walked into Bob Holland's office and broke down in tears. She told Holland, her boss, "They're taking my husband." That was not all she was losing. Grant and Tiger had to go with Reggie, or they would rarely see him, and both wanted to play for their father. Intellectually, Marisa knew that her sons going to Kentucky was the best thing for the family, but emotionally the decision was difficult to process. Even when Grant and Tiger were young, Marisa had fretted about the day when they left home. That made saying goodbye so much harder after she moved her family, including her father, Beau, to Kentucky.

Marisa made a lonely eight-hour drive back to Pittsburgh. When she got home, she was not ready to go enter an empty house. She grabbed a couple of Coors Light bottles from the garage refrigerator and returned to her car. She drank them as tears poured out of her eyes for the next hour and a half. "It was one of the lowest points of my life," she remembered.

Reggie dealt with angst beyond his and Marisa's long-distance marriage for the second time. The two schools that merged had been split largely along racial and socioeconomic lines. Muhlenberg North High School had a preponderance of white students from affluent families. Black students had made up the majority in Muhlenberg South High School. Many came from families that struggled financially. Bringing together players from rival schools was only part of Reggie's challenge. He had gotten the job over Muhlenberg North's coach Steve Sparks. During Sparks's successful tenure, his son, Patrick, had taken his place alongside Reggie as one of the greatest prep players in county history. The younger Sparks had started his college career at Western Kentucky before transferring to Kentucky for his final two years. The Sparks name was as big as the Warford name in Muhlenberg County basketball.

The hiring of Reggie caused hard feelings among those loyal to Steve Sparks, some of whom had money and influence. If the inherent politics made the job tougher for Reggie, so did the math. Six returning players, three from each school, had earned all-county honors the previous season. Plus, Grant and Tiger had been added to the group, and each could play well. Reggie tried to bring his players together during summer workouts, but it was all he could to keep them from clobbering one another. "Every practice there was a fight," he said.

His first test came when Muhlenberg opened play on the summer-league circuit. On the bus ride to the game, Joe Gabbard, the team's best player, taunted some of his teammates because their families were not nearly as well off as his. After a fight nearly broke out on the bus, Reggie benched Gabbard. That did not sit well with some parents, including Gabbard's. His mother, Carla, was on the school board. His father, Paul, had played against Reggie in high school and been an all-conference player. Reggie's tough stance fueled rumors that Joe would transfer. Paul Gabbard told Reggie that he did not want to meddle but was miffed that Joe had not started the first summer-league game. Reggie told him he could not play Joe if he was going to be divisive. Paul Gabbard had a talk with his son and squelched transfer rumors, but Joe remained a hard-nosed and headstrong player. Tiger often guarded Gabbard in practice since he was the team's best perimeter defender. Each tried to make a point when going up against one another. "I didn't want people to resent me for my dad being the coach," Tiger said. "I wanted to earn my way there. I was hardheaded with a lot of people but particularly with Joe. We dang near fought about four or five times."

Muhlenberg won a lot of games on sheer talent that season, but a cauldron of racial tension, parochial rivalry, and outside sabotage roiled beneath the surface. It boiled over after the biggest win of the season.

Owensboro Catholic, the top-ranked team in the region, visited Muhlenberg, and four thousand fans crammed into the gym for the showdown. Muhlenberg relentlessly pressed its bigger opponent and wore out Owensboro Catholic, winning by 24 points.

Reggie was so charged up that when Tiger walked past him in the locker room, he gave him a hard whack on the behind, as if to say *Way to go, Son!* The elation over the victory was short-lived. Two police officers came to Muhlenberg's locker room to tell Reggie that he and his family needed to stay put because a threat had been made against him. Then four players, including two starters, abruptly quit the team. They walked out of the locker room laughing.

Reggie had never experienced anything like it in all his years of basketball. After an hour, the police officers assigned to Reggie and his family and another player were the only ones remaining in the locker room. That player was Joe Gabbard. When Reggie stepped into the hallway to gather his dizzying thoughts, Gabbard emerged from the locker room. "Coach, I swear I didn't know this was going to happen, and I didn't have anything to do with it," Gabbard said. "I'll play however you want me to play. I'm yours." He hugged Reggie. The rest of the team followed Gabbard's lead, rallying around their embattled coach. Muhlenberg reeled off one win after another until it was one victory away from rarefied air.

No team from Muhlenberg County had advanced to the state tournament in twenty years. Making it there was no small feat, and not just because Kentucky is as synonymous with basketball as Texas is with football. There is just one state tournament in Kentucky, meaning schools with three hundred students might have to go through ones with three thousand students to win a state championship. The sixteen teams that qualify for the state tournament first navigate a gauntlet of single-elimination district and regional tournaments.

Muhlenberg's season looked as if it would end in the regional finals. Its opponent, Apollo High School, had four players who were at least 6-foot-5, including a 7-footer. Along with imposing size, Apollo had a slick point guard who made everything go.

Before the game, Reggie gave Tiger explicit instructions regarding Apollo's point guard. "I don't want him to be able to inhale." Tiger stuck to the kid like sunburn. Gabbard, with limitless shooting range, made one basket after another. Center Lamont Gregory helped Muhlenberg hold its own on the boards. Grant also played a terrific game but was an unlikely player to put the exclamation point on one of the biggest wins in Muhlenberg County basketball history.

Because of chronic injuries, Grant had played his senior season on faltering knees. They had robbed him of his explosiveness and sometimes failed him off the basketball court. During the week leading up to the game, Grant had stayed home from school one day because he simply could not walk. None of that mattered after he caught a pass behind the Apollo press late in the game. With adrenaline coursing through him, the player with the knees of a sixty-year-old man threw down a two-handed dunk, putting an indelible stamp on Muhlenberg's 64–50 win and a wild, wacky season. "This is the greatest gift you could have ever given me," a jubilant Dale Todd told Reggie after the game.

Close to one hundred cars led the team bus on the forty-minute ride back to Muhlenberg County. Some drivers laid on their horns the whole way home. Marisa honked her horn so much she blew it out. It was a price she gladly paid for a night her family would never forget.

Muhlenberg's season had unspooled like *Remember the Titans* meets *Hoosiers*. Then came the first game of the sixteen-team state tournament at Rupp Arena in Lexington—and a defeat that hurt Reggie as much as any he had experienced in college basketball.

What haunted Reggie most about the 73–63 loss to West Jessamine: his belief that he could have prevented it. Before the game, Louis Stout, who had been his mentor at the University of Kentucky, warned him that Muhlenberg might struggle with outside shooting in its first game at Rupp Arena. Adrenaline would mingle with nerves. Also, the players would have to adjust to the depth perception with fans seated much farther away than in high school gyms. Reggie trusted Stout, and he believed Muhlenberg, with players who were bigger and quicker than the opposition, could wear down West Jessamine.

But Muhlenberg had shot so well during its stirring run that Reggie said to one of his assistant coaches, "Let's go with what brought us here." Stout's prediction played out, though, and Muhlenberg struggled from the outside. It trailed by a point with five minutes left in the fourth quarter when Tiger knocked the ball away from the player he was guarding. After a scramble for the loose ball, Tiger found himself under a pile of players. To Reggie's chagrin, Tiger was whistled for a foul. West Jessamine made two critical free throws on its way to victory.

Reggie took the loss as hard as his players. He knew he should have reigned in the outside shooting. "We took thirty-two threes," Reggie said. "Ten too many." Joe B. Hall attended the game. Afterward he told his former player what Reggie already knew: "Reg, you're a great coach, but you should have gotten the ball to Grant," Hall said. "They couldn't stop him."

Despite the disappointing end, the season brought many from a fractious community together. Twenty-nine tour buses carried fans to the game in Lexington. Many others drove to it. Of the nineteen thousand fans in Rupp Arena for the game, twelve thousand were from Muhlenberg County. Paul Gabbard, Joe's father, told Reggie that he had been the right man for the job.

Had all this happened in a movie, Muhlenberg's riveting run to the state tournament would have united the community long past that feel-good time. But real life rarely follows a two-hour script with a happy ending. The palace intrigue that had come with Reggie's job devolved into gossip that was as malicious as it was baseless.

Some internet message boards claimed Reggie was having affairs with various women. That would have made Reggie laugh had he not already experienced the damage the written word can do to a reputation. He had to go before a judge after someone anonymously reported him for child abuse—Reggie's whack on Tiger's behind.[1] Apparently, the person who reported Reggie omitted the all-important context: Muhlenberg High School's biggest win of the season when a charged-up Reggie gave his son an exuberant *Atta boy!*

Reggie had been warned that such nastiness might happen. Denise Harris, one of Reggie's closest friends, had tried talking him out of taking the Muhlenberg coaching job because of the inevitable divisiveness after the two high schools consolidated. She did not want to see Reggie get sucked into an unrelenting vortex. After he took the job, *she* got sucked into it. Harris was at Sunday school when others in the class started bashing Reggie simply because he had been hired over Steve Sparks. Harris said that Reggie was one of her best friends and asked them to quit talking about it. They apologized but then started right back up on the subject. Harris stood up and said, "I told him not to come to this hellhole!" She stormed out of the room and vowed never to return. She did not go back for six months.

Most disheartening to Reggie was that he and his family dealt with racism that was worse than anything he had experienced at the University of Kentucky in the early 1970s. Bricks were thrown through windows of the house they rented. Ku Klux Klan threats were deemed serious enough that the state Attorney General's Office investigated. The Warfords were assigned a security detail after games even though they lived just two miles from Muhlenberg High School. "Two sheriffs would get in front of us. They would have another guy drive around the perimeter of the parking lot every day to make sure there weren't people setting up with guns," Reggie said. "Grant and Tiger experienced racism in Kentucky that I didn't experience. I thought what I had done and what other guys who came along with me had done had paved a way that was smooth enough for them to come through. Tyler was called 'ni—er' more than I was."

Sometimes, Tiger was called this name by students who thought they were complimenting him. "They'd get real close and say, 'You know, you're not like them other niggers. No offense or anything,'" he remembered. "I just kind of laughed it off and said, 'Thanks . . . I guess.'" Such remarks would have been anything but a laughing matter to Reggie, so Tiger shielded his father from some of his experiences as the biracial son of the head boys' basketball coach. "It wasn't until Tiger graduated that he told me how many times he had been called 'ni—er' at school, and he wouldn't fight because he didn't want to get me in trouble," Reggie said. "He told me how many times people told him he wouldn't be playing if it wasn't for his dad coaching and how he carried that around with him. I apologized to him because I never would have thought it. Because I never addressed it, they never felt like they had a sounding board for things that were happening."

Despite such ugliness, there was often hope. The white sheriffs who guarded Reggie and his family after the Ku Klux Klan threats

wore shirts that said, "We've got your back." Another close friend
had his back every bit as much as Denise Harris. Jolly Jernigan, who
had been best friends with Reggie's older brother, Billy, went to every
Muhlenberg High School basketball game and walked with Reggie
when there were credible threats against him.

Ultimately, the actions of some did not cancel out the warmth
of so many, and Marisa took a real liking to the southern hospitality
she experienced when visiting her family. "The majority of the people
were just terrific, friendly and lovely," she said. "They would bring
fresh-baked bread and homemade pies. Just very friendly. I appreciate
it way more now than I did at the time."

Nothing better symbolized the dichotomy of the quaint community support the Warfords enjoyed and the vitriol they also experienced
than after someone left a tin of cookies on their front porch. There
was no name attached to it, and no one wanted to be the first to bite
into a cookie. They went into the garbage.

Reggie spent five years in Muhlenberg County. That period mir-
rored the surreal script that had been his life. There were highs and
lows. Through all of it, Reggie stayed true to himself and his convictions, which is ultimately what led to his firing. After his first season,
Dale Todd pressured him to hire an assistant who had recently been
a head coach. Reggie saw the request as his boss wanting a head
coach in waiting, but he agreed to it anyway. After three seasons, the
situation became untenable. Todd gave Reggie the opportunity to
resign. Reggie, having made a promise to the kids that he would not
leave the program after Grant and Tiger graduated, refused. "I said,
'No, I'm not walking away,' " he remembered. "I made him fire me."

He left the job with a 66–28 record and the victory that had
propelled Muhlenberg to the state tournament. Reggie was just as
proud that he had never lied to his players. He never coached again
and soon faced his greatest challenge yet. It was the fight for his life.

12

Fight for His Life

The day Grant Warford reversed roles with his hero started with nary a hint of drama. Grant, a student at the University of Kentucky with no afternoon classes, had just settled down for an afternoon nap in February 2014 when he received an urgent phone call.

Jolly Jernigan, one of Reggie's oldest friends, told Grant there was a medical emergency.

Reggie, no longer coaching but still teaching at Muhlenberg High School, had woken up that morning disoriented and dizzy. He almost fell several times in the shower.

Reggie called Dr. Barry Hardison, and they planned to meet at a nearby medical clinic. A storm had dumped a foot of snow on Muhlenberg County. The steep, winding driveway to the house where Reggie was living was a swollen ribbon. There was no way Reggie's car could make it to the street. Snow had so paralyzed the area that paramedics could not send an ambulance.

Reggie called Jernigan, whose monster truck with cartoon-size wheels plowed through the snow. Reggie was so weak that Jernigan had to lift him into the passenger's seat. With no room to maneuver, Jernigan had to back down the driveway in reverse.

Not long after they got to the clinic, tests showed Reggie to be in stage 4 kidney failure. Because the kidney failure might be related to his chronic heart issues, he needed to get to a hospital that was equipped to handle all his medical needs. One in Nashville, Tennessee, was closer. But Reggie's heart doctors were in Pittsburgh, so it was better to return there.

After meeting his father and Jernigan at a gas station, Grant tied a white handkerchief to the radio antenna of his car to alert police that he was speeding because of an emergency. Jernigan then gave Grant explicit instructions before the 420-mile drive: "You need to make sure he stays awake the whole time," Jernigan said. "He cannot go to sleep."

Dr. Hardison had called hospitals in Cincinnati and Columbus, Ohio, to give them Reggie's medical history in case he could not make it to Pittsburgh. As Grant drove close to ninety miles per hour, he realized that he might lose his father. "It was something I never really tried to think about because my dad had always been Superman," Grant said. "I never felt there was this moment of hopelessness until that moment where there was this fear that things won't work out." Grant was not ready to say goodbye, and the drive gave him time to think about his relationship with his father. "He epitomized all the virtues I saw as being a good man, a good person," Grant said. "I saw the way he treated people."

Grant had struggled with anxiety and depression in high school, much of it having to do with his physical health. When he was in seventh grade and collided with another player on the basketball court, he heard a pop but played through the pain. A couple years later, a growth was discovered on the left side of his leg. Doctors removed a tumor the size of a fist, but the operation robbed Grant of explosiveness in his jumping-off leg. Overcompensating with his other leg caused the tendons in that knee to deteriorate.

The knee issues forced Grant to confront that he might never realize his dream of playing basketball at the highest levels. Self-doubt crept in, and it was exacerbated by confusion over his sexuality. Grant battled suicidal thoughts, and his struggles were such that his friends would not let him be alone. Their support saved him, and Grant finally decided to tell his parents that he was gay. His parents were deeply religious, and Grant had no idea how they would react. Reggie and Marisa said he was young and that he should keep an open mind, but they also told him that they loved him unconditionally. A couple days later, Reggie sat Grant down for a talk. "He said, 'I've had gay friends. I have friends who have gay sons, and I'm completely OK with that. But I found myself struggling with it when it was my own son. That's not right, and I'm sorry for that. I don't know if it's ultimately a sin, but, if it is, if you were to go to hell for this, then I would take your place, so you could live your life and find happiness,'" Grant remembered. "My feelings of self-doubt all sort of faded away after that."

Just as his father had done for him, Grant was determined to be there when his father needed him most. His insides were roiling as he sped toward Pittsburgh. He drove with one hand on the steering wheel and the other across Reggie's chest to keep him from slumping forward. As Reggie drifted in and out of consciousness, Grant started singing Bob Marley's "Three Little Birds," a reggae tune they both loved about how things are "gonna be alright." Reggie joined him. That song and father–son talk carried them all the way to Pittsburgh.

A drive that should have taken six and a half hours was completed in a little more than four hours. The crisis seemingly had been averted, but any relief was soon tempered.

Doctors at UPMC Presbyterian Hospital determined that Reggie's kidneys were shutting down because of congestive heart failure. Reggie was placed on a heart-transplant list and began meeting with doctors and specialists. The goal was to sell himself, much as he would to a potential employer. He had plenty of experience doing that. Only this time he was interviewing for his life.

Tom Piccione met Reggie while they were in the hospital awaiting heart transplants. Something about Reggie's smile captivated Piccione, a retired judge. They started talking one day, and it was as if they had known each other for years. "Reggie turned out to be an inspiration to a guy who was maybe just looking for something," Piccione said. "I had faith and my family, but he just added an additional layer to it."

He and Reggie needed all the support they could get. The process preceding a heart transplant is an emotional roller coaster. Many factors come into play for potential recipients, all of them pointing to the same thing: "It's whether or not you're a good match and a good risk," Marisa said.

When a heart becomes available, multiple candidates are prepped for surgery. Reggie went to the hospital twice hoping to get a new heart, only to learn it had gone to someone else. That happened several more times after Reggie was in the hospital full-time, a lengthy stay that almost broke his spirit.

He spent more than two months in the cardiac intensive-care unit, largely confined to his bed. Marisa visited every day, filling his room with balloons and more than five hundred get-well cards. Music also helped Reggie stay positive. When nurses helped him walk the hospital hallway, he always played "Three Little Birds," the song Grant had sung to him. One day Reggie sang it for doctors making their hospital rounds. They started singing with him.

But Reggie was existing, not living. He finally reached a breaking point. He just wanted to go home. He knew telling Marisa this might be the hardest conversation of his life. That morning he told his nurses not to interrupt them. As he and Marisa talked, he pleaded with her to let him live what time he had left on his terms. "Whatever happens, we'll live with it," Reggie told her. "I'm just tired."

Marisa was exhausted, too. While Reggie was in the hospital, she left for work at six in the morning and worked until noon. After that, she went to the hospital and stayed with Reggie until 10 or 11. Her days blurred together, but they also strengthened her conviction to keep fighting for Reggie. "When I was growing up, I always thought there was something important I was going to have to do," Marisa said. "I'm a caregiver. I'm really good at making sure Reggie gets through this situation and that situation and somehow knowing the right questions to ask the medical providers and knowing when to push him and when not to push him."

As Marisa and Reggie talked, it became apparent to her that she might not be able to negotiate that delicate balance. She pleaded with Reggie to think about the kids. She begged him to think about her. Reggie remained firm in his desire to go home. Marisa did not know what else she could say.

Both were crying when there was a knock on the door. Three nurses were outside Reggie's room. *Jesus.* Hadn't he told them to leave them alone while he talked with Marisa? "Not right now," he said tersely. One of the nurses said she had a message from Tom Piccione. Reggie did not know that Piccione had just gotten a new heart. To get rid of the nurse, he asked what Tom had said. "Tell Reggie it's worth it," the nurse said. It seemed nothing short of divine intervention, especially after Reggie and Marisa heard the whole story. Piccione had woken up from surgery and had no idea how badly Reggie was struggling. As disoriented as he was, he thought about his good friend. Five years later, Piccione, with tears in his eyes, said, "I don't have an explanation for it."

His words pulled Reggie back from the precipice. And two weeks later, everything aligned for getting a new heart. "They found a perfect match, and [Kentucky men's basketball coach] John Calipari posted to his million [social media] followers, 'He's getting a new heart! ' " Marisa remembered. "Everything was great."

And then it wasn't. The transplanted heart was badly bruised; doctors could not get it to start. Dr. Christian Bermudez faced a serious dilemma. If the heart was not good, Reggie, whose chest had already been opened, would likely die in surgery. If Reggie did not get a new heart soon, he would die anyway. Bermudez sent word to Dr. Dennis McNamara, Reggie's thoracic cardiologist, who rushed to the operating room. He called off the transplant before they reached the point of no return. "We'll find him a better heart," McNamara said.

Marisa found no consolation in those words. As she and Bermudez talked, Bermudez said he had never encountered this situation before. He was so upset that he cried with Marisa. She returned to Reggie's hospital room and curled up in a windowsill. She bawled as her father, Beau, consoled her. "That was probably one of the most devastating moments of my life," Marisa said.

As Reggie transitioned to consciousness, he dreamed that he was on a crucifix, probably a manifestation of his extreme pain. He was in a haze as doctors explained the situation but alert enough to under-stand the gravity of their words. "You're telling me," Reggie said in a hoarse whisper, "that I don't have my heart." Text messages flooded Marisa's cell phone. She did not know what to make of them or her own feelings.

Two weeks after Reggie's aborted surgery, a new match was found. The ensuing operation was successful, but Marisa knew that *success* was a relative term. A breathing tube protruded from Reggie's mouth, and wires and tubes crisscrossed his body. Everywhere Marisa looked, there was blood—on his pillow, on his sheets, on his hospital gown. Reggie had bled out during the surgery—twelve pints of blood were pumped into him—and his kidneys had shut down.

The dissonance between Marisa's fears and the congratulatory messages she received after Reggie made it through surgery made her head spin. She left the hospital after ten o'clock that night, completely drained. She had slept a total of fifteen hours the previous five nights. She got home at eleven and was asleep as soon as her head hit the pillow. Three hours later her cell phone rang. It was one of Reggie's nurses. "You need to come back," she told Marisa. "How soon can you get here?" Marisa, still half asleep, did not grasp the urgency of the call. She took a quick shower and was driving to the hospital when the nurse called again. She said Marisa needed to get there immediately. It might be her last chance to say goodbye.

Reggie's blood pressure had plummeted, and the doctors used a defibrillator to restart his heart. Perhaps most problematic, they could not stop the bleeding. Reggie, with his chest still open, needed more surgery. Marisa arrived in time to kiss him on the forehead. Then he was wheeled into the operating room, where doctors stabilized his heart.

Marisa stayed by Reggie's side after the surgery, not leaving the hospital until midnight because there was a six-hour period then in which doctors did not make rounds. Marisa returned the next morning at six o'clock. She had her laptop computer and set it up next to Reggie's bed. Only Marisa, her family and friends would marvel. "Work gave me a sense of normalcy," she said. "It grounded me, and the folks I worked with were so supporting and amazing."

One colleague supported Marisa when she needed it most. Vita Fontana regularly dropped off care packages at the hospital. Sometimes she packed small bottles of wine at the bottom of the bag for Marisa. She arrived with her warm, live-out-loud personality at lunchtime that day, bringing a sandwich and bag of potato chips for Marisa. She stayed the rest of the afternoon. Marisa had fashioned a makeshift office, using the top of a Hazmat garbage can for her laptop. Fontana set up next to her.

The cardiothoracic intensive-care unit was a big room with heart monitors and medical equipment everywhere. A hive of activity buzzed around Marisa and Fontana as they watched in bemusement. One nurse, after checking Reggie, yelled, "You just had a heart transplant, Reggie! You need to rest!" What struck Fontana as odd was that Reggie had not woken up from the surgery. He *was* resting.

Marisa and Fontana's suppressed giggles spilled into all-out laughter over something relatively banal. After fluid bags toppled off a cart near Reggie, people walked around them as if nothing had happened. Marisa and Fontana started laughing, and they could not stop. It did not make any sense. Or did it? "It was her release," Fontana said. "Marisa is so strong and just holds it together, but sometimes you need to let it all out. I feel like God put me there, with my personality, for her." "I badly needed it," Marisa said, "because otherwise I would have just cried and cried."

Marisa would be forever grateful to her friend for providing a respite for her frayed nerves. Reggie regained consciousness four days after surgery, but his responses initially caused Marisa more angst. A doctor asked Reggie what year it was. He said, "Nineteen eighty-six." Marisa's heart sank. *Now he has amnesia?*

Reggie's memory quickly returned, but his body needed more time. He could take only two or three steps at a time. He spent five weeks in a hospital rehabilitation center.

He finally returned home—for the first time in more than one hundred days—and enjoyed a quiet evening with Marisa. They ordered steaks, smothered with onions and mushrooms, and buttered baked potatoes from Outback Steakhouse. Reggie got a reminder of life with a new heart when he had to order his steak well done instead of his preferred medium rare.

On the way home from the rehabilitation center, Reggie called his doctor's office and talked to a physician's assistant. He asked if it was safe to be intimate with his wife. She told him the only thing to avoid was heavy lifting. This gave Reggie and Marisa a green light to renew their love after his interminable stay in the hospital and rehabilitation center. "We had a wonderful, special night," Reggie said.

Tiger Warford did not know the depth of his father's basketball life until he was in high school. Reggie rarely talked about it with Grant and Tiger, wanting them to forge their own paths. Most mementos and pictures from Reggie's playing career collected dust in a box, underscoring his indifference to self-promotion. To Marisa, that indifference was alternately one of his biggest strengths *and* one of his biggest weaknesses.

She loved her husband's humility but sometimes wanted to scream at him for it. That was especially true during the interview process that preceded his transplant. Marisa implored Reggie to sell himself to the doctors when they asked why he deserved a new heart. She sometimes did it for him, rattling off all he had done in his life, including pulling two people from a burning house.

Tiger knew that his father had played basketball, but he had always seen him as Coach Dad or Dad, not as a player. He laughed when Reggie told him he had once gotten scores of recruiting letters and scholarship offers, thinking it must be a joke. One day, though, Tiger got a glimpse of the player his father had been.

They were at Bethel Park Community Center when Reggie started shooting. There is a difference of opinion about where he shot from. Tiger remembers the foul line; Reggie recalled it being closer to the three-point line. Not in dispute is what happened next: Reggie started making one shot after another, his left-handed stroke still maple syrup. The streak of made shots stretched into the thirties. "And he made like forty more in a row," Tiger said.

The sublime shooting display stopped only after Reggie had had enough and walked off the court without a miss. As he and Tiger were leaving the community center, Tiger glimpsed another side his of father he had not seen—or had refused to see. As they climbed a flight of stairs, it was a struggle for Reggie, even with a cane. Tiger got impatient. Reggie told him that walking up the stairs was as physically demanding for him as a two-hour workout was for Tiger. He pressed down on Tiger's shoulders. "Now try to go up the stairs," Reggie told him. "That's what it feels like to take every step."

The heart transplant that saved Reggie's life had taken a tremendous toll on his body. Having his chest cut open four times, including the quintuple heart bypass back in 2006, ravaged his vascular system and eventually led to a dire situation with his kidneys. He was on dialysis, a process in which blood is taken out of the kidneys and cleaned before it is recirculated. However, his veins started collapsing, making it impossible for him to continue dialysis. His kidneys went into failure.

Around that time, Marisa, too, had a health scare. Stabbing midsection pain led her to the emergency room. Doctors discovered a grapefruit-size tumor and feared she had liver cancer. The tumor was benign, but it precluded Marisa from donating a kidney to Reggie. Ronnie Warford, Reggie's older brother, and Beau Bolinski, Marisa's father, offered to donate, but Ronnie was battling cancer, while Beau's age and health issues ruled him out, too.

The search for a match led to one of Marisa's colleagues. Shelley Trondle's desire to help went beyond her friendship with Marisa. Six years earlier, a cousin with whom she was close had needed a new kidney. Trondle had not been a match and never forgot how helpless she had felt. Her cousin eventually got a transplant, but the wait for a kidney had been excruciating for the family. Now, Trondle offered one of her kidneys to Reggie. "For me, it seemed illogical not to do something that could save someone's life," Trondle said. "I'm a person of faith, and I believe that God created all of us like puzzle pieces where we all have gaps and all have these extras and that they were designed that way to fit together to fill in each other's gaps. I just happened to have two kidneys that worked really well, and Reggie needed one."

If only it were that simple. Six factors determine a donor match, including blood type. Reggie and Trondle were thought to have different blood types, something that should have made her altruistic gesture a nonstarter. However, Reggie had undergone so many blood transfusions during his heart transplant that his blood type had changed. It was now the same as Trondle's. "That was an incredible coincidence or a miracle," Trondle said.

Everything else fell into place, and Trondle never wavered. The one person who tried to talk her out of the decision to donate a kidney was the one with the most to gain from it. "Reggie actually made a couple of special calls to me, saying, 'You know you can be on the gurney headed to the operating room, and you can still say no. I will understand. You don't have to do this,'" Trondle remembered. "Reggie and Marisa were just so sensitive to me. As desperate as they could have felt to want this to happen, they kept making sure that I knew I did not have to go through with it, and we would still be friends and everything. They were incredible through the whole thing."

The transplant succeeded, giving Reggie another lease on life. Nothing made Trondle feel better about it than after Grant Warford left a message on her voicemail. He thanked her and said how much it meant to him. As Trondle, who also has a son, listened to Grant's message, tears streamed down her face.

13

Call to the Hall

Reggie's health problems took him to many places, including back to his days at Pitt in one instance. Joey David, a sharpshooting guard, had played for Pitt from 1982 to 1986. His relationship with Reggie had been strained—at least that is how David perceived it. He played the same position as Brian Mitchell, whom Reggie had recruited from Lexington, Kentucky. Because a different assistant coach, Seth Greenberg, had been David's primary recruiter, David felt that Reggie pushed for Mitchell to play rather than him.

There was another layer to the tension. David had played at nearby Upper St. Clair High School in an affluent suburb of Pittsburgh. David's father, a priest, made only $18,000 a year, but the Davids lived in Upper St. Clair because that is where the church house was located. Reggie did not know this, and David felt that he had seen him as a pampered rich kid.

After graduating from Pitt, David went to physical therapy school and eventually opened his own practice in Mount Lebanon. In another interesting twist to Reggie's life, he started working with Reggie following Reggie's heart and kidney transplants. One day he told Reggie, "I just wanted to let you know where I came from, and it wasn't where you thought I came from. That kind of always bothered me." Reggie looked at him and said, "Joey, I had no idea." Something about the way Reggie said it struck David, and the sincerity in Reggie's eyes washed away any hard feelings that David harbored. "It was no longer the Reggie who kind of didn't understand me," David said. "It was Reggie, and we took that and grew from that."

The two assumed roles that were opposite of what they had been at Pitt. David was now the coach, pushing Reggie. Meanwhile, Reggie approached physical therapy the way he had played basketball. He attacked it. Reggie never complained when David put him through the paces, never begged off from anything, no matter how bad he felt. "I really enjoyed getting to know him on a deeply spiritual level, watching him fight," David said. "Reggie is just a great man, and anything I can do to help him, I would do."

Reggie's fight after heart and kidney transplants became even more challenging in 2018.

He knew something was seriously wrong after he and Tiger returned home from hitting golf balls at a driving range. As he walked upstairs, he had to stop halfway up the steps to catch his breath.

Reggie went to a neuromuscular specialist, who inserted a long needle into his calf. The needle probed different parts of Reggie's body with electric charges to see how quickly the nerves responded. Reggie had twice endured having his chest opened for heart transplants. He had once spent days in the fetal position before passing a kidney stone. Never had he felt pain like this.

The test produced more bad news. The muscles in the back of Reggie's legs had withered away, becoming like clumps of beef jerky. He was diagnosed with sarcopenia, a degenerative disease that erodes the muscles. There is no cure for sarcopenia. It can only be slowed through a combination of diet, medicine, and steroids. "I never saw it coming," Reggie said. He and Marisa struggled to glean even a glimmer of hope from doctors. "It was the first time we were told, 'We really can't do anything for you. We're just trying to keep you from getting worse,'" Marisa said.

Curtis Aiken, whom Reggie had recruited to Pitt, sent him a package with a generous check, moving Reggie to tears. Jack Givens and other Kentucky teammates pooled $5,000 to buy him a motorized wheelchair, which allowed him to return to Kentucky for a Blue–White basketball game and reunite with his teammates. Looking forward to such events kept him going, as did a phone call he received in February 2019. The news he received overwhelmed him. He started sobbing. His tears of joy were for good reason: Reggie Warford was getting immortalized.

Jerry Hancock spent more than a year researching and crafting the argument he submitted to the Kentucky High School Athletic Association (KHSAA) Hall of Fame nomination committee.

Hancock, who grew up in Muhlenberg County, was in middle school when Reggie starred for Drakesboro High School. Hancock could not take his eyes off Reggie during games. Reggie rose so gracefully on his jump shots and so effortlessly knocked them down. He was the first player Hancock saw who could play above the rim. "Reggie was different," he remembered. "As a little boy, I loved watching him play and would try to emulate him."

Hancock was a high school senior when he met Reggie and was legitimately starstruck. He looks back on the experience as the first time he met someone famous. Years later, he got to know Reggie on a different level. He was an assistant athletic director at the newly merged Muhlenberg High School when Reggie coached the boys' basketball team. The fact that Reggie led Muhlenberg to the state tournament in his first season only cemented his rock-star status in Hancock's eyes.

Fast-forward to April 27, 2019. An hour before the KHSAA Hall of Fame induction dinner, Hancock recalled what the KHSAA's executive director Julian Tackett told him after he had called Reggie three months earlier: "I have never been so moved by telling someone they had made the Hall of Fame."

Reggie had already been inducted into the Muhlenberg County Hall of Fame and the Pittsburgh Basketball Club Hall of Fame, but this was different. This honor was coming from the entire state, *his* state. "Finally, I feel like he is where he needs to be," Hancock said in the ballroom of the Lexington Hyatt Regency hotel.

Family and friends from all over joined Hancock to celebrate Reggie's big night. Reggie's brothers Ronnie and Derrick flew in from Texas and Arizona, respectively. Twin sisters Velma and Thelma came from Texas with Sharon, the youngest Warford sibling. Like Reggie, Velma had battled heart disease for years. She also had multiple forms of cancer. Two years earlier, she had been so sick that her daughter had moved up her wedding so Velma would be alive for it. Yet here Velma was for her big brother, still fighting, still leaning on her faith. She was a Warford. Reggie's family was part of a celebration that seemed straight from the TV show *This Is Your Life*.

Dr. Stuart Brown, a renowned veterinarian whom Reggie had mentored as a teenager, and his fiancé, Jen Roytz, were there, as were Patty Eyster and her husband, Burt. Through the years Reggie had become as fiercely protective of Eyster as she had always been of him. Before she married Burt, Reggie and several former Kentucky teammates told Burt that if he ever hurt Patty, he would answer to them. They had been only half joking.

Denise and Ricky Harris and Karen Walters made the drive from Muhlenberg County for the celebration. All had been classmates with Reggie at Drakesboro High School. Glenda Harper, the wife of Reggie's late high school basketball coach, Roby Harper, also represented Muhlenberg County.

Reggie's eclectic entourage also included his attorney and good friend Larry Roberts as well as longtime friend Debbie Reed. Reed's family had owned a restaurant in Lexington when Reggie was a student at Kentucky. He had become family to them. Reggie and Marisa helped Reed after she lost her teenage daughter in a car accident. Reed's mother called Reggie one day and told him Reed had become a shut-in. No one could get through to her. Reggie visited, and they talked for hours. Their concern for her did not end there. "Out of the blue, Reggie and Marisa would call, or they would show up at the door," Reed said.

Reggie and Marisa were also close with Roberts. He and Reggie had teamed up to sue the *Lexington Herald-Leader* for libel; the case still stoked Roberts's fire. At one point, he saw Reggie giving an interview to a Lexington TV reporter who had backed out in the middle of giving a deposition for Reggie during the lawsuit because he had feared the repercussions to his career. Reggie had long ago buried any hard feelings over it. Not Roberts. "I wouldn't spit on that guy if he was on fire," he said.

Dr. Tom Brown and James "Doc" Mendelsohn drove from Pittsburgh that day to attend Reggie's induction. The two had become good friends with Reggie when he coached at Pitt and represented another part of his life that had come together for him.

Then there was Kentucky basketball. Former teammates Jerry Hale and Larry Johnson were there. So was Lavon Williams, who arrived at Kentucky the year after Reggie graduated. Williams had struggled adjusting to a school where there were so few Black students and credited Reggie with helping him make it at Kentucky. Williams frequently texted Reggie. It was not unusual for Williams to add a goat emoji to signify GOAT, the "greatest of all time."

Former Kentucky men's basketball coach Joe B. Hall also attended the dinner, a welcome surprise. Hall, who was ninety years old, had not been feeling well, so Reggie did not expect him to make it. "My gosh I'd walk ten miles in my condition to be here," Hall said. "He's an inspiration. He truly is. He's like a son."

Reggie's family and friends filled six tables in the ballroom. It was the biggest contingent among the honorees. The alphabetic order of presentations meant Reggie spoke last. With Marisa, Grant, and Tiger standing behind him, he delivered a vintage Reggie speech. It was genuine, spliced with humor, and from the heart.

I've met a lot of people I'd like to thank. First and foremost, my mother and father, who are not with us, Reverend Roland and Valencia Warford. They gave me a foundation that made me want to work hard and do things the right way. I owe a lot to what my family instilled in me. My brothers Billy, Ronnie, and Derrick were my major competitors growing up. Ronnie, my oldest brother, and Billy were 210 pounds and 6-3 and much bigger than me. They beat the living heck out of me. That made it easier when I got into organized ball, and my younger brother Derrick played with me my junior and senior year as a varsity player.

Other people that affected me were coach Roby Harper, who is also in the high school athletic Hall of Fame. Roby was a good man. He never used profanity on the court. He believed in the two–three zone. Kept me out of foul trouble. One thing that he did that made it really nice for me, he said, "Shoot the doggone ball, son." And I did.

There's two more people I want to mention that especially had something to do with my development. The first is Louis Stout. Mr. Stout was a friend of Coach Hall's when I was being recruited by Kentucky. One of the things he instilled in me from the very first time that I met him was, "Son, this is going to be bigger than you. This is going to be bigger than anything you do on a basketball court." He said, "You don't understand it yet," and he was right. I didn't understand it, but over the years his counsel proved to be great for me.

I had other people that I love and cherish that bought me my first suit so I could attend the banquet where Coach Hall came down to sign me: the people of Drakesboro and Muhlenberg County, I really thank them. My coach Roby Harper was a great player in his own right, and for years he held the county scoring record until Patrick Sparks came along and broke it. He would scrimmage and play with us, so when he was having a kid from a town of eight hundred people being recruited by Kentucky and Indiana and Notre Dame, he was really excited.

The first time he came to Kentucky, on our visit we were going to meet at a Big Boy restaurant. They had television cameras out there and everything. They were all ready for us. Coach Hall was there. He comes up to us and says, "How are you doing, Coach? I'm Joe B. Hall. Pleased to meet you." He stuck out his hand, and my coach got so excited that he forgot his name. He said, "I'm Roby Joe Harper. No, not Roby Joe. My name is just Roby Harper.: It was a funny, "Who's on First" moment. That was my introduction to being recruited by Kentucky.

You hope for certain things during the course of your life, thinking, "If this could happen, that would be pretty nice." I've been to a number of Hall of Fame [ceremonies] where other people were being inducted. I can remember sitting there as a young man and a young coach and watching these guys, some of them in wheelchairs and some of them walking poorly. Now I am that guy. I'm the guy in the wheelchair. I appreciate it so much more because I'm still here.

The athletic director at Muhlenberg County, Jerry Hancock—and we worked together—started researching some of the things I had done as a player. As he started to go back and research it, he called me one day and said, "I'm going to present your name to the KHSAA for consideration for the Hall of Fame." He was in his car on his way to Lexington, and I said, 'You know, Jerry, that would be really nice.'

Sure enough, a year later I get the call from Julian Tackett, and I thought he was calling me to encourage me because of my failing health. He called to tell me that I had been voted into the Hall of Fame. I cried for the next three minutes because it's the greatest honor that I've ever received. And I'm receiving it while I can still smell the flowers, and my sons know that I did something that was OK, and this includes my wife, Marisa.

The crowd rose after Reggie finished speaking. They stayed on their feet, applauding as Grant and Tiger presented their father with his Hall of Fame medallion. Tears slid down Reggie's cheeks; Marisa dabbed at her eyes. Tingles zipped up and down Tiger's spine. "I was just so happy for him because it was such a special moment that even the other people getting inducted were touched," he said. "It was amazing to see how many people were asking about him and how many new faces I got to see that really respected him."

Marisa wanted nothing more than to freeze time, especially after everyone retired to the hotel bar. Surrounded by family and friends, swapping stories, Reggie was at his happiest. His voice and laughter often rose above the din. Even in his weakened condition, Reggie could still carry a room.

By the end of the night, Marisa was exhausted. She, Reggie, and her father, Beau, had arrived in Lexington on Thursday night. His brothers and sisters had arrived the next night, and they had talked and laughed into the morning's wee hours, so Marisa had slept only a couple of hours. She did not sleep much more the night of Reggie's induction, but she was feeling the best kind of tired. "Seeing how many people showed up to celebrate with him was amazing," she said.

Not long after his Hall of Fame induction, Reggie wrote what he titled "Lions to Lambs." He texted it to his brother Derrick one morning at three o'clock.

> My name is Reggie Warford and I used to be a lion. Most of you remember what that's like. You are the king of your jungle, you have strength, pride, and presence. You are in control and the master of your destiny.
>
> There are so many things you feel as the lion, until one day when you become the lamb. It's been a slow process, a slow revelation for me. It wasn't one day I'm a lion and the next I'm a lamb, it was more gradual than that. It was the slow erosion of things you used to take for granted, things like needing help to do the most menial of things.
>
> You surrender those things a little at a time until one day you wake up and you need help getting in the shower, then help getting out. You need assistance getting dressed, you go from a cane to a wheelchair. You need assistance to stand, walk, feed yourself. Your strength, pride and presence is gone. You are different as a lamb.
>
> You become more humble, less combative, more aware of all your vulnerabilities. As a lamb you can no longer be the leader of your pack. You surrender their protection to the new young lions who have become you. You become different than what you were. Most have a hard time accepting it as

you start to realize what's happening. You resist, you try to reclaim your place in the pride as those around you take up more and more slack of the things you used to do as the lion.

So you try to adjust. You become grateful for the lion and lioness taking you out. Getting you to a seat in the restaurant or getting you to a handicap section in the arena. Sometimes they cut up your food because your hands don't work. Your lioness packs the suitcases whenever you have to travel. You realize that you take a role that is unfamiliar to you.

For all the things you lose as the lion as you become the lamb, you still love as hard and as fiercely as ever. You try to make your presence as less intrusive as possible. You become the follower. You become the lamb. The lamb is a symbol of the meek (gentle) who God said "would inherit the earth." An obedient, and gentle spirit gives strength and support to the lion.

Derrick read it—again and again. It resonated beyond his brotherly bond with Reggie: Derrick had survived multiple heart attacks and beaten cancer. Sometimes when he was struggling, he called Reggie and asked him to tell a joke. "No matter how he feels," Derrick said, "Reggie can make me feel good." Derrick paused and fought back tears. "He's never not given me time, no matter what I ask him to do," he remembered, his voice choked with emotion. "When I saw him in Lexington, I was encouraged, but I knew that my brother was struggling. We were lions, there is no question about it. But there is more to life than physical presence. The character he showed in what he has gone through has inspired and helped me. What has been the centerpiece of our lives is our connection to God and what our parents instilled in us. That has been the cement that has gotten us through tough times personally and professionally. Faith does not make things easy. It just makes things possible."

Reggie continued to fight, but his struggle was constant. One day he cried for almost an hour because of the suffering. Doctors tried to find the right combination of medication to soothe the pain, but the process was trial and error. Some medication made Reggie so sick that he struggled to keep even tea down. "The insidiousness of this ailment . . . it just slowly chops away at things you don't normally think about," Reggie said. "You don't [normally] think about walking to a refrigerator. For me, that is a major, major move. There are days when you feel like you would do yourself a favor by getting out of everybody's way. But I don't want my son to find me or my wife to find me. If I don't want them to find me, don't do it."

Reggie felt well enough, relatively speaking, in August 2019 to fulfill a promise he had made to Keith "Lefty" Moore to attend an Iowa State basketball reunion. Reggie had recruited Moore to Iowa State in the late 1970s, finding this gem of a point guard at a remote junior college in Amarillo, Texas. Reggie was just four years older than Moore, so the two engaged in epic one-on-one games after Iowa State practices. There was a long-running argument about the outcomes of these games (Reggie said he never lost; Moore said *he* won half the time). There is no dispute over how their battles shaped Moore. "He made me toughen up and understand what it took to play in the Big Eight," Moore said. "He was a tough, strong guy and a really good midrange shooter. And you don't play point guard at Kentucky without knowledge of the game. I just wondered why he didn't pursue a playing career more."

Moore, who grew up in Detroit, had some idea of what Reggie had endured at the University of Kentucky. His mother and father were from Mississippi and Arkansas, respectively, and he often visited relatives there as a youngster. "It was like a whole different world, Mississippi from Detroit," Moore said. "Reggie telling me about some of the things he had to endure and some of the things that happened at Kentucky made me appreciate him more as a man. It made me appreciate him opening doors for other people to have those opportunities."

Although close in age, Moore refused to call Reggie by his first name. "It was 'Coach Warford' and always will be," Moore said. Coach Warford was one of the people Moore most wanted to see at the fortieth reunion of the 1978–1979 Iowa State men's basketball team.

Getting to Ames was not easy for Reggie, who was on oxygen full-time. His and Marisa's flight was delayed leaving Pittsburgh, and they missed their connecting flight from Minneapolis to Des Moines. They did not get to Ames until two o'clock in the morning, five hours later than expected. Yet any lingering fatigue turned into a good kind of tired during Reggie's first extended stay in Ames since he had lived there.

Reggie reunited with his former secretary, who was still working at Iowa State. He and Marisa attended an alumni basketball game and a cocktail party; she was surprised at how many people knew Reggie or knew about him. The highlight of the trip came during a gathering of the 1978–1979 team in which all twelve former players there picked a teammate and said what they had liked best about his game. Moore and several other players selected Reggie.

One testimonial especially moved him. It came from 6-foot-9 forward Chuck Harmison. "I remember the first time I saw Coach Warford, and it was in the gym, and he was playing." Harmison said. "I remember thinking I never saw a man play that hard in my life. It was just a pickup game, and he tried to teach us by example of what we needed to do."

As Harmison talked, Reggie's eyes misted up.

"As an assistant coach, you don't have the wins that you get on your résumé," Reggie said, "but you do have the measure of the young men that you coached, and it's about the young men that you coached being good, moral people. I've seen that in a lot of the guys that I coached. There were some guys that lost their way and had some troubles. But there's also a lot more, like the guys at Iowa State, that were great people. They said none of us has been perfect during this journey, but they were taught how to try, and they appreciated that."

14

Reckoning for Reggie

By the mid-1990s, Reggie had become an expert on Pittsburgh gangs through his security company. He frequently conducted intakes at Shuman Juvenile Detention Center in Pittsburgh to gather information about gang activity. He was working intake one day when a white teenager was brought to Shuman. He had dragged a Black kid with his car, severely injuring him.

He swore at Reggie repeatedly and called him "ni—er." Reggie ignored the vitriol but told the kid with lightning-bolt tattoos on his neck to get it out of his system. "I actually pissed off two guards who were Black because they thought I should have tuned him up a little bit," Reggie said. "The kid was scared, and I thought it was so much bravado."

The juvenile was placed in a unit drawn along racial and gang lines. He refused when offered a cell that could be accessed only by the guards. It did not take long for the kid to receive a brutal beating. "He was in the infirmary for quite a while," Reggie said, "and I started working with him." Reggie never held a grudge for what the kid had called him. They talked a lot, and the kid came to consider Reggie a friend. Before leaving Shuman, he hugged the man at whom he had hurled slurs nine months earlier. "I know some things about him changed," Reggie said. "The last time I saw him, he was looking to get the Aryan tattoos removed from his body,"

That Reggie was able to get through to a kid seething with hatred and prejudice reflected his ability to connect with juvenile inmates from all backgrounds. He did not just try to befriend them; he told them harsh truths, too. In an exercise he conducted with Black inmates who were teenage fathers, he would ask if they were going to take care of their child. He would get a resounding yes. He would ask if they would do anything for their child, including rob and kill. Again, a resounding yes. "Then," Reggie said, "I hit them with, 'OK, would you go to school and stay out of trouble for your son? Would you show up every day to make sure he's doing his homework? Would you stay out of prison so you can be there for your son? Would you do the good things? Would you do the really hard things?'" Reggie wanted to make the point that having a gun or belonging to a gang did not give them power. "To me, gangs are just another form of slavery," he said. "You always got some pushback, but there were some guys that listened."

Reggie also told them something that probably surprised many of them: he could identify with them because he was a Black man with a criminal record. In 1991, he was charged with aggravated assault after a fight in a tournament basketball game. He was playing for a friend's team in Herminie, a rural hamlet about twenty miles east of Pittsburgh. Reggie and Marisa got lost driving to the gym and arrived late. Reggie quickly made up for lost time, scoring 20 points in six minutes.

The more Reggie dominated, the angrier an opposing player became. He called Marisa a "ni—er lover." That was still on Reggie's mind when he made a steal. He said, "Beep, beep!" to the player who had cast the racial slur and scooted away for an easy layup.

Reggie was called for traveling a little later. He patted the ball with a smile, knowing he had picked up his pivot foot early, and bounced the ball to a referee. As soon as the ball left his hands, the player with whom tension had been building knocked Reggie to the ground. To Reggie, the man had just started a fight. "He was a big guy, and when I came up from the ground, I was under him," Reggie said. "I hit him and caught him on the left cheek. He tried to grab me, but he couldn't swing. I ran him into the wall, which was about eight or nine steps away, because I didn't know how many of his friends were going to jump on me."

The two were quickly separated, and Reggie was thrown out of the game. He and Marisa could not get out of there fast enough. Two days later, when Reggie got home from a Pittsburgh Steelers game, two state police officers were at his house. He had broken the man's jaw and was later charged with aggravated assault. He reluctantly pleaded guilty to misdemeanor simple assault after the plaintiff settled for $20,000 in damages instead of his original demand of $120,000 (Reggie had to pay an additional $10,000 for medical bills and lost wages). The plea bargain kept Reggie out of jail—he faced up to three years in prison if convicted—but it required that he admit he had committed a crime.

During his allocution, which was witnessed by an elementary school class on a courthouse tour, Reggie tried to say he had been pushed first. The judge quickly cut him off. There was no getting around the allocution. Reggie's attorney made that clear when he stood up and fixed a hard stare on his client. "They had to pry it out of me," Reggie said. What bothered Reggie most about the ordeal was that it left him with a permanent record because his skin color criminalized what he always contended was self-defense. "It confirmed what I had been told: that a Black man had hit a white man in Herminie, Pennsylvania, and I was going to catch hell for it," Reggie said. "It didn't make any difference that my argument might have been right."

April 2019 brought a cruel reminder that if Reggie did not have bad luck with his health, he would have no luck at all.

What had started at the new year as a minor cut on his right foot almost cost Reggie his lower leg. An infection that spread after his foot was improperly bandaged turned tendons and tissues into a ghastly mash like rancid ground beef. He was fortunate that doctors did not have to amputate his lower right leg. They removed only part of the heel, then he landed in Bridgeville Rehabilitation Center.

One day in a small room bursting with balloons, Reggie sat in his bed, talking on the phone. As he spoke with good friend Jack Givens, the concern in his voice was palpable. A former Kentucky basketball player had posted suicidal ideations on Facebook. Reggie and Givens talked about making sure they and others reached out to the player in his greatest hour of need. Reggie had not been a teammate of the man (his name has been withheld to protect his privacy), but they were Kentucky basketball players, part of a brotherhood. That meant something to Reggie. It always had, especially after what he experienced in 1988.

That year, Reggie had attended the funeral for Bob Fowler after his former Kentucky teammate died suddenly at the age of thirty-one. There were so few people at the funeral that Reggie and several funeral home employees had to serve as pall bearers. "That made a terrible impression on me," Reggie said. He had vowed that no other Kentucky basketball player would ever receive such a lonely farewell.

One of Reggie's greatest fears was that no one would show up for his funeral. That explains why he kept in touch with scores of former Kentucky basketball players—and reached out when one of them was in need. That might seem at odds with Reggie's Big Blue experience. As the player most responsible for integrating Kentucky basketball, he had endured a daily struggle unlike his teammates' experience. Life at Kentucky got easier as more Black players followed him there, but it was never easy.

When Reggie was introduced before his final home game at Memorial Coliseum, he thrust a closed fist into the air. It was not a political statement, just Reggie showing emotion after becoming a starter and team captain following three seasons of minimal playing time. Some fans took it as a "Black Power" salute and booed.

When Kentucky played an exhibition game in Jefferson County one time, an older Wildcats fan approached Merion Haskins afterward. He told Haskins that his ancestors had owned slaves, among them Haskins's ancestors. Haskins was livid, but Reggie and Larry Johnson could not resist teasing him about it. What struck Reggie was that the man meant no malice. He sincerely thought their family histories gave him a connection to Haskins. To Reggie, the encounter was emblematic of a patronizing attitude that prevailed during that time. He never questioned whether his white teammates had his back, but he sometimes wondered whether some did only because he was *their* Black player.

After his freshman year at Kentucky, Reggie spent a week with roommate Bob Guyette in his home state of Illinois. They went to Chicago, where Reggie, the country kid, nearly got whiplash from staring up at all the skyscrapers. But that visit to Guyette's home was a notable exception. Early in his career, Reggie had minimal social interaction with his Kentucky teammates. He could not remember going out to eat with any of them. The sting of that exclusion never left him, no matter how much he loved the University of Kentucky. Was it because their acceptance of him only went so far?

Reggie questioned whether they genuinely liked him or supported him only because he was a teammate. There is ample evidence that they cared, or maybe Reggie changed perspectives. Maybe it is both.

The night before Reggie had quintuple heart bypass surgery in 2006, he received a phone call from Jimmy Dan Conner. Conner had arrived at Kentucky a year before Reggie, and he could have been a poster boy for Wildcats basketball. Reggie had played for three seasons behind Conner, and the two were friendly but never close friends. As Reggie lay in his hospital bed, Conner told him, "Don't worry about a thing. You have my word: if something happens, I'll be there for your family."

Such support had been the norm from Kentucky basketball since Reggie's health started to deteriorate. On two different occasions, Jack Givens and Jerry Hale had planned basketball reunions around times Reggie was going to be in Lexington. Guyette flew in from Arizona, where he was a renowned plastic surgeon, to attend one of them. Mike Flynn drove from Indiana for the gatherings, at which Reggie was the honored guest. "All of these guys showed up, and they didn't show up because I had been an All-American and made everybody look good," Reggie said. "They didn't show up because I was a thousand-point scorer and had my jersey number hanging in the rafters. When you bring somebody into your orbit as a friend, it's because you feel that person had added value to you in some capacity. That's the way I was received by the guys at Kentucky."

Still, the scars from growing up in an area where Black people were treated as second-class citizens ran deep. His brother Ronnie recalls working as a janitor at an appliance store and some people defecating on the floor so that he would have to clean it up. Wanton racism like that stung. And Ronnie, even though he has a PhD in theology and is a minister, still struggles with forgiveness because of what he experienced.

And because of what he continues to see. "I don't really have a great deal of delight in UK [basketball] or the state of Kentucky. Maybe that's the first time Reggie's heard that," Ronnie said while visiting his younger brother at Bridgeville Rehabilitation Center. "A rigid unwillingness of people to change and consider people for just being people is not something that's embraced, to me, in the state of Kentucky. They can rally around Big Blue Nation, but after that season is over, there is still what I would term the racist expression of the societal norms in the state."

Ronnie once bore the brunt of an ugly racial incident that para-doxically had shades of hope. Drakesboro High School was playing a basketball game at Bremen High School, and Ronnie and Billy Warford were the only two Black players on the court. They were the target of slurs all night. After the game, when Ronnie went into the stands, a brawl almost broke out.

The police were called, and Drakesboro's team was whisked away to its bus. Shirley Hill, the wife of Drakesboro coach James Hill, draped her arms around Ronnie and walked him to the bus. The Hillses' daughter Denise (now Denise Harris) was a classmate of Reggie's. "I think that Denise was really proud of her mom for doing that because it took a certain amount of courage," Reggie said.

James Hill vowed never to play a game at Bremen again. He resigned rather than reconsider his stance. The ironic twist to this story is that one of the fans who had taunted Ronnie and Billy later coached Derrick, the youngest Warford brother, in baseball. Lilburn "Ray" Harper and Derrick won a Pony League state championship together and became close. "Derrick loves him to this day," Reggie said in 2019, "and Derrick knows what [Harper] did to our older brothers."

Sports brought the two together; Derrick believed they helped change Lilburn Harper. He said Reggie also helped bridge the racial divide in Muhlenberg County because of his brilliance on the basketball court and effervescence off it. "The county, as a whole, embraced our family, and I think a lot of that had to with the quality and character of Reggie," Derrick said. "We always said that Reggie was a little bit different. What Reggie did was amazing to me. Reggie had appeal to not only the Blacks in the county but a lot of the whites, and he had that early on in high school. You put a lot of people in a room together, and they are going to find common things they enjoy. One of the things for us was sports. That eventually, I think, broke down the barriers."

Sports eroded some barriers but not all of them, even after Reggie became a successful basketball coach. When he was on a recruiting trip in Louisiana in the early 1980s, he stopped at a restaurant. While there, he went to the bathroom and returned to see a card next to his plate that read, "You have been visited by the Ku Klux Klan." Reggie laughed it off, certain that he could handle himself against the anonymous coward who had threatened him. Not funny was when he received threats from the Ku Klux Klan after returning to Kentucky in 2009 to coach the Muhlenberg High School boys' basketball team. Reggie was not angry so much as saddened that such hatred still existed during a time when the United States had its first Black president—and that his sons had to experience it.

How does one square such experiences with the community response after Reggie went into heart failure and had to be rushed back to Pittsburgh in 2014? Reggie, no longer coaching but still teaching, could not finish the school year. He needed that fifth year to become vested. His fellow teachers donated enough sick days for Reggie to get credit for the entire school year. Among them was Steve Sparks, the former boys' basketball coach at North Muhlenberg High School who had been passed over for the job that went to Reggie after the two county high schools consolidated. Had Reggie not become vested, which guaranteed five years of disability pay, he and Marisa might not have been able to pay the mortgage on their

Pittsburgh house and lost it. "I'm forever grateful to that community for that," Marisa said. "That was one of the most thoughtful things I had ever seen."

Reggie had many white friends who would have done anything for him. When he was dealing with prejudice at the University of Kentucky, there were people who did things for him that he never forgot. Team doctor V. A. Jackson put his hand on Reggie's shoulder and squeezed it in support after some students yelled "darkies!" during the singing of the school song. Patty Eyster treated Reggie like a son from the day he set foot on campus. For many years, Eyster was the closest woman to Reggie next his mother. "Listen, if you're taught to be guarded against a certain race of people because you think they may not treat you fair, then all of the sudden you run into a person like Patty," Reggie said. "She not only treats you fair but with respect and doesn't fear you. She was always willing to give people a chance regardless of their background."

Joe B. Hall gave Reggie a chance, and the two integrated Kentucky basketball. It was not always easy. There were misunderstandings, some rooted in race. There was a rigidity in Hall's coaching that Reggie felt was a product of his time and tinged by race. But the two became close as can be, having learned from one another. Their relationship evolved into that of a father and son.[1] "Everybody told me I had to recruit a superstar," Hall said on his role in Reggie becoming the second Black scholarship player in program history. "I didn't believe that. I wanted an all-around good kid, and Reggie was that. He was a hard worker and loved by all of his teammates. I had coached Black kids in high school, and I knew the right kid could make it work the way it should. I didn't make a mistake."

Neither did Marisa. She grew up outside of Wilkes-Barre, Pennsylvania, in the northeast part of the state and had very little exposure to other races. She can remember only one Black family in the area. Dating Reggie and eventually marrying him opened a new world to her. She could never have imagined the challenges they would face together, which often had nothing to do with race. But as the deeply spiritual and religious Marisa would probably say, "We plan, and

God laughs." "I never would have envisioned myself in an interracial marriage because I didn't know that, but I'd never want anyone else," she said. "He's so much the yin to my yang. He's my best friend."

In April 2019, during a discussion that included his brother Ronnie and Marisa, Reggie shared his mixed feelings on the racial climate in the United States. "I believe there is more to race than just race," Reggie said. "Have I spoken out on things? Yes. I wanted to improve the situation for my kids and any grandkids that I might have. I would like to say that love is enough. I would like to say that forgiveness is enough. But I don't know that I can just say that. There is a generation coming along that says, 'You know what? I don't want prayers and sympathies. I want action. I want results.'"

Fourteen months later, that generation erupted. Ignited by the death of George Floyd while he was in police custody, it started something not matched in conviction since the 1960s. Another civil rights movement quickly swept across the nation.

The movement led Reggie to do some soul searching through the lens of a Black man. It infuriated him that he could have been George Floyd. It scared him that his sons, Grant and Tiger, could be George Floyd. He had been stopped numerous times by police officers while driving in Pittsburgh, ostensibly because he was a Black man driving in an affluent area. One time after getting pulled over, Reggie called Marisa on his cell phone so that she could listen to what was happening. That is how much he feared for his safety.

When Reggie taught Grant and Tiger to drive, he emphasized what to do should they get stopped by police: put their hands flat on the steering wheel and look as nonthreatening as possible; place their wallet on the dashboard; do not make any sudden movements; do not talk back to the police. To Reggie, such instructions were a matter of life or death, the same as telling them not to drink and drive. "An African American man could be in his car not even doing anything wrong, and if a policeman shows up, he has a chance to die," Reggie said. "That's a problem. There is a pervasive attitude that it's acceptable to watch the insanity of Black men being killed. The same thing happens over and over, and nobody's trying to change. And if you fight for change, you're fighting against police."

For years, as owners of R&D Security, Reggie and his brother Derrick worked closely with police. Each was acutely aware of the risks law enforcement officers face. "We put people in uniforms," Reggie said of R&D employees who later became police officers. "We understand, but it's bad when you have a whole system that thinks, 'Well, you don't like America because you're talking about police being bad.' We tend to deify law enforcement because they do sacrifice. We should make sure they are treated fairly and equally, but we also must demand that they treat others the same way."

Reggie said Tiger had been stopped by police while jogging in the mostly white neighborhood where the Warfords live. To Reggie, that was an example of institutionalized racism. So were things that had seemed funny when they happened. Reggie was cutting his grass one day when a man stopped his car. He complimented Reggie on how nice the yard looked and asked how much he charged. The implication was unmistakable: if a Black man was cutting grass in their upscale, mostly white neighborhood, he must be a landscaper.

As June 2020 meandered toward July, the protests and demonstrations showed no signs of abating. Reggie was encouraged at the number of white faces he saw among the protestors and at the prominent white athletes and coaches who publicly voiced their support for the Black Lives Matter movement. That NBA superstar LeBron James took a leading role in advancing social justice cemented the respect that Reggie had for him as a man. "LeBron James is putting his own effort and stamp on something in an effort to bring light to something, that enough is enough," Reggie said. "LeBron is a Black man, and he's got kids, and they're going to be driving nice cars in places where police will pick you up. Every time his kids go out when they're not with a bodyguard or somebody that can mitigate the situation, he's going to be scared as hell. And he becomes, with all the money that he has, just another Black man in America."

That perilous situation, to Reggie, highlights one of the fundamental truths in America: white people do not have to think about race, but it permeates every aspect of all Black people's lives—whether rich or poor, educated or uneducated, famous or obscure.

Reggie's life was about breaking down barriers. And fulfilling that purpose went beyond what he did at the University of Kentucky. Reggie treated others the way he wanted to be treated. He did not look at race or religion or sexual orientation. His group of friends included many white people, and he moved as easily among them as his Black friends.

"If Reggie Warford is the angry Black man, there's something wrong with this world, then this is a bad time," Reggie said. "I'm on my way out, so I can't do a lot of good. I hope I can do for someone what some people recently did for me, and that's made me more aware. People are right when they say all lives matter. They are. But when young Black men and women are being killed over and over, we need to bring attention to that."

15

Fighter to the End

In December 1974, Jack Givens was playing in just his third game for Kentucky. The Wildcats had traveled to Indiana University, where the sloping sides of Assembly Hall made it seem like spectators are sitting on top of the court.

Amid a cauldron of red-clad fans, Givens experienced his welcome to major college basketball. After getting a step on Indiana forward Scott May, Givens thought he had an easy layup, but the Indiana forward swatted his shot from behind. Quinn Buckner scooped up the loose ball, igniting a fast break that Bobby Wilkerson finished with a thunderous dunk. With the crowd going wild, May said to the reigning Mr. Kentucky Basketball, "Boy, don't you bring that weak shit in here no more." A cowed Givens looked at Kentucky coach Joe B. Hall and started pointing at himself. It was the universal sign of a player telling his coach that he needed to come out of the game. "Joe B. turned around and started looking up in the stands," Givens said.

Laughter filled the living room of the Warford house as Givens delivered the story's climax. Givens, his wife, Linda, and James Lee, another former Kentucky player, had driven six hours from Lexington to Pittsburgh to visit Reggie. A meat-and-cheese tray sat on a coffee table in front of the couch. Marisa brought in a plate of deviled eggs. Her father, Beau, popped into the room to say hello and remind everyone about the steak dinner that he and Marisa were preparing.

Reggie, Givens, and Lee spun stories, transporting them back to the halcyon days that had turned them from teammates into brothers.

Lee had been a supremely talented but ornery player. During one practice, Hall, frustrated with Lee's lack of effort, asked why he couldn't be more like Reggie or Givens. "I said, 'Well, Coach, I'm not Jack. I'm not Reggie. That would be like me saying, 'Well, Al McGuire does it like this.' Joe B. just threw up his hands." More laughter filled the cozy room where Reggie, clad in a black Kentucky basketball shirt and wind pants, sat in a recliner, his oxygen tank nearby.

Reggie lived for times like these. By October 2020, when that visit occurred, he did not know how many he had left. Six weeks earlier, doctors had given him a couple of months to live. Even though he felt as if he had already been on borrowed time, the news was a gut punch.

He would find himself in everyday situations, such as riding in the car with Marisa, knowing that the passenger seat he was occupying would be empty sooner rather than later. He tried not to dwell on it, but it was impossible for him not to think about Marisa's life without him. "You don't talk to her about that, but you want to talk to her about that," Reggie said. "I can't tell her what I'm thinking because I want her to have the happiest life that she should have."

Not that Marisa would have entertained such talk, anyway. Even after they received Reggie's bleakest medical prognosis, she stayed hyperfocused on what they could do next. To her, this focus was not denial or wishful thinking. Every time it had seemed as if Reggie were at the end of the line, something—or someone, in the case of Shelley Trondle and the kidney transplant—came through for them. Why couldn't it happen again?

Even though Marisa stayed relentlessly positive, she started going to counseling to work through any advance grief. She also dutifully, albeit reluctantly, went with Reggie to buy headstones and burial plots. Nothing hit her harder than when she and Reggie went to the funeral home to pick out a casket. She felt as if she were going to vomit. "I can't do it anymore," she told Reggie after he selected a casket the color of Kentucky blue. "I gotta get out of here."

Her abrupt exit was one reason why her father, Beau Bolinski, worried about her. He also worried about how his grandsons were dealing with everything. A religious man, he had increased the daily rosaries he had been saying for Reggie from one to two. Beau strongly believed that when it was Reggie's time, he would be in a better place and that his life would be celebrated because of how he had lived it.

Gregarious and irreverent, Beau had made his first meeting with Reggie an unforgettable one. Beau was living in Florida when Reggie flew down to visit Marisa and him. She and Beau were waiting at the arrival gate, and when Beau saw Reggie, he yelled, "Marisa, you didn't tell me he was Black!" Marisa wanted to shrink. "Everyone stopped," she said. "The place went dead silent." Beau had already seen Reggie on TV, of course, but this was his way of breaking the ice. His laughter sliced through any lingering tension, and he wrapped Reggie in a hug. Beau was overjoyed when Marisa married him in 1990. A couple years later, he was on his way to the Seychelles Islands, off the east coast of Africa, when Marisa called him. Their babysitter had suffered a stroke and could no longer help care for Grant, who was less than a year old. Beau, just shy of his sixtieth birthday, offered to stay with her and Reggie until they found another babysitter.

He moved in with them and never left. Almost thirty years later, he joked that he was like Uncle Charley from the TV show *My Three Sons*. He and Reggie became so close that Beau did not refer to him as his son-in-law but as his best friend. He told Reggie that he wished he had had a father like Reggie when he was growing up. "I can't allow him to go," he said before Reggie died. "This family needs him. This world needs a guy like him! Reggie's a good man. He's a *good* man." Beau paused and turned away. As he wiped away tears, he said softly, "Nobody ever said life was fair."

Tiger, the younger of Reggie's two sons, had been grappling with that reality for years. It hit him hard one time when he was at the gym. Tiger saw a man in his late seventies playing racquetball. His father, more than a decade younger, was on oxygen. "How can a man that lived a righteous life have such trouble?" Tiger said. "He never smoked, never drank, never did any of those things that people said, 'Oh, that's going to kill you.' That's what really hurt me for the longest time. He shouldn't be in the state that he's in, and it doesn't make sense to me."

It did to Reggie, especially when he read the Book of Job. That story is about facing hard times and suffering with faith and grace. When Tom Piccione, who shared a special bond with Reggie after each of them underwent a heart transplant, learned how badly Reggie was struggling physically, he broke down crying. *"Why you?"* Piccione asked.

Reggie's response: *"Why not me?"*

"God doesn't make something bad happen to you. What God does is give you the strength to overcome what you are going through. God may not come when you want Him, but whenever He comes, He's right on time. I believe that," Reggie said. "I wouldn't wish this on my worst enemy, but if ever there was somebody who should go through this, it's me. I think the way that I handled this situation turned it into an opportunity about faith and resilience and trusting in God. I don't want people to pity me. I want people to be inspired that I'm trying to show the strength to handle every situation put before me."

That outlook made Reggie an inspiration to many, including Kentucky men's basketball coach John Calipari. The two had coached together for one season at Pitt. Calipari never forgot the help that Reggie gave to a young coach, how he seemed to light up any room with his personality. When Reggie visited Lexington toward the end of his life, he was in a wheelchair, but to Calipari he was still Reggie. "I couldn't imagine what he was going through, but he had that Reggie Warford smile on his face any time I saw him or talked to him," Calipari said. "He knew he was in the battle. You could see it in his eyes, but he was just so gracious. That's courage. We're all going to die, but when you know it's imminent, it's a different deal. His thing is grace, being kind, worrying about the other guy more than himself, and he's just never changed."

That Reggie never changed explains the response after word circulated that his time might be running out. A group of Iowa State players got together with Reggie via Zoom. Former Pitt players visited him, including all-time leading scorer Charles Smith and former Panther greats Curtis Aiken and Sam Clancy. Pittsburgh Steelers legend Franco Harris called and told Reggie that the city of Pittsburgh was a better place because of him. Tears rolled down Reggie's cheeks after hearing that. One day Larry Roberts, Reggie's attorney and good friend, drove from Lexington to Pittsburgh. He spent the night with Reggie and left early the next morning so he could get back to work. "It's really nice," Reggie said of the widespread support, "because I want my kids to see that people respected the way that I lived. I still say I'm a man with enough shortcomings for multiple men, but I've tried."

Shortly before Givens and Lee visited, Reggie received a phone call that Marisa was convinced was the answer to their prayers. They had just made the agonizing decision for Reggie to go into hospice, where doctors would try to make him as comfortable as possible. Out of nowhere, Dr. Dennis McNamara, Reggie's chief cardiology doctor, called. He had been reviewing Reggie's medical charts and believed Reggie could live months longer than he had been given. McNamara said he understood if Reggie did not want to keep fighting, but there was a sliver of hope.

That was all Reggie needed to hear. Hospice plans were canceled. "We pray every day, and miracles come through people," Marisa said at the time. "A miracle isn't some thunderbolt coming out of the sky. It's the people that are put in your path that have an answer for you if you're willing to listen."

It would have been easy for Reggie to have given up on listening. His body seemed to be in constant revolt. Twice it shut down, and he blacked out on his feet. Fortunately, Grant, who had moved home from Lexington, was there to catch him or help him up. Breathing was such a struggle that Reggie always felt like someone was sitting on his chest. He often yawned just so he could get an extra gulp of air.

Shortly after Christmas in 2020, Reggie contracted COVID-19 and landed in the intensive-care unit of Presbyterian Hospital in Pittsburgh. Doctors did not intubate him, though, because they feared he would never come off the breathing tube. What made the situation worse was Marisa could not visit him because she had also been diagnosed with COVID-19. She spent tense days at home, praying and sending text messages and emails asking others to pray for Reggie. Around noon on December 31, Marisa got word that Reggie had been moved out of intensive care and could go home on January 2.

Not long after 2020 turned into 2021, Reggie had a dream that he was playing basketball. Such dreams had become more frequent as his health deteriorated. In this one, he was the Reggie of his youth. He was playing against guys who were 6-foot-5 and 6-foot-6 and talking like his idol Muhammad Ali—and then some. "I was cussing," Reggie said laughing, "and I don't even cuss."

The game may not have been real, but at that time it may have been as significant as any Reggie had ever played. It allowed him to feel like Reggie again. He ran the dream back in his mind over and over the next day.

Oscar Combs is arguably the preeminent University of Kentucky sports historian. He covered all Wildcats sports for years as publisher of the *Cats Pause,* traveling with both the football and basketball teams. After semiretiring, Combs embarked on a series of podcasts about former Kentucky athletes. Combs did 101 of them. His last one, with Reggie in 2019, may be his most memorable. "I don't think I did one that had more to offer Kentucky history than the one I did with him," Combs said. "It's so emotional, even if you don't know him."

That podcast reminded Combs of something he saw after Reggie had graduated from Kentucky. The Wildcats were playing at Mississippi State. Before the game, Combs and Kentucky guard Dwane Casey went to a drug store to get a snack. Casey was refused service. "This was 1977, and I did not expect that," Combs said. "I had never run into that growing up in eastern Kentucky. That was some of the things those early guys faced. I wonder how I would have felt if I was Reggie at the time."

Reggie gave his thoughts on that climate in the documentary *Reggie Warford: Fight of His Life,* which was released in late 2019. Directed by Dick Gabriel, a longtime sports journalist who has covered Kentucky basketball since Reggie was a player, narrated by former Wildcats All-American Jamal Mashburn, and produced by former Kentucky guard Cameron Mills, the documentary delivers an unflinching, poignant look at Reggie's life.

The Emmy Award–winning documentary examines the barriers Reggie challenged at Kentucky and the cavalcade of health problems he experienced later in life. Not long after it aired, Reggie received letters from two of his former teammates. One came from Bob Guyette, his roommate in his freshman year, and the other from Jerry Hale. Each expressed regret that they had not recognized the loneliness Reggie had dealt with as the team's only Black player his freshman year. Reggie's revelations in the documentary had surprised them, and they apologized. "When we would leave practice, we'd go back to the dorm, and we may go to eat, but after you ate and you went back to your room or went out with friends, what was Reggie doing?" Hale said. "It didn't dawn on me to think about what he was doing, or if he was walking across campus, is he walking by himself? Those are the kind of things I reflected back on and didn't really comprehend as I do now."

As much as Reggie's arrival at Kentucky has been framed as something bigger than basketball, Reggie did not look at it that way until later in life. He went to Kentucky to play with the best and play against the best. He may have been a naive country kid, but he was hardly in awe of Kentucky basketball.

He proved as much shortly after he got to campus. Adolph Rupp had been forced into retirement but still occupied the biggest office at Memorial Coliseum. Before Reggie played a minute at Kentucky, he asked the legend a pointed question: "Coach, why didn't you recruit more colored players?" Rupp told Reggie that he had not needed to because he could get "the best white boys in America."

Reggie got along with Rupp and came to see him as a product of his time. In the summer of 2020, when there was a push to remove Rupp's statue from Kentucky's campus, Reggie defended Rupp, saying he himself would not want his enemies to define his legacy. He thought of Hall the same way—and that Hall evolved from coaching players like Reggie.

After becoming a starter his senior season, Reggie emerged as the undisputed leader of the Wildcats. Kentucky would not have won its final ten games of the 1975–1976 season, capped by an NIT Championship, without Reggie. "I showed I could play at Kentucky," Reggie said.

But at what cost? That question is why some closest to Reggie have or had no love for Kentucky. They think he did not receive a fair opportunity or was thrust into a no-win situation because of a system stacked against him.

For *Fight of His Life,* Jolly Jernigan, one of Reggie's oldest friends, gave an interview while wearing a fleece-red Louisville pullover. Jernigan's sartorial choice was not a coincidence. "Loves me," Reggie said, "hates Kentucky."

Denise Harris, Reggie's high school classmate and close friend, felt the same way for years. "People have no clue what it was like for Reggie coming from nothing to UK and then not being loved like [he would have been if he] were somewhere else," Harris said. "Reggie's a saint, and he's made me feel better about it. For years I couldn't stand Kentucky, and now I love it."

Among Reggie's white friends, Stuart Brown may have understood the best what Reggie experienced at Kentucky. Now world renowned for his work with horses, Brown attended the College of Veterinary Medicine at Tuskegee University in Alabama. It is a historically Black college, and Brown said it "was the world turned out" for him. He was able to acclimate and thrive because of what his friendship with Reggie had ingrained in him. "I never saw Black or white," Brown said. "I attribute a lot of that to Reggie. He never made it about any of that stuff. He'd pick me up and take me to places, and it was just Reggie. To this day, I have no idea why he took an interest in me."

Reggie connects people like Brown with the Black basketball players who followed Reggie in Lexington. That is a huge part of his legacy.

Do Merion Haskins and Larry Johnson go to Kentucky if Reggie bails after his freshman year? Do Lexington natives Jack Givens and James Lee, the nucleus of the 1978 NCAA Tournament championship team, follow Reggie if his career at Kentucky ends abruptly? Does young Stuart Brown lose his way if Reggie does not come into his life? What happens with them and many others if Reggie does not push through struggles at Kentucky that even those who saw him every day could not fully understand?

"There was never more a perfect person for the most difficult situation of coming to Kentucky when they were breaking the racial barriers than Reggie," said former Wildcats All-American forward Kevin Grevey, who was a year ahead of Reggie. "He was a good student. He was a good athlete and good enough to play at Kentucky. The thickest, toughest rope that is made that you put up when you're docking a huge boat, that's the fiber that Reggie has been built with. If he hadn't had all these life experiences, he wouldn't be able to handle with the grace and dignity that he's handling things right now. You can't teach that. You have to experience it."

Reggie's Kentucky experience was far from perfect, and he was the least charitable about his legacy there. He often joked that they do not retire jerseys of players who scored only 220 career points, as he did. But there is ample evidence that Reggie transcended basketball at Kentucky.

Dirk Minniefield, a star Wildcats guard in the early 1980s, grew up in Lexington. He told Reggie that Reggie had given him hope that Minniefield, as a Black player, could one day suit up for the hometown Wildcats. Ed Davender, another standout guard from that era, chose number 15 after he went to Kentucky. That was Reggie's number, and Davender said it was a tribute because of what Reggie had done for players like him.

"Black, white, yellow, green, he's just a good guy." Guyette said. "Being the first Black player to spend the four years [at Kentucky], to get a degree, says a lot about his strength and I'm sure how he was brought up. His story goes beyond Kentucky. It goes to the history of our sport, our country."

"Coach Hall knew what kind of quality young man Reggie was, and he was a hell of a player," said Detroit Pistons coach Dwane Casey, who played with Reggie for one season at Kentucky. "Reggie was an intelligent young man that represented the team, his family, the city of Drakesboro, and the University of Kentucky well. He is one of the classiest guys to ever put on a uniform at the University of Kentucky."

And one of the toughest. "He just had a lifelong struggle," Oscar Combs said, "and kept fighting back, fighting back, fighting back." In November 2021, Reggie was still fighting with everything he had. That fighting spirit seemed nothing short of miraculous. Alas, it did not make Reggie's daily life any easier.

Reggie had almost as many doctors as fingers on his hands. They included a pulmonologist and neurologist as well as his primary-care physician and heart, kidney, and pain-managements doctors. "These are people who see him regularly," Marisa said in 2021. Reggie's breathing had become so compromised that he sometimes was too weak to make it, even with a walker, from the family room to the motorized chair that carried him upstairs to his bedroom. He and Marisa talked about buying a wheelchair that could be converted into a bed at night so Reggie could stay on the main floor of the house. Reggie, even with the aid of an oxygen machine, felt as if he were constantly trying to catch his breath. Doctors told him his diaphragm muscles were too weak to properly circulate oxygen throughout his body because of sarcoidosis. "Every day, it feels like I'm about to cry," Reggie said, "just the discomfort. It would be like someone getting you in a bear hug. Sometimes it makes my eyes twitch."

Support from all over continued to sustain Reggie and Marisa. His faither-in-law, Beau Bolinski, continued to say multiple rosaries for Reggie every day, even as Beau himself battled myelodysplastic syndrome, a blood disorder that can progress to leukemia and is treated like cancer. Kentucky men's basketball coach John Calipari, a devout Catholic who attends Mass regularly even when the Wildcats are on the road, texted a couple of times a week. He let Reggie know when he had lit a candle and said a prayer for him. Reggie also had what he called "prayer warriors" praying for him all over the country. One group was from a church in San Antonio, Texas, that Reggie had attended while visiting his sisters Thelma and Velma.

What also helped keep Reggie going was a quest to right what he saw as a wrong or at least a gross oversight. Reggie wanted to help a fellow pioneer find his way back to the University of Kentucky.

Tom Payne, the first Black player to attend Kentucky on a basketball scholarship, once elicited comparisons to Lew Alcindor. He is largely obscure in basketball annals because of what happened after the 7-foot-1 man-child left Kentucky. After averaging 17 points and ten rebounds a game in 1970–1971 and earning All-SEC honors, Payne declared hardship and entered the NBA draft. The Atlanta Hawks took him with the second overall pick of the 1971 supplemental draft. He played one season, but then he was arrested for rape.

This happened in March 1972, about four months before Reggie arrived in Lexington. A series of rape convictions led to Payne spending most of his adult life behind bars. Since getting paroled in 2018, Payne has worked in ministries and tried to atone for his past.

He and Reggie have always been linked, especially in news stories about race and Kentucky basketball. They had never talked or corresponded before Jim Andrews connected them in 2021. Andrews is a former teammate and friend of each, though at one time he would have been an unlikely nexus.

For most of the 1970–1971 season, Andrews and Payne, both centers, battled for one starting spot. Payne was so athletic that he could run with guards and never hesitated to use his immense size. He also played with an edge, something that undoubtedly could be traced to the times. Payne's skin color and size made him an easy target when Kentucky played on the road. He was taunted with racial slurs and spit on. Payne, largely isolated on a campus with so few Black students, did not feel much more welcome at home in Lexington. Basketball was an outlet for what anger and frustration simmered beneath the surface. "Sometimes Coach Hall would have to stop practice and take Tom off to the side," Andrews recalled. "He'd say, 'Tom, you're not interested in playing basketball. You're interested in breaking his nose. You need to play basketball because you can't play like that in a game.' And Tom would back off. We had some good battles."[1]

Those battles were still on Payne's mind years later while he served time in Green River Correctional Complex in Central City, Kentucky. Alan Cutler, a well-known Lexington TV sports anchor, interviewed him at Green River. After they were finished, Cutler asked Payne if there was anything they had not covered. "Yeah," he said, "I want to talk to Jim Andrews."

That request got back to Andrews, who was part of a ministry that visited prison inmates. When Andrews told a group that included former Major League Baseball player infielder Doug Flynn and former Wildcats baseball coach Keith Madison about Payne, they simultaneously said, "Road trip." Andrews and Payne reunited that week. They have been in contact since then and become good friends. Andrews attended several of Payne's parole hearings as a character witness. "I've never shied away from the fact that I have a relationship with Tom," Andrews said.

As 2021 drew closer to its end, Reggie found himself wanting to talk to Payne, if only to "compare notes." Andrews gave Reggie a cell phone number that led him to Payne—and a conversation that would have taken place decades earlier had Payne had his way.

He and Reggie hit it off immediately. How could they not? Each had dealt with prejudice and depths of loneliness to which few could relate. That is why Reggie shook his head knowingly when Payne made a literary reference during this phone call between the kindred spirits. "I remember reading *Invisible Man* by Ralph Ellison," Payne said of the groundbreaking book published by the acclaimed Black author in 1952. "I was sort of like that in a lot of ways. I was nonexistent to a lot of people." He does not blame that for the crimes he committed. He owns his actions and accepts that some people may define him by them, no matter how much he has changed.

"I didn't come from bad roots," said Payne, who had loving parents and whose father was a career army man. "I have eight other brothers and sisters, and they're all college graduates and doing well in society. There were just some things that happened in my life that I wasn't able to really deal with in the right manner. I'm just really returning home to where I'm supposed to be."

Payne went far from his native Kentucky after getting paroled in 2018. He moved to Michigan and later relocated to Oregon where he finally feels at home in the Pacific Northwest, working in a ministry with other like-minded pastors and mentoring at-risk youth. "One of my best friends is retired, and he was the first Black police captain here, and he's really been a good mentor since I've been out," Payne said. "I'm around a bunch of good men. They don't know me for basketball. They know me for my ministry. They know I played basketball, but it's not a big deal to them, so I really don't talk about it too much."

That does not mean Payne has put basketball completely behind him, especially the year he spent at Kentucky. "For a long time, I wanted to be back and wanted to feel like I did try to contribute something," Payne said. "I thought I did have some fair games and showed that we, as brothers, could come into a system and play on a high level. That's all I ever wanted was a little appreciation for that, but things fell differently for me. I don't have negative feelings toward anybody."

When Reggie heard how Payne felt, he saw an opening. He rallied support for Payne with the hope that the latter would be invited to return to Lexington for a Kentucky game in 2022. Reggie knew there might be pushback because of Payne's past, but, to Reggie, Payne had paid his debt to society. Forgiveness was at the heart of who Reggie was, and he wanted to see Payne recognized at a Kentucky game. "If I'm physically able to be there," Reggie said, "I will do that and ride out onto the court with him."

Payne told Reggie how much he admired the example he set for the Black players who followed him, how he paved the way for players such as Larry Johnson, Merion Haskins, Jack "Goose" Givens, and James Lee. Reggie was just as sincere when he said that no matter what had happened after Payne left Kentucky, nothing had changed the fact that he was the first Black scholarship basketball player in program history. "We need to pay homage to the original," Reggie told Payne. "I'm not the patriarch of Kentucky Black basketball. Tom Payne is, and I will happily surrender that title. Whatever your journey was, you're finished with that, and you can start a new chapter." He paused and added, "You are loved."

Reggie called it the "long dash": what transpires between a person's birth and death. Reggie's dash was longer and fuller than most.

Reggie is a member of three Halls of Fame and has a park and street named after him in Muhlenberg County. He coached the Harlem Globetrotters and at the highest level of college men's basketball. He received the Kentucky Medal of Valor. He earned a master's degree in education from Murray State at the age of fifty-five. He pulled all-nighters writing papers even as his health was faltering. It makes little sense that he would put himself through such rigors at that age, but he wanted to show that anything can be accomplished if you put your mind to it.

"This guy has done so much," said Dr. Ronnie Warford, Reggie's older brother. "Any African American athlete that graduates from the University of Kentucky is standing on the shoulders of Reggie. Regardless of the greatness they achieved, it is on the shoulders of what Reggie could do and dealt with at Kentucky. He's such a maverick with his accomplishments and achievements in life. I want others to recognize and realize what he's done and what he's doing."

What makes the man as much as his achievements is the stuff that does not stand out in the long dash. That is why Bob Holland is a vital part of Reggie's story. Reggie and Holland became close friends while coaching together on youth basketball teams. It did not matter that Reggie was far from coaching in Madison Square Garden or the Carrier Dome, as he had done at Pitt. Basketball was never about the brightest lights and biggest stages, though he had found both of these things as a player and a coach. Reggie's love for basketball was as pure as falling snow, his passion for it contagious, as Holland learned.

"One of the most remarkable things that Reggie did is he taught the kids how to play, but he also taught them how to love the game," Holland said. "Our kids were incredibly close, and a lot of them still are today. That's because of the connection Reggie had with them and the connection they had with each other because of the way he coached them and made them better people. I put Reggie in the category of great people that I've ever met in my life."

He does the same with Marisa, who works for Holland's company as a human-resources and benefits consultant. He said Marisa is the best hire he has ever made and marvels at how she juggled work while also serving as Reggie's primary caregiver. "There isn't anything she can't do," Holland said. "I always describe her as a pioneer woman. She's a huge part of his story."

"I have no idea how she does it," said Shelley Trondle, the friend who donated a kidney to Reggie. "She is one of the strongest if not the strongest person that I've ever met. She is so incredibly positive, maintains so much personal spirituality and faith through what have to be some of the darkest times anybody can face for years on end. She is so inspiring and has made me a better person. I really owe her a lot."

Trondle's connection to Reggie is also a big part of his story—in part because of stretches in his long dash that he would never have wished on anyone, and not just from a health standpoint.

His college coaching career came crashing down when he was a rising young assistant who seemed destined to lead a big-time program. Reggie got caught in the dragnet of a newspaper exposé, one in which agendas and twisted words led to accusations that nearly drove him to suicide. He got vindication after the *Lexington Herald-Leader* settled a protracted libel lawsuit, but his coaching career never fully recovered. "Let's hope that [the attack on Reggie] was not based on race, but that could be the fact," Calipari said. "I say all the time [that] white privilege or being white played a big part in the success I had. I've had opportunities that maybe he didn't have because he was Black, and it's not fair. Many times, if you're Black, you get one shot. You may be in a bad situation. Things may have happened that had nothing to do with you, and you don't get a chance to redeem [yourself]. In Reggie's case, I hope that's not what it was, but you can't discount that."

Rod Baker, who hired Reggie as an assistant when he coached the Harlem Globetrotters, said college players whom Reggie might have coached lost out as much as Reggie did after his coaching career stalled. "What parents in their right mind wouldn't want their son to be under his watch?" Baker said. "He's a principled man and the right model you would want your kid to play for and to be instructed and led by. You can take out the adjective *college coach, pro coach, high school coach.* He is just a good coach."

Several opportunities to resume his college coaching career were derailed in a Lucy-pulling-the-football-away-from-Charlie-Brown fashion. One happened in 1988, while Reggie was in the middle of his lawsuit. Dwane Casey was on the brink of getting the head coaching job at the University of New Orleans and was going to take Reggie to the Big Easy as an assistant. Right before Casey was hired, though, he was accused of making an improper payment to a recruit, something that later was proven false.

Casey rehabilitated his coaching career overseas and broke into the NBA as an assistant in 1994. He became head coach of the Minnesota Timberwolves in 2005 and the Toronto Raptors in 2011. Both times he wanted Reggie on his staff, but he did not have full control over hiring or needed assistant coaches with NBA experience. Casey, who became head coach of the Detroit Pistons in 2018, said, "Now I get to a point in my career where I'm in a position to hire him, and his physical ability doesn't allow him to do the job. Reggie could have easily coached in the NBA. It's a few years too late."

How Reggie handled such hard luck defines him as much as his success. "He was always that one little step away from being able to make a career and a great living out of the game of basketball," Holland said. "One of the things I love about the guy is he's not bitter about it. He never let it change him as a person. He's always been upbeat. He has a love of the game, a love of coaching, a love of other people."

Pride kept Reggie from reaching out more when he was trying to get back into college coaching. But there was something else at work, too: his indifference to self-promotion, even at the expense of self-interest. "He never looks at 'What can I get out of this?' He never has," Marisa said. "Not many people do that, and maybe that's why he made me try to be a better person because I'm always looking at the business side. He doesn't think like the typical person would think, 'Oh my gosh this is an opportunity for me.' I think that's been his star and his cross. He's never manipulated a situation to his advantage since I've known him."

After Reggie pulled two people out of a burning house in 1985, he quietly left the scene. He did not think of himself as a hero. He had done what his father and mother had raised him to do. "They had to track him down to figure out who he was," Larry Roberts said. "He doesn't go out and try to exploit anything even though it's worth exploiting. He doesn't live like that."

Another of Reggie's defining characteristics was his capacity to forgive. He never held grudges for some of the stuff he endured at Kentucky or even against the newspaper that almost ruined him with specious claims. When he and Marisa were driving home after his KHSAA Hall of Fame induction in 2019, a reporter from the *Lexington Herald-Leader* called him. A few questions into the interview, the reporter confessed that he liked Reggie too much not to be honest with him: he was writing Reggie's obituary. Marisa was furious, especially at the timing of the call. She and Reggie were still basking in one of the best weekends of their lives. Of all the newspapers to call, it had to be the *Herald-Leader*? Reggie laughed it off and calmed her down. He knew the reporter was just doing his job. He respected him for it and appreciated the work the reporter was putting into the obituary.

"Reggie is a better person than I am," former Kentucky forward Lavon Williams said. "I can hold grudges. I know stories, the things that happened to Reggie when he was at UK, and he forgives everybody. Never have I ever heard him say a bad word." Roberts said, laughing, "Reggie doesn't hold a grudge. That's his one failing as far as I'm concerned. I respect him more than anyone I know, particularly for what he's gone through with all of the medical problems."

If not for social media and Reggie's vast network of family and friends, most would not have known the depths of his medical travails. Reggie did not want people to pity him. But once people heard what he was fighting through, it only confirmed what they already knew about him. "He's had a very strong support group, and that is another side to his story," Kevin Grevey said before Reggie's death in

2022. "Rope will eventually break no matter thick and tough it is, and he's got an amazing wife and kids. He's got friends from all different circles, from coaching, teaching, playing, from all over the country. And he's got us. His teammates for life. I know he's going through hell, and he needs to know that I love him and his teammates love him and we're there. He's proud, and he's tough, and he's not one to call and say, 'Hey, Kev, can you help me here?' He knows we would drop [everything] and do what needs to be done."

They proved as much at an American Heart Association fundraiser in Lexington in 2017. Reggie and Marisa attended the event organized by Dr. Stuart Brown. During an auction, Jack Givens announced, "I want to donate $1,000 in the name of my teammate Reggie Warford." Former teammates Jerry Hale and Jim Andrews followed Givens's lead. So did others. Another man said he would donate $20,000 for every person who donated $1,000 in honor of Reggie. By the end of the night, the event had raised more than $1 million. That is one of countless examples of how people rallied around Reggie.

As his daily struggle just to catch a breath continued in 2022, Reggie also dealt with more heartache. His brother Derrick—the youngest of the four Warford brothers—died at the age of sixty-five in Arizona. Like Reggie, Derrick had been an athletic marvel whose body had betrayed him in just about every way it could and robbed him of his golden years. He had suffered multiple heart attacks, and Reggie knew how weak he was by the end.

Reggie participated in the funeral virtually, and on January 15, the day Derrick was buried with military honors in San Antonio, Texas, he suffered more loss. Joe B. Hall, the beloved former UK men's basketball coach, died at the age of ninety-three.

Joe B. had been so much to so many Kentucky players of a certain generation, none more so than Reggie. The two integrated Kentucky basketball, and a direct line can be drawn between that seminal moment and Kentucky winning Hall's only national championship in 1978. Neither Hall nor Reggie could have possibly known what to expect when the latter arrived in Lexington as a wide-eyed, stick-thin teenager who just wanted to play basketball.

It could never be simple, and Reggie and Joe B. had a complicated relationship for most of Reggie's time at Kentucky, in part because of forces outside their control. Time and life experiences gave each a better understanding of the other. The respect and admiration the two shared morphed into unconditional love. Reggie saw Joe B. as a father figure, and Joe B. saw Reggie as a son.

The three days Reggie and Marisa spent in Lexington for Hall's goodbye answered any lingering questions Reggie had about whether he deserved a place in Kentucky's rich basketball history. Florida State coach Leonard Hamilton, the first Black assistant basketball coach at Kentucky, talked about how Reggie had paved the way for him—and for the other Black players who had been part of the core of Kentucky's 1978 national championship team. Just as meaningful to Reggie: Hall's son, Steve, told him that he was his dad's favorite player.

The farewell to Joe B. was a bit surreal. The time Reggie spent swapping Joe B. stories with former teammates and others who had played for him, such as Kenny "Sky" Walker, also validated Reggie. Even if he was the last to truly grasp it, he *had* mattered in Kentucky basketball. "I couldn't believe some of the things that were said about me. I was as proud as I've ever been," Reggie said. "I was glad I was alive to hear it. I was really glad Marisa was alive to hear it."

Reggie made another memorable trip to Lexington a month later. A slew of former Wildcats gathered for an alumni weekend, and Reggie did more than share laughs and memories with Wildcats basketball players. The day before Kentucky's game against visiting Alabama, he attended practice, and Coach John Calipari had him address the team. Reggie may have been far removed from his coaching days, but he did not hold back when talking to some of the players. "You don't have to wait for shots to come to you," he told guard Kellan Grady. "Your range is in the city of Lexington. Shoot the ball, man." He also had high praise for Oscar Tshiebwe, one of the best players in the country. He compared the junior center to former NBA great Moses Malone: "You're one of the best rebounders I've ever seen."

The next day Grady drilled seven three-pointers on the way to a team-high 25 points in a single game. Tshiebwe scored 21 points and grabbed fourteen rebounds in what had become a typical performance in a breakout season. The Cats also got 18 points from Keion Brooks Jr., whom Reggie told he had looked like the "next DeMar DeRozan" in Kentucky's 90–81 win over the Crimson Tide.

His final two Lexington visits gave Reggie a preview of what people would say about him after his fight—the fight that had inspired countless others, the fight that he had won several transplants and many years ago—was finished. "When I'm gone, I want people to remember that I loved God, that I had a belief that sustained me through all my hardships," Reggie said. "I want people, enemy or friend, to say, 'Yeah, he was a good man.' That's what I want my legacy to be, that they recognize that I lived to try to be a good man and that I truly, truly begged forgiveness for my shortcomings." Reggie paused. His voice cracking, he added, "I want my kids to want to be like me. And I want Marisa to think that I was the love of her life."

Epilogue

My journey with Reggie came full circle on May 25, 2022. Tom Brown, my cousin and Reggie's close friend, had gotten us together in 2019 to talk about turning Reggie's surreal story into a book. Three and a half years later, Tom and I again met at Reggie's suburban Pittsburgh home. Only this time we had come to say goodbye.

Reggie had called me at the beginning of the week to say he had only days. The inevitability of his death had loomed over our project from the day we started it. Still, his call jarred me. Some closest to Reggie, including Wildcats legend Jack "Goose" Givens, had driven from Lexington, Kentucky, to Pittsburgh the previous October to say goodbye. That was a couple of days after Detroit Pistons coach and Reggie's former Kentucky teammate Dwane Casey had called me to ask if the situation was as dire as he had heard. And yet Reggie had staved off an imminent move to a hospice care facility because, well, that is what Reggie did. He *always* rallied. It is the predominant theme of his life.

But this time there was a faintness in his voice, a finality in his words. I texted Marisa later that day. She had remained relentlessly positive, countering one bad medical turn after another with prayer and unwavering belief in the power of it. Her incredible strength and can-do attitude had helped keep Reggie alive. But this time she could offer little hope. "Every day is a gift," she texted back.

Two days later Marisa prepared Tom and me for the worst. Reggie was with a hospice nurse in their bedroom and very weak. Stories and laughter, Marisa told us, were the best medicine. I had seen Reggie in bad shape before. Never had I seen him when simply talking was such a struggle.

Not long after Tom and I settled into seats next to his bed, Reggie in his inimitable, eloquent way said, "I've run my race." He gamely sat up during the visit for as long as he could, even eating a piece of cheesecake and some fruit that Tom had brought for the family. He still had one vintage Reggie moment for us.

I started telling Tom, a Pitt graduate, a story from when Reggie coached. Two Pitt players had been going after one another verbally one day at practice, and Reggie became so exasperated by the jawing that he put them in boxing gloves. They danced around, each promising the other a beating. Finally, a disgusted onlooker said something and walked away. I told Tom, not knowing if Reggie was following the story, that I would have to paraphrase because I could not remember the exact quote from the onlooker. That is when a supine Reggie said, "One's scared, and the other one's glad for it."

Reggie drifted in and out of sleep over the next hour. Before leaving, Tom and I told him that we loved him. We were the last ones outside of family to see him.

Reginald Garfield Warford joined his Lord and Savior fifteen hours later. He died on May 26, the same day as his wedding anniversary. Thirty-two years earlier he had married Marisa at four o'clock in the afternoon. He died at four o'clock in the morning.

News of Reggie's death went national after Kentucky men's basketball coach John Calipari paid tribute to him on Twitter. "Reggie Warford passed away this morning at home surrounded by his loving family," Calipari wrote. "I know how much Reggie meant to Kentucky & how he inspired others. Reggie and I worked together at Pitt in the 80s and have remained friends. I'm going to miss my brother. May God bless you Reggie."

Three weeks before Reggie died, he had gone to UPMC Shadyside for the final time. He was in congestive heart failure. His oxygen needs had kept increasing until, Marisa said, they were at "ridiculously high" levels. His kidneys were shutting down. Doctors tried everything, but it became apparent that putting Reggie through more tests would do no good. After a week, Reggie told Marisa, "I want to go home." He had wrung every last ounce of life out of the body that first betrayed him when he was a sophomore at the University of Kentucky.

During his last full day, he and Tiger were sitting on his bed. "Dad, I love you so much," Tiger said. He wanted to take a picture of them. Reggie, weak as he was, flashed one of his vintage smiles. Tiger noticed how at peace he seemed.

Reggie's brother, Dr. Ronnie Warford, was in the air, flying in from Houston. Racing against time, he got to the house that night. He was with Reggie along with Marisa, Grant, and Tiger, father-in-law Beau Bolinski, and Matt Allison, Grant's partner, when Reggie took his last breath.

Those were the five people Reggie wanted in the room when he passed. He had also told good friend Larry Roberts during their final visit that he wanted to make it to May 26, the day of his wedding anniversary. That he held on long enough for Ronnie to be with him and for the date on which he married his soul mate confirmed that Reggie died as he had lived. On his own terms.

Reggie Warford would have turned sixty-eight on September 15, 2022. The night of his birthday, he gave his beloved wife a present. Marisa had not cried much during the day. The tears had come on September 14, and they had come in torrents. Marisa could not explain why she had cried so much the day before Reggie's birthday. But that is grief, impossible to predict when, where, and how it will hit.

Marisa was incredibly distracted on Reggie's birthday. She found it hard to focus on even the most mundane of tasks. Sleep brought clarity in a way that she needed. She dreamed about Reggie, a dream different from any she had had since he had passed. "I felt him hold my hand," she said. It was a sign that Reggie was still with her and was in a better place. That mattered to Marisa. She knew better than anyone how much of a struggle the last few years of his life had been.

She knew how much suffering he had endured just so he could be with her, Grant, and Tiger. And she knew that his suffering was over.

Still, coming to that realization was so damn bittersweet. "He worked so hard to be here, and it just got to the point where it was time, but we just miss him," Marisa said. "Oh my God, we just miss him so much."

Family members and friends sent cards and called on Reggie's birthday. Many had regularly stayed in touch with them since he had passed, but it still meant a lot to the family to hear from them on his birthday. Such support—including what took place just after he passed—would have warmed Reggie's heart.

Hundreds of people streamed into the Bible Chapel in the South Hills of Pittsburgh to say goodbye. The parking lot teemed with cars with Kentucky license plates. Countless others who were unable to attend accessed the live stream of what Reggie's family framed as a celebration of life. Reggie's fear that no one would attend his funeral proved to be as silly as people over the years had told him it was.

A recording of Reggie singing "I Can Only Imagine" filled the auditorium as family members, friends, and former Kentucky teammates settled into their seats. Most had glossy programs that the family had printed for the Celebration of Life Service. The cover was a montage of pictures of Reggie, and the program was filled with more pictures and other tributes to Reggie. One page was devoted to part of a famous poem by Robert Frost that framed Reggie's life.

> I shall be telling this with a sigh . . .
> Somewhere—ages and ages hence:
> Two roads diverged in a wood
> And I—
> I took the one less traveled by,
> And that has made all the difference.

Laughter commingled with tears during the service, which spanned two and a half hours. Marisa would have been aghast had someone told her it would last that long. She had instructed the five speakers that Reggie had chosen—Dr. Stuart Brown, Jack "Goose" Givens, Bob Holland, Larry Roberts, and his truly humbled biographer—to keep their tributes to Reggie to three to five minutes.

The speakers went way over their allotted times. In addition, Reggie's sister, Thelma Freeman, and Eric Harper, the son of his beloved high school basketball, Roby Harper, spoke before singing "His Eye Is on the Sparrow" and "Amazing Grace," respectively.

It did not take long for Marisa to realize that the ceremony would go way over the planned time of one hour twenty minutes. That normally would have caused angst for someone who is so detail and task oriented, but Marisa said the heck with it and stayed in the moment. She laughed and cried at the Reggie stories that spanned his life. She felt an enormous sense of pride as Grant and Tiger spoke together.

Grant is very philosophical, something Reggie and Marisa knew from the time he read *The Prophet* by Kahlil Gibran as a seventh grader. He and Reggie had some very deep conversations near the end. At the service, Grant talked about how Reggie had pleaded with him not to be angry at God after Reggie was gone. Tiger talked about how close he and Reggie had gotten. How one night he broke down crying, telling his father that he wished he could do something to take away his suffering or change places with him. Reggie told Tiger that he was glad he was the one in this situation, not his son. When Tiger asked why, he said, "Because I can handle it."

That courage, that strength coursed through his sons as they said a public goodbye to their father. "There was no way Reggie couldn't be celebrating, listening to what his sons were saying," Marisa said. "I was so touched."

Following a stirring eulogy by Ronnie, people packed into their cars for a drive to nearby Queen of Heaven Cemetery, where a short gravesite service was held. Grant and Tiger flanked Marisa as they said their final goodbye to Reggie. Her sons' arms swallowed her, and the three clung to one another, a metaphor for what they would need in life after Reggie.

In the weeks that followed, Tiger often visited Reggie's grave. Queen of Heaven is sprawling, even by cemetery standards, and the headstone had not yet been installed, but Tiger never got lost. He always found his way to Reggie.

During the final months of Reggie's life, he and Tiger had become particularly close. At night, Tiger would help Reggie to his bedroom, help him brush his teeth, and help get him into bed. It was a process, and Reggie often apologized to Tiger for inconveniencing him. Tiger thought about those times while lying on Reggie's gravesite and cried. "It was the best time of my day, just talking to him for that hour because it was so private with us," Tiger said. "He opened up to me, and I asked him about everything. I became a better friend with him in the last couple years of our lives together than I could have ever imagined we'd be. If I can be 10 percent of what he was, then hopefully I'll be good."

Grant felt the same way. "He had this amazing ability that when you told him how you felt, he could really understand. He could meet you where you were at," Grant said. "It was always easy to talk with him because you weren't trying to make yourself understood. I definitely miss that now. I find myself sometimes with decisions I want to run by him and get a piece of that sage wisdom. No one knew how to give it like him."

The start of 2023 could not come soon enough for Marisa, Grant, and Tiger. Even if a new year is merely symbolic of a fresh start, they needed it. They had still been in the early stages of grieving Reggie when Marisa's father died on November 6, 2022, at the age of eighty-six. Beau Bolinski—"Pop Beau" to Grant, Tiger, and even Reggie—had been dealing with some health issues, including myelodysplastic syndrome, a precursor to leukemia.

But his death was a shock as it came two weeks after a fall at home landed Beau in the Trauma Intensive Care Unit at UPMC Presbyterian Hospital. Beau had initially waved off going to the hospital, insisting he was fine. But one thing after another went wrong, and he never made it home. He passed away with his family by his side. "He was doing so well, even with the cancer," Marisa said, "and he had every intention of living a very long time."

Indeed, Beau liked to say that he would live to be one hundred, and he had shown few signs of slowing down even as he got closer to 90. He retained his outsize personality, which was exceeded in scope only by the size of his heart. As quick as Beau could be with a quip, he probably said just as many rosaries for friends, loved ones, and even strangers. That's just who he was.

Beau always had such a presence, especially in his grandsons' lives. Grant and Tiger could not remember life without him after he came to live with Reggie and Marisa when Grant was just eight months old and before Tiger was born. What was supposed to be a temporary solution when Reggie and Marisa needed child care eventually became permanent.

Beau helped hold the family together when circumstances forced Reggie and Marisa to live apart. He became a second father to Grant and Tiger. Even as they got older, they loved having him around. Tiger would have friends over, and they would sit around a bonfire in the backyard or swim in the family pool. Beau often joined them—at their request. Of course, he rarely if ever said no to Grant and Tiger. Sometimes after Tiger came home late, he knocked softly on Beau's bedroom door. He was hungry, and Pop Beau always loved to cook for him. After some initial grumbling, Beau would be in the kitchen making a full-course breakfast.

"He gave us so much character that without him we would not be who we are as a family," Tiger said. "He had so much charisma and creativity. He had so much animation and life in him. Every time he could make someone smile, he would."

The loss of Beau made Marisa, Grant, and Tiger's first Thanksgiving and Christmas without Reggie that much harder. "I miss Reggie every day and my dad. Every day," Marisa said. "This house is so empty. Thank goodness Tiger is here, and Matt and Grant come over often. Their [Reggie and Beau's] presence is here, but they are not, and you can feel that they are missing. It's so completely different."

A December trip to Lexington helped them make it through the holiday season. Kentucky honored Reggie and Florida A&M coach Clemon Johnson at a December 21 game at Rupp Arena. During the first TV timeout, Marisa, Grant, and Tiger were brought onto the floor. As Reggie's accomplishments flashed on the scoreboard, they were introduced to the crowd. After the game, they and other family members posed with John Calipari and caught up with the Wildcats coach.

Tiger wore Reggie's actual Kentucky warm-up jacket, and during one trip to the bathroom a handful of people told him what a great man Reggie was. An older fan stopped the family to thank them for Reggie. "It meant a lot that even after he was gone, they were still so heartfelt about his life," Tiger said.

Three days later the family celebrated, albeit with heavy hearts. Christmas Eve had always been Reggie's day. He had cooked steak, shrimp, and lobster. That was a family tradition, and Reggie loved making the meal after Christmas Eve Mass. Grant and Tiger took over that tradition, and the family did its best to do what Reggie would have wanted: celebrate Christmas with all the family traditions as if he were still there.

They did skip one of those traditions, though. From 2016 on, they had watched a video that Reggie had given to Marisa as a present. It contained pictures and footage from their wedding and of all the Christmases the family shared, including the one when Tiger had just started walking. Only thirty minutes, it was a lifetime of memories. It would again be a part of Christmas one day, but that year was just too soon for them to watch it as a family.

On New Year's Eve, Marisa went to dinner with some friends. It was still early when they finished, and Marisa did not want to go home. She went to nearby Hollywood Casino, where she felt like the only single person. She played the slots a little and returned home. As midnight approached, with a glass of champagne she turned to the NBC New Year's Eve special to watch the ball drop. Shortly before midnight, cohosts Miley Cyrus and Dolly Parton sang, "I Will Always Love You."

The tangle of emotions that Marisa had managed during the holiday bubbled to the surface. They crashed through an emotional dam as the song played, and she unleashed a primal scream. "I screamed and cried 2022 out," Marisa said. "Fortunately, no one was close enough to hear." She stopped as soon as 2022 turned into 2023. What felt cathartic also represented the new normal for Marisa, Grant, and Tiger.

One thing that helped as they continued to process such profound loss is they would not walk their respective journeys alone. All the people Reggie touched would not let them.

For all his achievements, the street in Drakesboro named after him, his place in several Halls of Fame, his lead role in integrating Kentucky basketball, Reggie mattered most because of who he was as a person and how he had always stayed true to himself, even in the most trying of times. "All of it came back to leave the place better than you found it, the genuine hope and belief in betterment and good even if the world turns against you, as it so often did with him," Grant said. "He never lost that genuine hope and belief in doing good for good's sake and doing good for people around him, to be a godly person and good person. Everyone he touched, I feel, is a kinder person, a more thoughtful person for it. That's what his legacy is to me."

Acknowledgments

So many people made telling Reggie Warford's incredible story possible. They start with Reggie and his family. When Reggie and I first started this project, I didn't know if we would have more than a couple months together. My original plan was to talk to him as much as possible during his remaining time and rely heavily on others to fill in the blanks.

Reggie, being Reggie, lived for more than three years after we began this project. He insisted that his life story be told exactly how it had transpired. He was, to best put it, an open book. His brutal honesty made my job easier, as did his good cheer, despite daily suffering, and talent for telling stories. I was floored when I learned after he passed away that he wanted me to speak at his funeral. Doing so was one of the greatest honors of my life. So was writing this book with him.

Like Reggie, his wife, Marisa, his sons, Grant and Tiger, and his father-in-law, Beau Bolinski, could not have been more welcoming and enthusiastic about this project. They were always generous with their time and help with the book. They have become family. Reggie's brothers, Dr. Ron Warford and Derrick Warford, and sisters, Thelma Freeman, Velma McKinney, and Sharon Greene, were so gracious to me. They not only helped with the book but made me feel like a part of the Warford extended family.

I also had help from so many others outside the Warford family who helped shape Reggie—and vice versa. I thank University of Kentucky legend Jack "Goose" Givens for writing a terrific foreword. I thank everyone I interviewed for the book (some multiple times), including Curtis Aiken, Jim Andrews. Dr. Stuart Brown, Dr. Tom Brown, John Calipari, Oscar Combs, Joey David, Patty Eyster, Vita Fontana, Dick Gabriel, Kevin Grevey, Bob Guyette, Joe B. Hall, Jerry Hancock, Denise Harris, Merion Haskins, Bob Holland, Jolly Jernigan, Larry Johnson, Michelle Johnston, James Lee, James "Doc" Mendolsohn, Keith "Lefty" Moore, Tom Payne, Tom Piccione, Patty Reed, Larry Roberts, Shelley Trondle, and Lavon Williams.

Thanks to Deb Moore and Eric Lindsey of the University of Kentucky Sports Information Department for their help with interviews and photos for the book. Finally, thanks to Ila R. McEntire, Ashley Runyon, Victoria Robinson, and Margaret Kelly of the University Press of Kentucky as well as copyeditor Annie Barva for the effort and care they put into the publication of this book. They made Reggie's dream of having his life story published a reality.

Appendix

When I think of Reggie Warford's legacy, the one word that comes to mind of tenacity. By definition, tenacity means determination. Reggie Warford showed tenacity not only in sports but throughout his life. He inspired others through his leadership as an athlete and coach. His accomplishments at Drakesboro High School, the University of Kentucky, and as coach of the Mustangs speak for themselves. However, for me the takeaway is the hard work and determination he put into reaching those accomplishments.

I play baseball and basketball for the Muhlenberg County Mustangs. I also just signed my National Letter of Intent to play Division I baseball at Morehead State University. My motto is No Excuses, Work Harder. I believe Reggie Warford embodied a similar spirit. As a student-athlete, I have to be tenacious on and off the court or field. Tenacity doesn't just apply to sports; it applies to all areas of life. In 2022, I played for a basketball regional championship. We were facing our rival, McLean County. As center of my team, I knew I had to step up. McLean County's center was one of the best players of the region. At the beginning of the game, I really felt the pressure and the nerves.

This appendix includes the essays written in 2023 by the two winners of the college scholarships given annually by the City of Drakesboro in honor of Reggie. The two winners have given Marisa permission to publish them.

As the game came down to the wire, I knew I had to dig in and be tenacious. I took one dribble and went right through their center's chest; I shot an eight-foot post hook. Not only did I make the shot, but I was able to come through for my teammates. I tell this story because it embodies the tenacious spirit of Reggie Warford.

In addition to being tenacious, Reggie Warford had a passion for helping others. Through my time as a Mustang, this principle is one that I try to instill through community service. I have volunteered at local basketball tournaments and umpired at youth baseball games. I also give hitting and fielding lessons after school to youth. When working with the younger generation, I attempt to teach not only fundamental skills, but also encourage them to be good teammates, lead by example, put their education first, and to be tenacious. It is important for me to give back to the community in more ways than just athletically. I volunteered during the 2021 tornado, unloading trucks, picking up debris, and delivering needed items to families. Through the National Honor Society, I helped organize a book drive to aid the flood victims in Eastern Kentucky. We also delivered food to families in need for Thanksgiving. Providing a helping hand to others in need is something so much bigger than what I do on the basketball court or baseball field.

There are certain characteristics that set great student-athletes apart from good student-athletes. Tenacity is one of the characteristics that every athlete needs to add to their arsenal. The greatest student-athletes are able to dig deep and find something they didn't know they had. Everyone is going to face tough times and challenges. As a student-athlete from Muhlenberg County, thank you Reggie for the example you have set and the legacy you have left behind.

Kaydin Ray

I don't think I have ever been as disappointed as I was on February 25, 2022. This was the night of our District Championship game. It seemed, at first, everything was going our way. All of a sudden, I heard a whistle blow. I looked up at the scoreboard; there were three minutes and twenty-four seconds left and we were up by fourteen. My eyes wandered to the referee as he signaled that I had just fouled number thirty-four. I had just received my fifth and final foul. That was it for me. I made my way back to the bench feeling like I not only let my team down but also my county. We ended up losing by one point, 60–59.

Muhlenberg County has a history of being dominant in basketball. Players like Reggie Warford are exactly why we have this reputation. I have grown up being taught that to play for a Muhlenberg County school is an extreme privilege that you should never take for granted because you are playing for a much bigger purpose than just your team. You have a whole county, with a rich history, you are playing for as well. This does not come without many hardships though because just like in my District Championship game, things do not always go the way that you want.

Reggie Warford was the first African-American player to ever graduate from the University of Kentucky. During his time as a Wildcat, he had to face many hardships. People were always telling him he couldn't do it, and that there was no way an African-American could graduate from a big school like Kentucky while also playing a sport. One statistic I find astonishing is the amount Warford played. His freshman year, he played in one game the whole season. His senior year, he played 507 minutes. He had to work to get to the place he wanted to be on the team. This is the definition of tenacity, to not give up when the situation is hard and when making progress is difficult. Tenacious athletes fulfill their potential, just like Reggie Warford.

It would be very easy for me to make excuses after my District Championship Game. I could blame it on the subs that came in after me, the refs' fault for a bad call. It could even be my coaches' fault for not putting us in the right defense. That is not what it means to be a Muhlenberg County athlete. Looking back on at my game, I only see ways I could have improved. Silly fouls at the beginning of the game that I could not have given up; I could have made all my free throws;

or even just played better defense. I know now, in my next game, when I am put in a difficult situation, that I am not going to give up. I am going to be a little smarter and work a little harder because that is what this sport is about. That is what Muhlenberg is about. That is what Reggie Warford was about.

Sarah-Cate Boggess

Notes

1. Strange New World

1. Daryl Bishop, who went to Kentucky on a football scholarship, was the second Black player to appear in a varsity basketball game at Kentucky. According to the University of Kentucky Sports Information Department, Bishop played in five games in 1971–1972, the year before Reggie arrived in Lexington.

3. A Shooting Star

1. Wallace, a Nashville native, stayed home to attend Vanderbilt despite scholarship offers from more than seventy-five suitors, including UCLA, which was in the midst of a historic run under Coach John Wooden. Wallace played for Vanderbilt from 1968 to 1970 and earned All-SEC honors his senior year while getting degrees in electrical engineering and engineering mathematics. He also distinguished himself beyond basketball. A graduate of Columbia University Law School, he taught law and served as an attorney with the US Department of Justice. He died in 2017 at the age of sixty-nine.

4. Staying the Course

1. Smith tragically died in a car accident in 1967, shortly after the Los Angeles Lakers selected him in the second round of the NBA draft. Smith and his brother and sister, who also attended Western Kentucky, had returned home to celebrate Mother's Day but left that night to get back to school for final exams. Rainy weather contributed to the car accident, which also killed Smith's sister, Kay, and seriously injured his brother, Greg. The tragedy rocked Western Kentucky, and the school posthumously honored Smith with his undergraduate degree. Smith, who scored 1,142 career points

and excelled academically, was inducted into the Western Kentucky University Sports Hall of Fame in 1995.

2. Kentucky's practices reflected its depth—and the desperation of a proud program coming off a .500 season. The first team, comprising Jimmy Dan Conner, Mike Flynn, Keven Grevey, Bob Guyette, and Rick Robey, was pushed—and sometimes beaten—in scrimmages by the second team, consisting of Reggie, Larry Johnson, Jack Givens, James Lee, and Mike Phillips. "The practices were wars," Reggie said. "There was a lot of blood."

6. A Coach Is Born

1. Jack Hartman went 589–279 as a men's college basketball coach. He won a junior college national championship at Coffeyville (Kansas) Community College and an NIT Championship at Southern Illinois University before moving on to Kansas State. He won almost 300 games at Kansas State, and a street near the school's basketball coliseum is named after him. He died in 1998 at the age of seventy-three. "I really respected him, and he and Joe B. were very much alike," Reggie said. "That is one guy I would not have minded working for because I could have learned from him."

2. Joy Woodruff (née Maxberry) attended Kentucky before transferring to Louisville to be at the same school as her future husband. Dwayne Woodruff played eleven seasons in the NFL, all with the Steelers, and won a Super Bowl ring while making thirty-seven career interceptions. He became a practicing attorney *while* still playing for the Steelers. Still living in the Pittsburgh area, Woodruff is an Allegheny County Court of Common Pleas judge and has been lauded for his work in family court.

8. Fall from Grace

1. As a youngster, Reggie had an "Aha!" moment after he heard his father say, "Charge it, Junior." Soon after that, he stopped at the store on the way to a baseball game to buy chocolate milk and a Twinkie. He only had a dime, so he said to charge it. That went on long enough for him to run up a $16 tab. When his father confronted him about it, Reggie said he did not owe any money because he had charged it. "My dad said, 'Son, if you charge it, you've still got to pay for it, you damn fool!'" Reggie remembered, laughing. "That ended that in a hurry."

10. Long Road Back

1. Grant looks back "fondly" on his acting days but still won't eat orange sherbet because of a commercial in which he appeared for the animated TV show *Rugrats*, which followed the adventures of babies. Ironically, the theme of the commercial was "Don't be a baby. Watch *Rugrats*." Grant was paired with a toddler actor, and, he said, "for the commercial we were walking and eating orange sherbet on a cone. He knocked his orange sherbet on the ground and started crying. I looked at him

and then looked at the ['Don't be a baby. Watch *Rugrats*'] tagline." The shoot had so many takes that it was the last time Grant ever ate orange sherbet. "I was really excited initially, but it wore off after two hours of eating orange sherbet," he said with a laugh. "And I never had to eat the cone because we never got that far."

11. Homecoming to Remember

1. When Tiger played for Muhlenberg High School, he wore a University of Kentucky shooting shirt during pregame warm-ups and a Kentucky T-shirt under his jersey. Each had belonged to Reggie. "I thought everything he did was golden," Tiger said. He learned the hard way that this was not always the case. Reggie had always guzzled cherry soda before high school games, so Tiger tried to keep a family tradition going, thinking it would help him play better. One game he cramped up badly while going up for a layup after a steal. He was in such agony that people thought he had broken his leg. Fortunately, that was not the case, but Tiger swore off soda before games.

14. Reckoning for Reggie

1. Tom Payne, the first Black scholarship basketball player at Kentucky, was also recruited by Joe B. Hall, then an assistant to Adolph Rupp. Payne, who played just one season in Lexington, said he never had much of a relationship with Hall and the other Kentucky coaches, but he attributed that to how busy they were running an elite college basketball program. Payne is still appreciative of the response he got after writing to Hall while he was in prison. "I just wanted to let him know how I felt about him, and he sent me a real nice letter back, and he remembered some important games when Adolph Rupp got sick and how I really performed for him," Payne said. "He remembered a lot that I didn't remember. He was a good person, a fair person."

15. Fighter to the End

1. Despite their rivalry, Andrews and Payne were the forerunners of Kentucky's "Twin Towers," which included Rick Robey and Mike Phillips as well as Sam Bowie and Melvin Turpin later. Andrews remembered, "When Coach Rupp had some health issues [in 1970–1971], there were six times that Coach Hall [played Andrews and Payne together], and one of the first times we did it, it was very successful. Coach Hall got called by Coach Rupp, and he said, 'Don't ever do that again.' We didn't understand why, but we think it had something to do more with what Coach Rupp thought needed to happen: 'Don't change what I've been doing and go with something else.' It was nothing against Tom. He [Rupp] didn't think two 7-footers playing together was the way to play basketball. Coach Hall saw differently, and obviously with Robey and Phillips [it] later on became a very successful way, and everybody did it for the longest time."

About the Author

Scott Brown has written nine other books, including *A Noble Knight: Dan Priatko's Story of Faith and Courage* (2020), *Hope and Heartbreak: Beyond the Numbers of the Opioid Epidemic* (2019), and *Miracle in the Making: The Adam Taliaferro Story* (2001, with Sam Carchidi), which is being turned into a movie. Brown is the editor of Steelers Depot, a website that covers the Pittsburgh Steelers. He lives in Greensburg, Pennsylvania.

Index

Race and Sports

Series editors: Gerald L. Smith and Derrick E. White

This series publishes works that expand the boundaries of sports history. By exploring the intersections of sports and racial and ethnic histories through the racial dynamics of gender, culture, masculinity, sexuality, and power as represented in biography, community, film, literature, and oral history, the series opens a new analysis of American sport and culture.